A Better Nation

A Better Nation

The Challenges of Scottish Independence

Edited by

GERRY HASSAN AND SIMON BARROW

Luath Press Limited

EDINBURGH

www.luath.co.uk

First published 2022

ISBN: 978-1-80425-014-3

The contributors' right to be identified as authors of this book under the Copyright, Designs and Patents Act 1988 has been asserted.

The paper used in this book is recyclable. It is made from low chlorine pulps produced in a low energy, low emission manner from renewable forests.

Printed and bound by Severnprint Ltd, Gloucester

Typeset in 11 point Sabon by Lapiz

Contents

CONTENTS

Acknowledgements

THIS BOOK IS an attempt to aid a better and more constructive debate on Scottish independence, examining the specifics that independence has to address, the wider context of the union, and Scotland's position in relation to the UK and wider world.

We have aimed in our planning and commissioning of this volume to explore the independence debate in as non-partisan an approach as possible. Contributors to this book come from a range of areas – with different expertise, authority and background, and different views. Some are pro-independence, some are anti-independence, others are neutral or undeclared. All come to this debate with an open-mindedness, something to contribute and a willingness to listen and engage with others who do not necessarily agree with them.

This book is the fourth book that the two of us have undertaken over the last six years, covering numerous aspects of public life and debate. The first three have examined the SNP's years in government, the first two decades of devolution, and the challenges facing Scottish society in light of the COVID-19 pandemic. We are proud of each of these books and grateful for our relationship with Luath Press, who have offered considerable support and encouragement.

Many people have assisted the creation and development of this book, while even more have offered encouragement. In particular, we would like to give our thanks to the following people: James Mitchell, Michael Keating, Philip Schlesinger, Kirstein Rummery, Dave Moxham, Ruth Wishart, Richard Walker, Andrew Wilson, Mike Small, Jordan, Shona and Oshin Tchilingirian, Ian Dommett, Doug Hynd, Deidre Brock, Douglas Fraser, Isabel Fraser, Alastair McIntosh, Verene Nicolas, Alex Bell, and Joe Lafferty. We would also like to thank the kind folk who took the time to read proofs of the final version of the book and offered us commendations: Stuart Cosgrove, Lesley Riddoch, Neal Ascherson and Elaine C. Smith. And we could not offer thanks and not take this opportunity to be grateful for the patience, fortitude and observations of our partners, Rosie Ilett and Carla J. Roth.

A major debt of gratitude is owed to Gerry's partner, Rosie, who (as with all of his publications and writings) read and proofed the text to near-final sign-off. The book and its contents are sharper, more focused and better argued for having the benefit of Rosie's professional editing skills and overall insights.

Many thanks to the creation and design of the cover from Allistair Burt of 'Hole in My Pocket' who has continued our tradition of striking, original covers: Allistair began this tradition with the cover of our first book: *A Nation Changed? The SNP and Scotland Ten Years* On and it is fitting that he has returned with his design for this cover.

Finally, we would like to thank the brilliant people who make up Luath Press. They are passionate about books, ideas and writers, and it has been a pleasure and privilege to work with them over the past few years, and in particular in the last two years, which have been challenging ones for book publishers and sellers, along with the rest of society.

We want to record our deep-seated gratitude for their support, and pay tribute to the wider contribution that Gavin and the Luath team – Eilidh MacLennan, Thomasin Collins, Lauren Grieve, Rachael Murray and Caitlin Mellon – have made to the public life and conversations of Scotland in recent years. Our country is a better, more vibrant, dynamic and interesting place thanks to their efforts – and we would like to play our part in acknowledging and celebrating this.

Gerry Hassan
gerry@gerryhassan.com

Simon Barrow
director@ekklesia.co.uk

INTRODUCTION

Independence and the Politics of the Long View

Gerry Hassan and Simon Barrow

THE FIRST DECADES of the 21st century will be seen as vital in Scotland's history: a time when the idea and possibility of independence came in from the cold and into the mainstream; a time when it became something normalised, attainable and attractive for many people, not least the young.

The scale of change in this direction has been remarkable. Just over twenty years ago Scotland did not have a parliament, a government or a democratic voice directly accountable to the people (Hassan and Barrow, 2019). That all changed in 1999. Equally, in the early years of devolution, the dominance of Labour in Scotland seemed unassailable. Today, the SNP has been in power at Holyrood for more than 14 years, while Scottish Labour has been polling at less than 20 per cent.

Two decades of tumultuous change, challenging what was once seen as unquestionable, puts the shift towards independence as a plausible possibility into context. Debates about process, legitimacy and timescales (as well as equally critical ones about practical details and policy specifics) need to be seen against the backdrop of wider political, social and cultural change throughout Scotland over the past 20 years, which we mapped in our earlier volume, *Scotland the Brave?* (Hassan and Barrow, 2019).

The scale of that change now makes it necessary (and, indeed, unavoidable) to question the conventions which have hitherto underpinned British politics, the UK state and how it is run. The same interrogation must also be brought to bear on the subject of self-government – whether in relation to the often ultra-cautious SNP leadership (Hassan and Barrow, 2017), or more impatient voices across the land demanding instant constitutional change. The degeneration of British governance, corporate life and the union state are also in the spotlight. This goes well beyond the current Johnson government and the chaos of Brexit – political disruption has been a global phenomenon over the past decade and more. In this, Scotland's turmoil is no exception, before we even get to the long-term effects of COVID-19 and the deepening climate emergency.

Much was written about Scottish independence before and since the 2014 referendum; however, there have been few attempts to examine the changing prospects and challenges for independence in-depth (aside from the recent academic example of Hepburn et al). This book aims to redress this lack. There are many strong arguments for and against independence but the press, broadcasting and social media-driven debate has too often remained shrill, fragmented and simplistic. This is not good for a healthy democracy. In a mature political community, people of different instincts and opinions need a solid understanding of, and respect for, different perspectives.

Understanding the Case for and Against Independence

In surveying the whole landscape of debate we can identify at least seven main arguments for Scotland becoming a new, self-governing state:

Democratic expression: The Scottish people are best placed to decide their own future. Scotland should not have Westminster Governments it did not vote for imposed upon it, limiting or distorting its choices and possibilities.

Economic justice: The UK, and the form of capitalism it represents, does not work for Scotland (or the majority within the union).

Social justice: Despite being the sixth richest country globally, the UK is one of the most unequal countries in the developed world with a punitive welfare system that punishes the poor and does not suit Scotland.

Psychological development: Having decisions made for Scotland elsewhere harms its collective wellbeing; whereas taking full responsibility for its future can be a major positive and can unleash untapped potential.

Moving beyond the imperial mindset: The UK is not a fully-fledged political democracy, but an empire state defined by militarism and conquest across the world – something which has also had a detrimental effect domestically.

Becoming a modern country: The UK increasingly shows that it trapped by an unresolved past and outdated structures; Scotland has the potential to be forward-thinking and outward-looking, shaped by a progressive vision.

A new internationalism: Scotland can chart its own, positive course on the international stage – transitioning away from being a nuclear power and towards supporting conflict transformation, human rights, cooperation and democratic engagement around the world.

There is also a case for the union, which has to be properly recognised and responded to – particularly by those who are instinctively pro-independence. The seven key arguments for remaining in the union revolve around:

Financial issues: The UK, via the Barnett formula, engages in financial transfers to Scotland – which would stop in the event of independence. Other economic benefits of UK integration would be lost.

Border questions: An independent Scotland would require a harder border between Scotland and England, harming our ability to travel and trade.

Money concerns: What currency would an independent Scotland have, and how strong could an independent currency be? What would happen to pensions and mortgages established through the pound within the UK?

Europe: The terms and timing of EU re-entry – or any other arrangement, such as a European Economic Area (EEA) one – could present obstacles and problems.

Identity: What to do about those who feel British in identity and who think this is being taken away from them by departing the UK?

Solidarity: workers, families and companies need fewer barriers, not more in Britain and beyond, it is argued.

Risk factors: An independent Scotland might be attractive as an idea, but involves too many risks, uncertainty and transition (in economic, security and other forms). The interruptions created by the Russia – Ukraine crisis are certain to be part of this debate.

Eleven Observations About the Scottish Debate

If we are to have a far better conversation about these issues – one that rises to the substantial challenges of the 21st century – there are several significant matters that need to inform the debate on Scotland's future.

ONE: A conventional reading of this debate is that the pro-independence side has to address details, and acknowledge the difficulties and downsides inherent in the first years of an independent Scotland. In this view, the anti-independence side is seen as inert, passive and having no cause to prove itself. All the pro-union side has to do is be a sceptical friend to the status quo, pouring cold water on the hot passions of independence.

However, this is a mistaken view. It ignores the fact that the union is not a static entity. It is continually evolving, and at some points degenerating. Hence there is risk and uncertainty *on both sides*. Ignoring this downplays one of the key drivers of the debate – the emotional, instinctual pull that makes some people pro- and others anti-independence. This has been long neglected by the No side in the run-up to 2014 and beyond.

TWO: Independence has now become part of mainstream politics and how we see ourselves. For many people under 40, there is little memory of Scotland before the Scottish Parliament. Taking decisions here, rather than in distant Westminster, just seems natural to them. Hence – as polling amongst the young shows – for many, independence should be a natural state of affairs. This is particularly so in light of Westminster's oft-perceived disregard for Scotland and the contemptuous attitudes of successive Tory governments, elected at UK level without a majority in Scotland for over 60 years.

On this, union defenders have up to now chosen to fight a defensive war; to pursue an argument in long-term retreat, on terrain not of its choosing. This leaves that argument in a poor position to define and win the debate. Retreating armies fighting defensive engagements rarely win conflicts, including political ones. Moreover, the union argument has chosen 'transactional nationalism' as one of its main positions. This is based on an independent Scotland facing significant financial constraints, due to the withdrawal of Westminster transfers. That is an important issue but a very narrow defensive line to pitch your tent on – particularly in a country with abundant natural resources and technical and scientific know-how.

THREE: Tone and language matter. There need to be fewer messianic, evangelistic voices – particularly from the independence side – and a dialling down of certainty and self-righteousness on all sides. This requires not just rhetorical self-policing, but also much greater self-awareness and understanding of the multiple Scotlands that exist, including those populated by the unconvinced, the wary, the uncertain and the sceptical. We all need to develop more nuanced languages and approaches; Just as not all pro-independence voters are nationalists, not all pro-UK voters are necessarily unionists. As pro-independence blogger, Southside Grrrl, has pithily observed on Twitter: 'There is no such thing as No voters, only people who voted No.' That is true of many Yes voters, too.

FOUR: The union argument has to understand that this debate is not exclusively about Scotland, but also about the nature of the UK, the British state, wider society and capitalism. It touches upon the role of government and the utilisation of democracy to address major concerns; the potential for self-government; and how all these are manifested in an age of interdependence, globalisation and the power of global capital.

FIVE: There is the nature of centre-left politics and social democracy in Scotland, the UK and its wider state across the West to contend with. There is too prevalent an assumption that social democracy in Scotland is somehow exempt from its malaise across the world, or rests too easily on its apparent resurgence in the Nordic countries. It involves comparing ourselves in Scotland favourably with the state of English social democracy, and cites the negative examples of New Labour and Blairism to show our moral superiority. So ex-SNP MP, George Kerevan, is able to assert that: 'The Scottish electorate is the most social democratic in Europe, despite 40 years of neo-liberal propaganda' (Kerevan, 2021). This oversimplifies things considerably, and sidelines questions about whether, and to what extent, Scotland is really a social democracy.

SIX: Related to this is the legacy of neo-liberalism, and its capture of mainstream British politics in recent decades. Scotland has not been immune to this, and nor has the SNP. On the one hand, the party has used neo-liberalism as a dividing line between Scottish and British politics. On the other, in office, it has sometimes embraced neo-liberal ideas while projecting a social democratic outlook. Thus, we have had the SNP Sustainable Growth Commission, chaired by Andrew Wilson, backing a conservative approach to public finance; or remarks made by Alex Salmond about the Scots and Thatcherism in 2008, when he was First Minister: 'We didn't mind the economic side so much. But we didn't like the social side at all.' These are comments he had to backtrack on (Hassan, 2009). For all the commentary on Nicola Sturgeon being more centre-left and social democratic than her predecessor, many would argue that too much of the shift within the SNP has been mood music. They appear less overtly pro-business and pro-corporate, but despite co-operation with Greens and individual progressive policies, the fundamental disposition of the party makes it open to corporate capture.

SEVEN: The independence debate is often framed in terms of Scottish versus English and British nationalisms, and even (at times) Scotland versus England. However, historian Colin Kidd has pointed out in that Scottish and English nationalism exist in relationship to one another – reinforcing each in their respective territories. 'English and Scottish nationalisms are not only antagonistic but co-dependent: the rise of the SNP has provoked an English nationalist response that in turn appals Scottish opinion, and so the spiral of instability continues', he observes, while adding: 'English nationalists' pride in the prestige and idea of Great Britain is largely vacuous, ill-informed and accompanied by festering resentments of the largesse enjoyed by their fellow Britons.' They also 'cling possessively to British institutions, regarding them as their own – as 'English in all but name" (Kidd, 2021).

EIGHT: Simplistic caricatures can gain significant traction when sweeping generalisations are deployed. There is the attempt by some pro-union voices to pose a monocultural Scottish nationalism that is anti-English, othering England and the UK. This was laid out bluntly in a *Times* article by Kenny Farquharson after the Euro 2020 football tournament, which saw Gareth Southgate's England team get to the final, lose to Italy, and gain numerous plaudits for its stance on racism and 'taking the knee'. He wrote:

> The only time Scottish nationalism allows English-ness a human face is when it is ugly. The English must always be defined by the worst instincts of their most regressive minority. So the English can be toffs, racists or raving, swivel-eyed, right-wing loons. They cannot be black British midwives in east London or retired Cadbury factory workers who are now lollipop ladies in Birmingham (2021).

Farquharson went on: 'The impression must be fostered that there is one Scotland when in fact there are many Scotlands ... Scotland must not be talked about as a place where there are a variety of viewpoints ... Similarly the truth that there are many Englands must not be acknowledged' (2021). This convoluted argument even cited the audacious work of Momus and his *The Book of Scotlands* (Momus, 2018), which maps 156 parallel universe Scotlands. Yet it is suggested that there is only one Scottish nationalism – essentialist, monochromatic, and scared of a more progressive England glimpsed through Gareth Southgate. Farquharson has not noted that he has done to Scottish nationalism what he claims it does to the English – reducing it one variant with no agency and diversity, in order to dismiss it.

NINE: Similarly, there are some parts of Scottish nationalism that present a simplistic version of the UK and the British state. They assert that the UK is only an imperial construct, a warfare state, a modern advocate of neo-liberalism, and nothing more. Hence, the UK as a state goes from being the force for good of official UK accounts to being a force that can do no good, and has only upheld empire, colonialism, racism, and holding peoples and nations down. The development of the welfare state across Britain is glossed over. Even the defeat of Nazism and fascism and role of Winston Churchill in this (backed by Labour and Clement Attlee) can be downgraded in order to present the UK as a perpetual villain.

TEN: These essentialist takes on Scottish, English and British nationalisms not only reinforce the worst dynamics between them, they also reduce the terrain of common ground and shared political language. Instead, we need to encourage the kind of debate that allows for the widest diversity of political perspectives and voices. This ranges from facilitating a spectrum of views within the various nationalisms (resisting those who try to pigeonhole and corral them into singular worldviews), to encouraging a politics of self-determination and social change which is not just reduced to the claims of competing nationalist outlooks. It can be – and is – about left and right, green aspirations, peacemaking, equality, feminism, and other radical views too, reshaping the narrow contours of current politics (Barrow and Small, 2016). In particular, the determination of a resurgent far-right to capture political territory through manipulating competing nationalisms needs to be resisted by a larger politics of internationalism on all sides.

ELEVEN: Scotland needs a debate that moves beyond the claims of different nationalisms. But we also have to challenge the notion of an entirely binary debate: one with two mutually antagonistic camps who have nothing of significance in common. This is not how most voters see or experience Scotland. The politics of post-nationalism – of a shared, pooled, contingent sovereignty – has particular relevance to the 21st century, to Scotland and to the UK (or whatever might come in its wake by way of a polity for the British Isles). As George Bernard Shaw wrote in his play *Pygmalion*: 'Independence? That's middle class blasphemy. We are all dependent on one another, every soul of us on earth' (quoted in Keohane, 2021: 292).

Post-nationalism – the explicit mindset of many who advocate Scottish self-government – has been advanced in the influential writings of Neil MacCormick, and could offer pan-British Isles architecture for an independent Scotland, and for Northern Ireland and Ireland (MacCormick, 1999). This would avoid the cul-de-sac of UK-wide federalism frequently floated by Gordon Brown post-office (Brown, 2021). Instead it will aspire to practical, confederal, co-operative arrangements between self-governing nations.

The challenge need not be, as some suggest, the choice between a romantic Scottish nationalism ill-equipped for the modern age, versus a reactionary English nationalism peddling an absolutist, purist sovereignty – as seen in the politics of hard Brexit. Long before the 2016 EU referendum, Orwell biographer Bernard Crick accurately described this uncompromising sovereignty as 'the English ideology', predicting that it could lead to the eventual break-up of the UK (Crick, 2008). Post-nationalism and confederalism (independent nations and more autonomous regions voluntarily entering co-operative agreements) point the way beyond competing nationalisms, one of which – a unitary state nationalism – fails to comprehend that *is* a form of nationalism, let alone to acknowledge the make-up of the UK as a supposedly voluntary union of four nations.

Beyond 'Process Politics'

Practical questions that focus on process issues need consideration, but these are really about a number of fundamental things – how politics is done, issues of perception, how a political project is co-produced by a political community and movement, and wider issues of ownership of the goal of independence.

The question of timescales is central to all ideas of political change. Post-2014, and even more so post-2016, independence has been a live, contemporaneous political topic. Yet over this period there has been conspicuous wariness by the SNP leadership to be explicit about timescales and strategies – the former to keep their options open, and the latter to keep UK government guessing. This has led to claims about a perceived lack of clarity and communication, to conspiracy theories about true aims and objectives, and to political infighting and posturing. Process has become politicised in some pretty unhealthy ways, aided by frustrations about the slowness of progress towards resolving the constitutional question.

Understanding timescales and how they relate to political objectives is fundamental to political change. An independence referendum is the means to an end, not the end in itself, and there are numerous ways in which this end can be advanced while focusing on a future vote. A politics of timescales would explicitly lay out short-term, medium-term and long-term goals and see these in relationship, with such an approach aiding a wider ownership of the idea of independence, but so far post-2014 such candour has been missing (see Crick, 1984). It is almost as if arguments about process have been a proxy (and in some instances phoney) war, while the larger political issues are passed over. The important point here is that process for determining major decisions needs to respect both the fabric of democracy and its participants. The Johnson government in Westminster has hardly been helpful in this regard, obstinately refusing to acknowledge the democratic mandate of, and within, the Scottish Parliament. But this is also a challenge to political leadership in Scotland as a whole, and that of the competing political parties. There are also recognisable pressures on political leaderships across the developed world: tensions between short and long-term political goals, winning popular support, and charting a strategic direction in parliamentary terms that last but a few years (Heffernan, 2020).

This is the context in which independence as an idea has continually had to adapt and evolve in order to avoid becoming ossified (and ultimately constrained) by its own myths. The extent of political education, understanding, and literacy is critical to the determining the issue of independence and the quality of debate around it. The 2014 Independence referendum (or indyref) was, in fact, one of the greatest examples of political education, citizenship and engagement ever seen in Scotland. It saw grassroots groups challenging the political monoliths; it put questions of power and legitimacy centre stage, shining a light onto areas of public life never previously examined, coinciding with a long-term decline in traditional authority (the Church of Scotland, the Labour Party), alongside a more immediate crisis of once powerful institutions (RBS, Rangers, the BBC) (Hassan, 2014).

One problem area in 2014 and since has been the rise of hyper-partisanship: the pushing of conspiracy theories and disinformation, against a backdrop of the decline of mainstream media, the previously educative role of political parties, and trust in political institutions. An element of the debate has bought into questionable takes on the recent history of Scotland, particularly those emphasising betrayal. Points of contestation and overheated passion include the supposed burying of the McCrone report on oil (commissioned by the UK government as a briefing paper and circulated in 1974), the 1979 referendum and its 40 per cent threshold rule, and the Blair government's moving of the maritime boundary between Scotland and England. Over-determined, simplistic or inaccurate readings of the recent past matter, because they justify bad political takes in the present: why can Scotland not just make a unilateral declaration of independence (UDI), or SNP MPs withdraw from Westminster, as Sinn Fein did in 1918? Such positions seek to short-circuit the complexity of negotiating political change, and the need to engage a divergent popular will, rather than bypass or ignore it. They also take discussion away from crucial present issues that look very different to the past: a post-carbon economy, rather than a fossil based one; the capacities and limits of devolution; and the future of Scotland's maritime industry after Brexit and how to address that.

There has also been an alarming retrenchment in political life following the 'Big Bang' of the 2014 independence referendum – unsurprising from such a high point of participation, and part of which has been an attempt by traditional agents to reassert their role. How, in such a context, do we shape politics, public life and discussion for the better? How do we stand up to conspiracy theorists and peddlers of fake news, while genuinely respecting opposing views and facts on such high-octane issues as Scotland's constitutional future? The issue of upping our political game and challenging a culture of 'thought silos' and over-simplification of issues seems even more important in the aftermath of COVID-19, with all the hurt and loss it has occasioned. There is a need for healing, and politics cannot and should not ignore this. Indeed, it is the voice of the arts, of writers and poets who perhaps need foregrounding to make a better way possible (Hassan and Barrow, 2020). Here we are talking about political process in terms of civic engagement and debate – citizens assemblies being just one example of how to bring contesting views and experience into an arena where something new can emerge, notwithstanding the distorting issues of power and wealth which also need to be confronted.

Beyond Binary Choices and Understanding Scotland's Long Revolution

In assessing the political contours of the immediate future, it is important to unpack the weary tropes that describe Scotland as divided and trapped in irresolvably confrontational politics. On Scotland's future and many other questions, public opinion is actually much more fluid and changing than many political actors wish to allow.

This belies the notion of two warring camps facing each other in a never-ending stand-off.

First, there is an unchallenged assumption in much commentary that any future vote must be a simple repeat of 2014 when other options are available, including a sequential vote and multi-option referendum. Moreover, the chance of another three-year campaign is close to zero, there is much talk of there never being another 'Better Together' campaign (particularly in Labour circles), and even 'Yes Scotland' (which to many outside the SNP was seen as a front for the party) may end up taking a very different shape. Citizen's juries, 'human libraries' (connecting people through an organised system), community forums and other mechanisms can and should emerge.

Second, 'the missing Scotland' and the 'missing million' – the voters who had not voted in a generation, but who turned out in 2014 – are always with us in one form or another. The complacency of the official campaigns that turning out to vote once trumps a generation of political disengagement and exclusion is threadbare. Rather, 'the missing Scotland' is continually present and changing, with voters moving in and out of non-voting, engagement and dis-engagement. Younger voters, working-class communities (the most usually ignored), the changing demographic of 'New Scots', and new voters – all need to be taken with fresh seriousness, and all suggest that the debate and campaigns from 2022 onwards can and should look very different.

Third, between those who are pro- and anti-independence there is a significant constituency of voters – one which the pro-union campaigning body Our Scottish Future calls 'middle Scotland'. They could equally be described as 'floating voters' or 'undecided Scot-land.' These voters are a key group that need to be addressed in a way that does not play to the certainties of the binary politics of Yes and No.

Fourth, rejecting simple binary divisions is about opposing poli-tics as a war of attrition, weaponised disrespect, and seeking to under-mine the legitimacy of the other side, or a different (or uncertain) view. It is about discovering and celebrating the common values and communal bonds Scots share together, despite differences concern-ing independence. Some of the supercharged rhetoric can sometimes forget the collective stories, histories and traditions that make us a people and nation. Equally, making the division about constitutional matters the only one that counts ignores the real issues of economic disparity and class which divide people over real life chances, not just opinions. In other words, there are real divisions in Scotland that are not well mapped or recognised by binary politics around independence.

Finally, those on the independence side who worry about limited action and progress since 2016 need to remember the larger canvas. This is the fundamental fact that one of the major drivers towards full Scottish self-government is the unequal, dysfunctional union that is the current UK – economically, socially, and democratically. Without dramatic reform, this makes the Scottish question an ongoing live issue. Pro-union commentator Alex Massie recognised this when he declared, 'the best antidote to Scottish nationalism is not British nationalism but a Britain that demonstrably works for all of its constituent peoples' (Massie, 2021). The late Nigel Smith, organiser of the 1997 pro-devolution referendum campaign, reflected: 'This is not a settled issue, but rather a live one which has to be concluded one way or another by at some point having another independence referendum.'

Thus, the independence debate is about more than timing, processes, or how and why any referendum is held. It is about more than the principle of whether Scotland should be independent or not, and the detail of any future set of proposals. It has to be seen against a much bigger backdrop: one concerning power, legitimacy and voice in Scotland and the UK; the nature of economic power; the challenge of how to face down the climate crisis; and the nature of democracy and society as whole. In this, the long revolution in Scotland that has transformed politics and the nature of society (through declining deference, the collapse of punitive authority and marginalisation of once omnipotent public bodies) has also seen the challenge of independence transformed. The writer Neal Ascherson took note of this shift when he cautioned, in 2020:

> Don't rush towards Indyref2. The polls majority for independence is still very frail. To unknown extent, connected to COVID – Nicola's leadership, Westminster's uselessness. In a ferocious, post-COVID campaign, that edge may well diminish. But meanwhile the big pot of national self- confidence and alienation from

old Ukania is cooking slowly and surely. Don't take it
off too soon. (Ascherson in Hassan, 2020)

That long revolution and perspective is further underlined when we
go back 70 years to writer Moray McLaren's observations about
Scottish self-government:

> There is another radical quality in the Scots. It is the
> self-respect; and from this self-respect comes the most
> valuable element in the movement for Scottish home
> rule, an element not usually to be found in a small
> nation struggling to reassert itself. The Scottish move-
> ment is not built upon a sense of superiority, upon fear
> or upon hate, but upon a desire for full self-respect
> (1951: 244).

This was written, the year of a UK general election when the two
largest parties – Labour and the Conservatives – captured their highest ever share of the UK vote: 96.8 per cent. It was a time when
the Liberals and the SNP were micro-forces. This was the most 'British' of all post-war UK elections, with a homogenised politics and
a national vote swing extending from the Highlands to Cornwall
and Devon. Yet, even then the self-government question could not
be extinguished.

Fast forward 70 years and 'UK politics' is no more, beyond the
artifice of the Palace of Westminster. There is no homogenised UK
politics and national swing. Instead, there is now politics across the
four nations of the UK – each evincing different dynamics, different
political pulses, different and dominant parties. This is the reality of
the 'Disunited Kingdom'. The fundamentals of the Scottish self-government debate are deeply rooted in that reality, and they will not dis-
appear until a new set of arrangements commands popular support.

In all this, Scotland needs new stories which link past and present, and imagine and create the future – part of a continual conversation for any nation and political community, its invention, and
ongoing reinvention. This is central to the outcome of the constitutional debate and to the shape and success, or otherwise, of the
independence cause. A 'futures literacy' is integral to our public life
and politics, and not something that Scotland has spent enough time
thinking about (see Godden et al., 2020).

The stories of a self-governing Scotland need ambition, humanity, a sense of belonging and connectedness, and a championing of many multiple Scotlands in the present, and potential Scotlands of the future. Our political narratives have to acknowledge this explicitly, rather than leaving it implicit. The latter is demonstrated by the words of musician and commentator Pat Kane, when he talks about 'the pragmatic normalism' of the SNP. He believes it is based on the conceit: 'Let us get to the starting block of nation-statehood, and we'll worry about the future when it comes.' This looks alarmingly like continuity independence, where the formal symbols and flags change, but little else.

It is vital that Scottish public life and the case for independence understands the pitfalls of believing in the existence of a single national story and monocultural nation. This mode of thinking has been adopted unhelpfully before – past examples being 'unionist Scotland' and 'Labour Scotland' with some on the independence side perhaps wanting 'nationalist Scotland' to be its latest expression (see Adichie, 2009). Such serial single story Scotlands, in different guises, cannot prevail, because they do not do justice to a much more complex and messy reality, which democratic politics has to negotiate.

The real world of many Scotlands has to have the maturity to recognise the power contained in multiple stories and voices, avoiding the pitfalls of narrative fallacy – that is, too easily falling for the most simple, evocative story that plays to our own prejudices and sounds best in our own echo chambers. In the words of the novelist Kim Stanley Robinson, we need to dare to tell 'the story of the next century' (Taleb, 2007; Krznanic, 2020: 222). This future Scotland is already present in the here and now but needs nurturing and encouragement to allow the new storytellers to emerge.

It has to recognise the long revolution Scotland has experienced and the long tail of current contemporary debates that did not just emerge when the SNP won in 2007 or 2011, or even when the Scottish Parliament was re-established in 1999. Our present independence debate has been framed and magnified by all of these, but there are deeper, historic forces affecting the changing nature of Scotland and decline of Britain and Britishness which are explored in this volume.

Viewing the Scottish debate from this perspective should give everyone involved in it – whether pro or anti-independence, unsure or undecided, a sense an understanding that this discussion is not going away and is not just about the appeal or anti-appeal of party. This means that we need determination and resilience to dig deeper, confront our own shortcomings as a society, address where we don't hold power to account, and identify where (for all the invoking of radicalism) the conservative mindset characterises too much of politics and public life exists. The latter can be seen in the defensive social democracy that defines too much of the SNP and Labour, and the unreflective modernity that was once the anchor of 'Labour Scotland' that has now become one of the reference points of 'nationalist Scotland'. In the Scotland of the early 21st century we must not cling to past shibboleths and ideologies – we need to be much more open-minded and ecumenical. we must embrace and take part in shaping the new world as it emerges.

References

Adichie, C. N. (2009), 'The Danger of a Single Story', *TED Talk*, 7 October, https://www.ted.com/talks/chimamanda_ngozi_adichie_the_danger_of_a_single_story

Barrow, S. and Small, M. (2016), *Scotland 2021*, Edinburgh: Ekklesia / Bella Caledonia.

Brown, G. (2021), *Seven Ways to Change the World: How to Fix the Most Pressing Problems We Face*, London: Simon & Schuster.

Crick, B. (1984), *Socialist Values and Time*, London: Fabian Society.

Crick, B. (2008), 'In conversation', *Changin' Scotland weekend*, The Ceilidh Place, Ullapool, 2 November.

Farquharson, K. (2021), 'A progressive England scares the hell out of the SNP', *The Times Scotland*, 14 July, https://www.thetimes.co.uk/article/a-progressive-england-scares-hell-out-of-snp-vn9mjx8wz

Godden, I., Sillittoo, H. and Godden, D. (2020), *Scotland 2070: Healthy, Wealthy, Wise: An Ambitious Vision for Scotland's Future Without the Politics*, London: College Publishers.

Hassan, G. (2009), 'The Legacy of Thatcherism North of the Border Thirty Years On, *OpenDemocracy*, 5 May, https://www.gerryhassan.com/short-journalistic-essays/the-legacy-of-thatcherism-north-of-the-border-thirty-years-on/

Hassan, G. (2014), *Caledonian Dreaming: The Quest for a Different Scotland*, Edinburgh: Luath Press.

Hassan, G. (2020), 'The Pressures of Success: What Independence has to do to win', *Sunday National*, 15 November, https://www.gerry-hassan.com/blog/the-pressures-of-success-what-independence-has-to-do-to-win/

Hassan, G. and Barrow, S. (eds) (2017), *A Nation Changed? The SNP and Scotland Ten Years On*, Edinburgh: Luath Press.

Hassan, G. and Barrow, S. (eds) (2019), *Scotland the Brave? Twenty Years of Change and the Future of the Nation*, Edinburgh: Luath Press.

Hassan, G. and Barrow, S. (eds) (2020), *Scotland After the Virus*, Edinburgh: Luath Press.

Heffernan, M. (2020), *Uncharted: How to Map the Future*, London: Simon & Schuster.

Hepburn, E., Keating, M. and McEwan, N. (eds) (2021), *Scotland's new choice: Independence after Brexit*, Edinburgh: Centre on Constitutional Change.

Kerevan, G. (2021), 'The SNP shouldn't quit Westminster – this is what they should do instead', *The National*, 2 August, https://www.thenational.scot/news/19483960.george-kerevan-snp-mps-use-time-westminster/

Keohane, J. (2021), *The Power of Strangers: The Benefits of Connecting in a Suspicious World*, London: Viking.

Kidd, C. (2021), 'The revolt of the English', *New Statesman*, 9 June, https://www.newstatesman.com/Englishness-Ailsa-Henderson-Richard-Wyn-Jones-Gavin-Esler-review

Krznaric, R. (2020), *The Good Ancestor: How to Think Long Term in a Short Term World*, London: W.H. Allen.

MacCormick, N. (1999), *Questioning Sovereignty: Law, State and Nation in the European Commonwealth*, Oxford: Oxford University Press.

McLaren, M. (1951), *The Scots*, Harmondsworth: Penguin Books.

Massie, A. (2021), 'Gove is right to say 'not now but not never'', *The Times Scotland*, 3 August, https://www.thetimes.co.uk/article/michael-gove-is-right-to-tell-unionists-not-now-but-not-never-v6vt-236kv

Momus (2018), *The Book of Scotlands*, Edinburgh: Luath Press.

Taleb, N. N. (2007), *The Black Swan: The Impact of the Highly Improbable*, London: Penguin Books.

Section One: Past, Present and Future

CHAPTER I

A Very Different Choice? The Impact of Brexit on Attitudes Towards Independence
John Curtice

JUST SEVEN SHORT years ago, Scotland voted by 55 per cent to 45 per cent to remain part of the UK, rather than become an independent country (Curtice, 2021). Portrayed by Alex Salmond as a 'once in a generation opportunity', the ballot gripped the attention of the nation and no less than 85 per cent of those who were eligible to vote did so. Yet, following the devolved election in May 2021, Scotland now has a SNP administration that, supported by the Greens, is committed to holding a second ballot once the COVID pandemic is over.

Have attitudes towards independence changed since 2014 such that another ballot might produce a different result? This chapter addresses that question. It examines how the level of support for independence has fluctuated since 2014, how far the character of that support has changed, and how people now view the consequences of independence.

It does so with particular reference to the one key constitutional development that has occurred since 2014: the UK's decision to leave the EU. This has played a key role in stimulating the SNP's call for another referendum. For over 30 years, the party's vision of independence has been one of 'independence in Europe'. Whether that vision could be realised was one of the key issues during the 2014 referendum campaign, with those on the No side arguing that an independent Scotland would have difficulty remaining in the EU. However, the outcome of the EU referendum two years later, in which Scotland voted by 62 per cent to 38 per cent to stay in the EU, not only undercut this argument but also appeared to substantiate the nationalist claim that, as part of the UK, Scotland is always at risk of having its democratic wishes overturned by the views of those living south of the border. When it became clear that Theresa May envisaged exiting the EU single market and customs union – not just the political institutions (May, 2017) – the Scottish Government indicated in March 2017 that it wished to hold another independence ballot (Sturgeon, 2017), a request that has remained on the table ever since.

Yet, despite these political developments, there is no guarantee that Brexit will have changed the views of voters. Perhaps for most of those who voted No in 2014 the UK's relationship with the EU matters far less than the maintenance of Scotland's ties with the UK. And maybe not all Yes supporters are necessarily enamoured of the pooling of sovereignty that would be entailed in an independent Scotland becoming part of the EU. But first we need to examine the legacy left by the 2014 ballot.

Trends in Support for Independence

Although a majority voted to stay in the UK in 2014, the result was closer than seemed likely beforehand. This is evident from Table 1, which demonstrates how people in Scotland have responded in most years since 1999 when the Scottish Social Attitudes (SSA) survey (Curtice and Montagu, 2020) has posed the following question: which of these statements comes closest to your view? Scotland should become independent, separate from the UK and the EU; Scotland should become independent, separate from the UK but part of the EU; Scotland should remain part of the UK, with its own elected parliament which has *some* taxation powers; Scotland should remain part of the UK, with its own elected parliament which has *no* taxation powers; Scotland should remain part of the UK *without* an elected parliament.

To simplify matters, the table combines under the heading 'Independence' those who gave either the first or the second answer, while those who offered the third or fourth response are brought together under the heading 'Devolution'.

Table 1: Constitutional Preference, 1999-2019.

	Independence	Devolution	No Parliament
	%	%	%
1999	27	59	10

(continue)

2000	30	55	12
2001	27	59	9
2002	30	52	13
2003	26	56	13
2004	32	45	17
2005	35	44	14
2006	30	54	9
2007	24	62	9
2009	28	56	8
2010	23	61	10
2011	32	58	6
2012	23	61	11
2013	29	55	9
2014	33	50	7
2015	39	49	6
2016	46	42	8
2017	45	41	8
2019	51	36	7

Source: Scottish Social Attitudes (SSA). The 2014 survey took place before the independence referendum, while the 2016 survey was conducted after the EU referendum.

Prior to the 2014 referendum, independence appeared to be very much a minority preference. On average, just 28 per cent said that they wanted Scotland to leave the UK. In particular, the advent of a SNP administration in 2007 did not herald a rise in support. If anything, the proportion who backed leaving the UK often appeared to be rather lower after 2007 than it had been during the early years of devolution. That the referendum produced a much narrower outcome than might have been expected is affirmed by the initial polls – taken in the first half of 2013 – of how people proposed to vote in response to the question that appeared on the 2014 ballot paper. On average, the 'yes' response to the question 'Should Scotland be an independent country' was selected by just 38 per cent of voters, seven points short of the final tally the following year.

Crucially, this proved to be a durable increase. In 2015, the first SSA survey to be conducted after the independence referendum reported (in response to its long running question) a record high of 39 per cent support for independence, while in the following two years the figure matched the 45 per cent reported in the referendum. True, the surveys in 2016 and 2017 were conducted after the EU referendum and may reflect its impact – an issue to which we will return shortly. But there is further evidence that the 2014 referendum had made a difference even before Brexit came over the horizon. This is demonstrated by those polls that continued to ask people – albeit somewhat episodically – how they would vote if presented again with the question that was posed in the first referendum.

As Table 2 reveals, for a year or so after the referendum these polls suggested that support for independence might, if anything, be even higher than it had been during the referendum – not far short of 50 per cent. However, by the time the EU referendum approached, the average level of support for independence had fallen somewhat to 47 per cent. Moreover, far from rising again in the immediate wake of the outcome of the EU referendum, the average level of support for Yes settled back in 2017 and 2018 to the 45 per cent level recorded in the referendum. In short, there was never any sign that the increased support for independence registered during the course of the referendum campaign had gone into reverse. At the same time, however, it was far from clear that Brexit was having the impact on public opinion that nationalist politicians had, perhaps, anticipated.

The Impact of Brexit

The absence of any post-Brexit increase in support for independence was, in truth, consistent with the evidence on how people had voted in the independence referendum in 2014 and in the EU ballot in 2016. These two plebiscites revealed that, despite the arguments during the 2014 campaign about whether an independent Scotland could be a continuing member of the EU, many voters did not see a link between the two issues of Europe and independence. The 2015 SSA found that those who either wanted the UK to leave the EU or who at least thought the EU should be a less powerful institution ('Eurosceptics') were in fact slightly more likely to have voted Yes in the independence referendum (49 per cent) than those ('Europhiles') who either wanted to keep things as they were, or wanted the EU to be more powerful (44 per cent). Meanwhile, according to the British Election Study internet panel, there was little difference between the proportion of 2014 Yes voters who voted Remain in 2016 (62 per cent) and the proportion of 2014 No voters who did so (60 per cent). Between them these figures gave little support to the idea that Brexit would have a significant impact on people's attitudes towards the constitutional question.

Table 2: *Summary of Polls of Indyref2 vote intention since September 2014*

	Yes	No	No. of Polls
	%	%	
Oct 2014–May 2015	49	51	17
May–Dec 2015	49	51	10
Jan–June 2016	47	53	13
June–Dec 2016	48	52	12
Jan–June 2017	45	55	20
June–Dec 2017	45	55	6
Jan–Dec2018	45	55	13
Jan–Dec 2019	49	51	12
Jan–Mar 2020	50	50	5
May–Dec 2020	54	46	17
Jan–Feb 2021	51	49	7
Mar 2021	51	49	11
Apr 2021	49	51	15
May 2021	48	52	7

Note: Those who said 'Don't Know' or refused to vote excluded
Source: Whatscotlandthinks.org database

Yet, within months of the EU referendum there were signs that the outcome was beginning to reshape the character of support for independence. Two polls by YouGov in August and November 2016 found that how people had voted on Brexit made a difference to their chances of backing the same side as they had in 2014. No less than 93 per cent of 2014 No voters who voted Leave in 2016 indicated they would vote No again, but the figure was only 74 per cent among those who had backed Remain. Here was evidence that the outcome of the EU referendum was serving to erode some voters' support for the union. At the same time, however, there was a countervailing movement among those who had voted Yes. While 86 per cent of those 2014 Yes voters who had backed Remain said they would vote Yes again, the proportion was only 65 per cent among those who had voted Leave. If these two patterns persisted then, while the level of support for independence might be unchanged, the issues of Scotland's constitutional status and the country's relationship with the EU would become intertwined.

Table 3 uses data from SSA from 2013 onwards to trace the level of support for independence (as measured by the question that was introduced at Table 1) separately among Eurosceptics and Europhiles. Between 2013 and 2015 there was little difference between the two groups in their level of support for independence. However, in the 2016 SSA, conducted after the EU referendum, support for independence among Europhiles was at 53 per cent – nine points above Eurosceptics. That gap then widened yet further to 16 points in 2017 and 19 points in 2019. Brexit may not have resulted in an increase in the level of support for independence, but it had seemingly changed its character.

Table 3: Support for Independence by Attitude towards the EU, 2013–19

% favour independence	Europhile	Eurosceptic
2013	30	29
2014	31	35
2015	39	41
2016	53	44
2017	56	40
2019	62	43

Note: Europhile: Respondent said that Britain's long-term policy should be to leave things as they are, or to stay in the EU and try to increase the EU's powers, or to work for a single European government. Eurosceptic: Respondent said that Britain's long-term policy should be either to leave the EU or to stay but try to reduce its powers.

Source: Scottish Social Attitudes (SSA).

However, a glance back at Table 2 indicates that, having been stable throughout 2017 and 2018, support for independence increased sharply in 2019 – when a perpetual Commons stalemate over the future of Brexit meant the issue was dominating the media headlines.

By 2020, support for independence was only a little short of 50 per cent – and indeed reached that figure by the time that Brexit was implemented at the end of January 2020. Meanwhile, as Table 4 reveals, this increase coincided with a strengthening of the link between how people had voted in the EU referendum and their propensity to vote Yes. In line with the figures from SSA, it was already the case by the second half of 2018 that, at 50 per cent, support for independence was 16 points higher among Remain voters than it was among those who had backed Leave. However, by the time of the 2019 UK general election campaign, support for independence had risen among Remain voters by five points (to 55 per cent) whereas it had fallen by four points (to 30 per cent) among Leave voters. Not only had the pursuit of Brexit changed the character of support for independence but it seemed it had now resulted in an increase in support such that it was no longer clear what the outcome of another independence referendum would be.

Table 4: Percentage Support for Yes in Polls of IndyRef2 Vote Intentions by 2016 EU Referendum Vote

Per Cent Yes	Remain Voters	Leave Voters	No. of Polls
June–Dec. 2018	50	34	8
Apr–Oct 2019	56	32	7
Nov–Dec 2019	55	30	5
Jan–Mar 2020	56	31	5
May–Dec 2020	59	37	10
Jan–Feb 2021	56	34	9
Mar 2021	53	32	7
Apr 2021	54	31	9
May 2021	55	30	7

Source: Average of polls conducted by BMG, Ipsos MORI, Lord Ashcroft, JL Partners, Opinium, Panelbase, Savanta ComRes, Survation, YouGov. Not all companies published a poll in each period.

The Pandemic

The rise in support for independence did not end there. As Table 2 shows, it came to reach an average of 54 per cent in the second half of 2020, making it the first time in Scottish polling history that the polls were consistently reporting majority support for independence over an extended period. However, Table 4 reveals that, in contrast to the increase that had been registered in 2019, this further rise was in evidence among both Remain and Leave voters – and thus cannot be attributed to Brexit. It occurred, of course, in the midst of the coronavirus pandemic when the Scottish Government's handling of the crisis was evaluated more highly by voters than the UK government's was (Curtice, 2020). However, as the Scottish Parliament election of May 2021 approached, support for independence fell back once more to just below 50 per cent. But, the division between Remain and Leave voters was just as sharp as it had been at the end of 2019. While the impact of the pandemic on support for independence may have been temporary, the impact of Brexit has so far proven to be durable.

Why Has Brexit Made A Difference?

Brexit has had a long-term impact on the level and character of support for independence, even though voters' views on the EU had hitherto made little difference to their attitudes towards how Scotland was governed. But in truth, this development should not come as a surprise. The UK's exit from the EU means the choice that would confront voters in a second independence referendum is significantly different from the one with which they were faced in 2014. Both sides of the debate were arguing that a vote for them was more likely to secure Scotland's continued membership of the EU – they were simply debating which was the better way of achieving an agreed end. Now, in contrast, those arguing for a Yes vote will claim that independence will provide a pathway back to EU membership, while those supporting the union will have to persuade voters that being part of the UK is a more attractive prospect than being part of the EU.

In short, a post-Brexit independence referendum will not only be a choice between being inside or outside the UK, but also a choice between two unions – the EU and the UK. Therefore, what will matter to voters is whether they think the consequences of being independent inside the EU are more or less favourable than the implications of being part of the UK but outside the EU. Thanks to the unpopularity of Brexit, this comparison will not necessarily be favourable to the unionist side – not least on the crucial issue of the possible economic consequences of independence.

For example, in 2019 SSA found that voters were more likely to be optimistic about the consequences of independence than they were the implications of Brexit (Curtice and Montagu, 2020). Only 18 per cent said that they thought Britain's economy would be better off as a result of leaving the EU, while 61 per cent believed it would be worse off. In contrast, 43 per cent said that Scotland's economy would be better off as a result of independence while only 33 per cent believed it would be worse off. In early 2021, although Panelbase found that slightly more voters felt that independence would result in Scotland being worse off (42 per cent) than better off (36 per cent), the balance of opinion was still less pessimistic than it was in response to a similar question about the impact of leaving the EU. On this, just 26 per cent reckoned Scotland would be better off and 44 per cent worse off. Meanwhile, an earlier Panelbase poll in 2019 reported that 45 per cent thought that Scotland would be better off economically as independent country within the EU while only 35 per cent reckoned it would be better off as part of the UK but outside the EU. And although in 2020 Survation reported that only slightly more disagreed (39 per cent) than agreed (37 per cent) that 'independence would be more damaging to the Scottish economy than Brexit', even this reading suggests that the No side may not draw the benefit it enjoyed in 2014 from what was a widespread pessimism about the economic consequences of independence at that time (Curtice, 2021).

Conclusion

Nobody can be sure what will happen if there is another referendum on independence. Much of the increase in support for the cause has occurred in the vacuum created by the Brexit stalemate, followed by the coronavirus pandemic. For the most part voters have yet to be exposed to the arguments that will be made for or against a choice that will have different ramifications from the one with which they were presented in 2014. However, prior to the 2014 referendum independence was still very much a minority point of view, whereas the legacy left by both that ballot and by the Brexit referendum means a second campaign would be addressing a much more evenly divided electorate, who would have to assess the relative merits of being either part of the UK or part of the EU.

Acknowledgement

This chapter was written while the author held a research grant from the Economic and Social Research Council (grant no. ES/T000775/1) as part of its 'The UK in a Changing Europe' initiative. Responsibility for the views expressed here lies solely with the author.

References

Curtice, J. (2020), 'COVID in Scotland: How do Scots rate their leaders in the pandemic?', *BBC News Online*, posted at: https://www.bbc.co.uk/news/uk-scotland-54973255

Curtice, J. (2021), 'The Scottish Independence Referendum of 2014' in Smith, J. (ed.), *The Palgrave Book of European Referendums*, London: Palgrave Macmillan.

Curtice, J. and Montagu, I. (2020), *Is Brexit Fuelling Support for Independence?*, London: NatCen Social Research, available at: https://whatscotlandthinks.org/wp-content/uploads/2020/11/SSA-2019-Scotland-paper-v5.pdf

May, T. (2017), 'The government's negotiating objectives for exiting the EU', Speech given by the Prime Minister at Lancaster House, 17 January, available at: https://www.gov.uk/government/speeches/the-governments-negotiating-objectives-for-exiting-the-eu-pm-speech

Sturgeon, N. (2017), 'Second independence referendum', Speech given by the First Minister, Bute House, 13 March, available at: https://www.gov.scot/publications/first-ministers-speech-bute-house-march-2017/

CHAPTER 2

The New Strategic Challenges of Securing A Yes Vote
Marco G. Biagi

UNSURPRISINGLY, MANY OF the great aphorisms about strategy come from military circles – 'ready to fight the last war' is one such phrase. Throughout history, one could find wizened generals in their army headquarters congratulating each other at their mastery of the prior conflict and nodding sagely at each comradely contribution. But this often came before a total defeat. Being deeply ready to fight the *last* war can leave you totally unprepared for the next one, especially if all of the conditions have changed in the interim. In politics as in war, the backdrop of situation, attitudes and technology can all shift.

A strategist for the next Yes campaign may, for example, arm themselves with a currency position that, on their life, they swear would not cause the same problems as the 2014 position did. But the main effect of the currency debate, pushed in 2014 by the No campaign, may simply have been the creation of an air of uncertainty. The second time around, opponents of independence could seek to create the same result by other means. Similarly, the economic prospectus set out in the Scottish Government's white paper is outdated in a variety of ways. The normal drift that gradually renders statistics out-of-date has been compounded by the changes in both the price and political acceptability of oil and, more recently, by the almost unprecedented bill the UK government has accumulated to weather the COVID-19 pandemic.

Certainly, the No campaign will have to wrestle with foundational shifts of their own. Brexit's effect on Scotland's more cosmopolitan classes, a very visible contrast between the handling of the pandemic in the two jurisdictions, and the third unpopular Conservative prime minister in a row have all made the next No campaign's job harder. The democratic case for independence was evoked by the Yes Scotland campaign's slogans: 'Scotland's Future in Scotland's Hands' or, more provocatively, 'End Tory Rule Forever'. 70 per cent of Yes voters agreed the most important reason for voting Yes to independence was 'the principle that all decisions about Scotland should be taken in Scotland' (Ashcroft, 2014), and this has been reinforced with every year that has passed since. But those of a different constitutional bent can explore the next No campaign's problems, of which there are many.

The Conditional Union

Nothing should worry those anti-independence strategists more than the flimsiness of Scotland's gut feeling about the union. In 2013 the SSA Survey made waves with the finding that, should Scots be, on average, £500 better off from independence, a substantial majority would vote for it (Curtice, 2013). A later poll by Progress Scotland (Survation, 2020) found similar results. A sense of Britishness, attachment to cross-border institutions like the monarchy, a project of building a union of nations – nothing that couldn't be bought out for around ten pounds a week. At its heart, Scotland is its own nation, and content to take on all the trappings that come with it. Indeed, it is easy to suspect that were independence just seen as economically neutral, the electorate would accept it. Support for the union only exists on the condition that the alternative is more costly.

Therein lies the Yes campaign's economic problem. The majority of voters have – rightly or wrongly – been more sceptical about the economic prospects of an independent Scotland than Yes campaigners would like. This makes the prospects for independence relative to the status quo. Even David Cameron once accepted Scotland could be a successful independent country by global standards, but would it be more or less successful now?

In the 2014 referendum, the Yes campaign put other choices in the foreground. They wanted people to go into the ballot box thinking about the shape of society, rather than the size of the economy. But, when it had to speak on the economic issue, the Scottish Government mainly felt it could meet its opponents on their turf. The annual Government Expenditure & Revenue Scotland (GERS) report, which estimates taxes raised in Scotland and compares it to total public spending, had been relatively healthy for several years.

GERS carries the National Statistics badge of neutrality, so it was accepted and quoted until people were tired of hearing about it. The UK government's own Department of Energy and Climate Change projections for the price of oil and ensuing revenue to a Scottish exchequer were buoyant. And, while several businesses were loudly sceptical about independence, the Yes campaign could always find businesspeople willing to go in front of cameras and say that there were plenty who supported a Yes vote too. Faced with all of this, the No campaign then emphasised not that Scotland was 'too poor' but that it ran the risk of losing out in the future if oil revenues changed, or it would be unable to pay for the extra services promised by the Scottish Government.

Perhaps this was sufficient evidence to leave Scottish voters nervous enough that on referendum day, they doubted the Yes campaign's promises and voted No. Since 2014, however, the situation has changed. With the exception of the hyper-obsessed on Twitter, this is a change that is not often talked about. With Brexit and the pandemic dominating the news over the last few years, the economics of independence are not much explored on a day-to-day basis – consciously or unconsciously, voters are generally weighing other factors when deciding on independence. Once a second referendum becomes a reality, however, the experience of 2014 shows us that people will be all too happy to grapple with the details. The No campaigners would be fools not to make a major issue out of the economic situation; the Yes campaigners would be fools to meet them on the same turf as before and expect a different result.

Fortunately, SNP strategists know this. The first attempt to solve this problem came via the creation of the Sustainable Growth Commission, which ran from 2016 to 2018 and was tasked with updating the economic case for independence. As well as setting out a transitional, unilateral use of sterling after independence, the report proposed that an independent Scotland should increase public spending each year but – crucially – by less than economic growth. If the economy grew by three per cent, public spending might grow by two per cent. That way the gap between how much the government would be raising in revenue and how much it would be spending could close over time without there ever having to be cuts. The authors of the case clearly believed they had squared the circle of acknowledging Scotland's issues while proposing a believable solution.

But the reception to the Growth Commission was cool, to say the least. The SNP was no longer the party of the early referendum campaign. After the No vote, tens of thousands of new members joined and, while the views of the new silent members may not have been much different to those of the old, the tenor of internal debate led by the membership's vocal elements became noticeably more restive. A party conference political floor fight over the commission's currency recommendation left the victors unclear but the damage obvious. The opposition attack line of a promise of 'a decade of austerity' was heard almost as often from the Yes side as the No. The commission chair who had unquestioned expertise and who may have been a good choice to reassure business, Andrew Wilson, turned out to be somewhat less effective at winning over a sceptical Yes movement. Today, few even in the SNP are caught defending the proposals.

Any good Holyrood Kremlinologist can see the Scottish Government dipping its toes in the water but with Western contrasts. Independence in the EU versus the UK's economic isolation after Brexit? That presentation has been featuring in speeches, articles and leaflets for some time. Does it hit home? The jury is out, and may well be so until the electorate actually votes.

This approach does offer some serious advantages. The 2014 economic message was based on citing the authority of a (supposedly) neutral bureaucracy. The ONS-approved statistics were used to challenge the belief of many voters that Scotland was, to put it bluntly, poor. The Brexit argument is instead an appeal to principles – t is a story rather than a statistic. Doubters who believe that independence is economically risky may also believe that Brexit is worse, and thereby they can be won over to independence by inviting them to connect sets of views they already hold and reach a new conclusion. That is much easier than trying to tell them they were wrong all along.

Such narrative approaches are more effective at persuading people than any statistics. The No campaign's talk of 'broader shoulders of the UK' and 'pooling and sharing' in 2014 were just this sort of story-based argument. They were statements that, rightly or wrongly, just seemed to be common sense to enough voters to deliver a No vote.

But there are other ways of building such an argument. Yes campaigners might argue that a Scottish Government would, by definition, be more focused on building Scotland's prosperity than would a UK government responsible to a wider electorate (and that this would yield rewards over the years through good stewardship). This would certainly accord with the gap in perceived competence that has been built up in the pandemic, and with the public's pre-existing belief that Scottish governments are the ones that care most about Scotland. In 2014, the Yes campaign's phrase 'A Scottish government working for Scotland' alluded to this, but did not lean fully into the economic dimension. Success would depend on people believing that governments are actually able to bring about economic growth – an untested proposition and one that recent decades may have shaken.

Another option might be to fully embrace an 'alternatives to GDP' approach. This would focus on levels of actual lived wellbeing in Scotland and seek to construct measures of a country's wealth other than those typically used when politicians debate economics. Gross domestic product (GDP) is a measure of the amount of goods and services being bought and sold in a country. It is a terrible measure of the said country's wealth or income but it remains the measure that is most commonly used as shorthand to approximate these concepts. Would this just seem too 'out there' for the nervous voters who won the last referendum? And how would they react if Yes campaigners decided to – tactically or sincerely – state that there might be an economic cost but invite them to consider that the benefits of independence would be worth it? Would this be seen as refreshing honesty or just the thin end of a wedge? This last would be the highest stakes strategy of all.

How the Scottish Government presents its economic case is the most important unknown of the next referendum. A good argument may not be enough to deliver independence alone but a bad one will certainly scupper it, and refighting the last war is not an option.

Uncertainty By Other Means

Choosing the economic case they should put forward is within the Scottish Government's power. But no government is omnipotent. Success also depends on the choices of others. In 2014, the opponents of independence used the currency proposals as a way of casting doubt on the whole prospectus. Listening to the Scottish Government, an independent Scotland would enter into a bilateral deal with the remaining UK government. The two governments would use the pound together, but publishing a currency plan that depended on both sides agreeing was a strategic mistake. All the other side had to do – and did – was say that under no circumstances would they sign up to it if independence went ahead. George Osborne did precisely that in a speech in Edinburgh in February 2014 and was subsequently backed by the opposition. Both conceivable UK administrations had publicly ruled it out. In fact, the very first line of attack from Alistair Darling in the referendum debates was currency. Even if they felt privately that they would have ultimately signed up to it, they were still able to put the Yes campaign on the back foot publicly.

However, to see the lesson here as the need to adopt a more robust currency plan is to miss the bigger picture. While there is an emotional attachment to the pound sterling, the intent of the No campaign was to stir up doubt and uncertainty about independence in general, to challenge the credibility of the public. Independence campaigners need to understand that mass publics are generally risk averse and tailor their strategies accordingly. A thought process of 'Growth Commission, unilateral sterling, job done' is a dangerous mistake to make. This time, the other side will have many fresh sources of uncertainty to tap into, based on the same reality that the Scottish Government is not the only actor who will be able to shape events. The next Yes campaign needs to take this risk seriously.

The 2014 campaign was, by and large, an SNP campaign. The Greens were visible in support but generally accepted that the Scottish Government had a mandate to describe the initial situation of an independent Scotland and did not seek to emphasise the two parties' divisions. Fortunately for the Yes side, the cooperation agreement signed between the parties in August 2021 should deliver a repeat of the strategic unity, albeit this time with greater Green influence.

In 2014, the many grassroots groups that sprung up organically generally also aligned with the official Yes Scotland campaign. Exceptions like the Radical Independence Campaign were vibrant but gained rather little mainstream media attention by comparison. The official campaign had a diverse board but by the end, no one close to the operation was in any doubt that it was being run not from its own headquarters, but from the SNP's.

This old world is gone and it is not coming back. The Yes movement no longer speaks with one voice, though the SNP's remains by far the loudest. In 2021, the Alba Party made a loud entrance to the political stage. Even though they gained only 1.7 per cent of the vote in the 2021 Scottish Parliament elections, they were constantly in the spotlight. A week before the last referendum George Galloway was invited onto stage at the Hydro by the BBC, presumably because he was seen as having box office appeal. Broadcasters regard Alex Salmond similarly and he will undoubtedly be given many platforms.

Even the SNP itself no longer speaks with one voice. Many of those who sympathise with Salmond's views remain in the party. High-profile MPs, such as Joanna Cherry and Angus Brendan Mac-Neil, have their own distinct criticisms of party strategy and followers. In addition, campaigners and commentators who were prominently part of the Yes campaign in 2014 now regularly use their platforms to submit the SNP leadership to sharp criticisms from multiple directions. Lesley Riddoch, Iain MacWhirter, Ruth Wishart, Kevin McKenna – even with the infamous Stuart Campbell of Wings Over Scotland having retired from blogging (for now), the list goes on. All these tensions have been compounded by coming at the same time as an emotive and highly public division over positions taken by the SNP on sensitive equalities issues.

Moreover, since the party has shifted efforts away from the economic case for independence, groups of members advocating unorthodox approaches have surfaced. Many have been given copious space in the pages of *The National*. Some decry GERS as a work of pure fiction, irrespective of its centrality to the 2014 independence case. Another growing group are the proponents of Modern Monetary Theory (MMT), an approach to economics based on using a country's sovereignty over its own currency to absorb and – allegedly – negate the effects of large deficits. To its adherents, it is the most exciting development in economics in decades; to its opponents it sounds a lot like a government paying its bills by printing money. The vacuum left by the quiet shelving of the Growth Commission has given MMT a space in which to grow its support among the SNP membership, though it has not become the position of the party's leadership.

At their worst, the dissidents are, to put it mildly, forthright about their criticisms of party leaders. Yet these leaders are the same people who, if a referendum is indeed called, will be the ones speaking for the official Yes proposition and will need to demonstrate their credibility to the public. Salmond has never shied from the limelight and will be similarly forthright in presenting different positions to those his former party will take. For example, Alba already openly entertains declaring independence without negotiations in extremis and Salmond has suggested renouncing any commitment to national debt accrued by Scotland while part of the UK. Whatever the merits of those policies, they are different to those the Scottish Government will present as the official line and they are unlikely to be the last such colourful interventions.

The SNP may seek to dismiss Alba as a breakaway fringe group made up of the embittered and disaffected. Opponents can reply by pointing Salmond's status as the man who would have been prime minister had the 2014 referendum gone the way the SNP wanted. And if the official Yes campaign finds itself using all its time defending its independence prospectus from what is ostensibly its own side, it will be caught in a mire, rather than free to put its energies to winning over voters – just as it found itself doing with its erstwhile currency plan.

Conclusion

The third unloved UK prime minister in a row, Brexit, and the prospect of endless Tory governments are all boosting the democratic case for independence every day. But the Yes campaign needs to realise the risk that people may yet go into the polling station torn between the merits of both a democratic case for independence and an economic case for the union. The SNP cannot repeat the economic strategy of 2014. Stakes are high: in a referendum campaign, support for a proposition can do down as well as up. And whatever approach the Scottish Government eventually take, they will be faced with an unprecedented level of hostility from those ostensibly on the same side. Will Yes choose and deploy an effective economic case? Will infighting be used to damage credibility, as with the currency debate before? Whether Scotland becomes an independent country or remains in the union depends on how Yes meets these challenges.

References

Ashcroft, M. (2014), 'How Scotland voted, and why': https://lordash-croftpolls.com/2014/09/scotland-voted/

Curtice, J. (2013), 'The Score at Half Time: Trends in Support for Independence':
https://www.scotcen.org.uk/media/270726/SSA-13-The-Score-At-Half-Time.pdf
Survation (2020), Poll for *Progress Scotland*: https://cdn.survation.com/wp-content/uploads/2020/10/19100958/Progress-Scot-land-Data-Tables-October-2020.xlsx

CHAPTER 3

A Future No Campaign:
Terrain and Challenges
Colin Kidd

THE 2014 REFERENDUM campaign was arguably more depressing for the winners than it was for the losers. While the Yes side enjoyed a festival of democracy (the result excepted), matters were less buoyant among No voters, who did not even celebrate victory. From personal experience and from the anecdotes of friends and relatives, I can testify that some of us in the majority that voted No were, on occasion, made to feel like a deviant minority – unpatriotic, immoral, insufficiently Scottish.

The Yes campaign itself behaved with propriety, but there was an oppressively loutish tail, both on social media and on the streets, that served to shut down fruitful discussion, sometimes to the point of intimidation. The most welcome event in 2014 came in the immediate aftermath of the referendum: the service of reconciliation at St Giles' Cathedral attended by Alistair Darling, the head of Better Together, and, to his credit, John Swinney, on behalf of the Scottish Government.

I say this by way of preamble. Although I am a convinced unionist and have serious anxieties about the future prosperity and social fabric of an independent Scotland, I feel very strongly that cross-party civility is more important than the union. As much as I dread independence, no political issue is – or should be – so overriding that it spoils friendships or drives colleagues into separate unionist and nationalist bubbles. It is a pleasure to contribute to a volume that brings together those pro- and anti-independence, as well as those undeclared – respectful disagreement is a vital sign of democratic health. The murder of Jo Cox MP during the Brexit referendum campaign and the incursion of a Trumpist mob into the US Capitol have shown us the fragility of democracy when partisanship turns into siloed tribalism. Can Scotland do better?

Perhaps an unseemly stramash is inevitable. Whereas arguments over matters such as the appropriate rate of taxation are amenable to compromise, two-option referendums on irreducible matters of identity lead inexorably to binary divisions. If only David Cameron had permitted the three-option referendum that Alex Salmond initially wanted in 2011 then, whatever the result, Scotland would be a less divided society than it is today. Indeed, it was my impression between 2016 and 2019 that Brexit significantly lowered the temperature of political debate in Scotland for, at this point, there was a four-way split in the Scottish electorate. Did unionist Remainers have a closer ideological affinity to nationalist Remainers or to unionist Leavers? We were unsure. Nationalist Remainers were surprised to find that about a third of Yes vote were Leavers, whether that meant Brexit or Scottish independence outside of the EU. But the conclusion of a Brexit deal (though not, of course, the Brexit saga) has prompted a return to binary divisions.

An ongoing 50:50 division on the most existential of political questions seems unsustainable in the medium to long-term. We need another referendum – a monsoon to clear the air. Whether the outcome is an independent Scotland or a decisive second puncture that deflates the case for independence, a result – however harmful economically – would at least allow Scots to return to practical matters of governance. There is only so much bandwidth in politics, whether for politicians or for the media and the electorate it informs, and it is difficult if not impossible to tackle the real problems we face in the midst of a continuing debate about nationhood. Among the most compelling of unionist sentiments is a preference to not have an argument about independence at all, given the opportunity costs. Does the very existence of the constitutional debate inhibit thinking about environmental concerns? Is it hard to see economic and social problems straight when we view them, as we do, through unionist or nationalist filters? Many so-called 'unionists' would rather be arguing about something other than the union.

This is not the only asymmetry between the cases for and against independence. Whereas many nationalists are fervently against the union, unionists – a few red, white and blue loyalists excepted – rarely think about the union as such. Scotland's reluctant, reactive and intuitive unionists are far from being the 'Brit Nats' derided by their opponents – at a conscious level, many of them are not even 'unionists'. These indysceptics are not so much for something as against – to a degree, apolitically – something else. Sensibly enough, they don't want politics intruding on more important things, like family, sports, hobbies, volunteering. Scotland might not be the wealthiest place in the world, but plenty of Scots perceive that, in their current circumstances, they enjoy a measure of comfort and personal freedom that many other people crave. Call it complacency if you will, many small 'u' unionists just want to be left alone. The division between nationalists and unionists is, in some measure, a gulf between the politicised and the apolitical.

This serves as a reminder that winning referendums requires very broad coalition building. The No coalition includes many supporters of the three main unionist parties: Conservatives, Labour and Liberal Democrats; most of those born in the mid- 20th century, who have lived their whole lives as part of the UK; and the apolitical. But it might also draw support from the indycurious – even from a smattering of SNP voters – sceptical of the economic prospects of an independent Scotland. While it seems unlikely that No can put together a predominantly young, progressive coalition, it should not spurn the possibility of making the broadest possible range of appeals, and to the most unlikely voters.

Lessons from 2014

Things were different in the 2014 referendum campaign. Better Together started with a substantial lead in the opinion polls and ran a cautious, safety first campaign that saw it safely over the line in the end, although not without a few stumbles. But the campaign had little cause to experiment. There was a premium on not making gaffes. The No campaign's flatness was, in part, structurally determined by the No side's substantial early lead.

Strategic flaws marred the campaign. Labour and the Conservatives appeared to share a common interest in preserving the union; therefore, it was sensible for Alistair Darling to lead a cross-party drive against independence. However, in its very conception Better Together was probably a mistake, albeit an understandable one. Gordon Brown, on the other hand, stood apart from Better Together and tried to run a separate No campaign pitched at Labour voters.

Notwithstanding Brown's efforts, the main consequence of the referendum debates of 2014 was large swathes of the Labour electorate being delivered to the SNP, which made winning a UK general election outright a virtual impossibility for the Labour Party.

The most pressing issue in any post-mortem on the 2014 No campaign relates to claims about EU membership. A second referendum on Scottish independence would take place in the shadow of Brexit. From the outset, any No campaign would need to open with a unionist apology: the argument used in 2014 – that independence would jeopardise EU membership – was not deliberately misleading, but it turned out to be spectacularly wrong. Nevertheless, the unforeseen result of the Brexit referendum in June 2016 made it appear that the No side had deceived the voters in 2014. I know my sentiments here will be unwelcome to many on my own side, but I strongly believe that the next No campaign should apologise for this inadvertent mistake.

Indeed, both sides should apologise for misleading claims made in the previous referendum campaign. The economic prospectus on the Yes side in 2014 envisaged a prosperous, oil-based, independent future for Scotland. Half a decade or so later, that economic case for independence now looks preposterously outdated, not only given vast fluctuations in the price of oil, but also because of the widespread recognition of the threat continued fossil fuel extraction poses to the planet. Should both campaigns be willing to apologise for claims made in 2014, it would enable a refreshing clearing of the air for a more plausible debate next time round.

The Yes side presented independence in 2014 as a straightforward matter of Scots enjoying continued prosperity and a fairer social democratic distribution of resources as an independent nation. There was no recognition that independence involved hard choices, not least a choice between independence and (at the very least) a risk to prosperity. There would be, it was argued, an immediate loss of Barnett largesse and also considerable uncertainty surrounding Scotland's future currency arrangements and – at that stage within EU regulations – about the status of cross-border pension schemes.

Moreover, there was no acknowledgement in 2014 that independence threatened the very argument for self-government. A newly independent state with no credit history would have to establish the credibility of its public finances on the markets. The whims and gusts of the market, not the will of the Scottish people, would determine an independent Scotland's monetary and fiscal priorities for the first few years, possibly first few decades, of independence. The Yes side offered an independent, social democratic Scotland, but it was all too probable that the markets would insist on Thatcherite measures in the first instance. Were the Scottish people forewarned about the bilious independence journey upon which they were about to venture, on choppy seas in a vessel whose seaworthiness had still to be proven? The 2014 campaign was, in many ways, a fraud on the public and the No side's mistaken claims about EU membership were the very least of the false advertisements clouding discussion and decision-making. Indeed, any realistic analysis of Scotland's immediate future economy was casually dismissed as 'talking Scotland down'.

The Next Time and Avoiding the Mistake of Better Together

Is it too much to ask that, next time around, the Yes side advances a soberly honest prospectus? There *are* serious arguments to be made on behalf of independence. We have no guarantees that a post-Brexit government of the UK won't appease its English nationalist base by ending the Barnett formula, or dismantle environmental standards in order to win trade deals with the US. Is the British welfare state best preserved within the UK or as the guiding ideal of an independent Scotland? That is, indeed, an open question. But the Yes option is not risk-free – far from it. The Yes campaign should inform voters that cuts – imposed with the gravest reluctance, not out of Thatcherite dogma – might well be necessary in the early years of independence to maintain fiscal credibility. Nothing would be worse than a narrowly decided vote for independence on a false prospectus, followed by deep austerity, serious falls in the value of savings, and bitter recriminations from deceived Yes voters. Nobody – and I include unionists here – wants independence to be a flop.

But how can we avoid the charge that unionist realism is not 'Project Fear'? I propose that both sides agree to set up a neutral panel of economic experts, all from outside the UK, who would inform the debate. This group would act as a kind of advisory body to the Scottish public, adjudicating on the economic claims and counterclaims of the Yes and No campaigns. Otherwise, I fear the voters will continue to be bamboozled by 'Project Unrealistic Optimism'.

Brexit has destabilised the union, but it has also functioned as a warning beacon. Voters have seen the difficulty faced by the UK in extricating itself from a 45-year-old union. How easy will it be for a small community of five million Scots to forge a new self-governing existence apart from an English state and economy with which Scotland was deeply intertwined for over three hundred years? Voters will want to know what Scotland's future relationship with the rest of the UK will be. They will also be reluctant to buy a pig in a poke: independence without a clear sense of how the negotiations with the remainder of the UK will proceed. There are very strong arguments that negotiations should precede an independence referendum, or that any deal should be concluded with a confirmatory referendum of the sort that was missing from the Brexit debacle.

Brexit has also erected a new obstacle to Scottish independence: the unavoidable corollary of the SNP's policy of independence in the EU is a hard trade border between Scotland and England, the latter the former's biggest market by far. Although neither Scotland nor the rest of the UK would want such a border, the EU would insist upon it as a way of protecting the integrity of the single market. The SNP doesn't have an answer to this, though in the recent Scottish elections, Alex Salmond's Alba Party advanced a more plausible policy for independence: that Scotland would be better advised to join the European Free Trade Area/European Economic Area rather than the EU. As Alba recognises, Brexit has narrowed the scope for a non-scary, non-hard Scexit.

In effect, the very fact of Brexit further restricts the already limited options of an independent Scotland. There is an arguable case to be made that, notwithstanding the absence of full sovereignty, a devolved Scottish government at Holyrood – unconstrained by the need to appease the financial markets and enjoying generous Barnett revenues – currently experiences more real freedom of action than an independent Scotland ever would. By the darkest of unspoken ironies, independence might entail a loss of practical freedom.

If a future referendum comes down to a straight choice between independence and the status quo, it would be very difficult, though not impossible, to make a persuasive case to the voters to stick with the devil they know. On the other hand, the case for the union would become much more attractive if the union itself were to be reformed – if the choice facing Scots was one between two kinds of change: independence, or continued participation in a new, reformed federal Union. This is something that Labour has thought seriously about but there is, alas, little appetite for major constitutional change among Conservatives. Thus far, the obvious open goal of transforming a superannuated, semi-feudal House of Lords into a Senate of the Nations has held little appeal. But will anxieties about going down in history as another Lord North – the prime minister who lost the American colonies – dislodge Boris Johnson's costiveness on constitutional reform? For it is important that Tories at Westminster – slow-learning muscular unionists, above all – appreciate what happened on 18th September 2014, referendum day, when a *sovereign* Scottish nation (whose sovereignty was implicitly conceded by David Cameron's government) decided to remain in what was now clearly a multinational 'union state', though one still to be explicitly federalised.

Next time around, there should be no repeat of Better Together. Rather the pro-Union parties, Labour, Conservatives and Liberal Democrats should each run their own niche campaigns speaking to their own voters. But what about the main No campaign? There is an obvious problem of leadership. Gordon Brown has retired from frontline politics; Ruth Davidson has gone to the House of Lords. For what it's worth, my own hunch is that unionists should make a virtue of the absence of an obvious political leader. Indeed, I would go further. There should be a non-partisan People's Campaign, headed by a nonpolitician, running a populist campaign against Scotland's pro-independence political establishment – not least against the SNP, who for too long have enjoyed the licence to pose as anti-establishment insurgents. My nomination for head of the People's Campaign would be Professor Ronald MacDonald, the expert in monetary policy and exchange rates at Glasgow University. Were MacDonald to head the People's Campaign, it would force the Yes campaign to address the issue over which it has so long and so evasively prevaricated: the currency question.

MacDonald estimates that the Scottish economy's balance of payments deficit would produce a 30–40 per cent depreciation in the Scottish currency within five years of independence. Of course, the technicalities of exchange rate policy are hard to convey to the general public in a campaign. But picture a contrast between two hairdressers, one in Dumfries and the other across the border in Carlisle, both in their thirties, both with a nest egg of £1,000. Speed up the film and watch as one sees her savings depleted by a third.

I envisage a campaign with two roles: the first explicitly political, to win the referendum; the second educative. There is a pressing need to educate the public and the political classes in the realities of modern political economy. Should an independent Scotland have an autonomous central bank? How would an independent Scotland attract capital inflows or build up currency reserves to defend the exchange rate? Discussions about grown-up questions will educate politicians and the public about the serious demands involved in setting up and running an independent state. If independence is the choice of a majority of the Scottish public, then unionists, notwithstanding their anxieties, want it to work.

Who says the Scottish public is too daft to understand such matters, or to grasp nuance? That, to echo a phrase, is talking Scotland down. As teachers, journalists and broadcasters know, there are ways of conveying difficult material to general audiences. With enough smeddum, wit, ingenuity and style behind it, a campaign to preserve the union could be not only educative, but also cool and affirmative. Imagine the scene, an adman's encapsulation of independence and its delusions: a psychedelic hippy trip to the tune – tellingly – of 'A Magic Carpet Ride', ending up the morning after with the detritus of a wild party and shrinking piles of money. Identifying with No is not definitively to don carpet slippers and become a curmudgeonly OAP. It could be about aligning with humour, flair and optimism. Picture another scene, the modernistic skylines of Britain's cities, then up close their youthful, racially-mixed populations: the UK as a young, energetic, multicultural country. Let the SNP beware – a future No campaign, however sceptical of a nationalist utopia, need not be despondently negative.

CHAPTER 4

The Challenge of Independence: Winning Over Unconvinced Scotland
Mark Diffley

REFERENDUM CAMPAIGNS ARE focused on, and often decided by, the group of voters who are initially undecided on the issue. For campaigns on either side, the decision to focus resources, research and effort on this group is both tactical, as they are most likely to be persuaded to their argument, and efficient, as it is seen as the most effective use of limited resources.

However, understanding unconvinced voters – where they are, who they are, what issues are important to them and what will swing their ultimate choice – is no easy feat. Numerically, the pool of undecided voters naturally declines as a referendum draws closer and voters pay more attention and are won over by different messages and policies. This was true in the long referendum campaign which culminated in September 2014.

When the Edinburgh Agreement was signed in October 2012, there were a significant number of undecided voters. Indeed, in the 29 polls measuring binary attitudes to independence during 2013 (Yes versus No), the average proportion of undecided voters was almost one in five (19 per cent). By the time of the referendum itself this had fallen significantly, with the average falling to nine per cent in the 19 polls conducted in September 2014 before the vote. In the interim period, both campaigns concentrated significant resources on attempting to persuade those yet to decide (What Scotland Thinks, 2014).

In this chapter, we briefly consider what happened in the 2014 campaign and what lessons we can draw from that in any future referendum. From there, we examine what we know about undecided voters in terms of their number, characteristics, and attitudes towards the key issues that are likely to sway the outcome of another independence referendum in one direction or the other.

What Happened in 2014?

From the moment the starting gun was fired on the first independence referendum, both Yes Scotland and Better Together understood that the ultimate result depended on each campaign's ability to persuade floating voters (Pike, 2015). As Better Together identified, at the beginning of the campaign, around 40 per cent of voters were committed to voting No, around 30 per cent committed to voting Yes, and the other 30 per cent up for grabs, as we have identified earlier. What both campaigns also did was reverse the long-term downward trend in turnout at electoral events. Turnout at Holyrood elections had been at around half of the electorate since the initial high turnout at the inaugural 1999 election, falling to 49 per cent in 2003, then 52 per cent in 2007 and 50 per cent in 2011. Similarly, at UK general elections, turnout had sunk to 58 per cent in 2001, 61 per cent in 2005 and 64 per cent in 2010 (Hassan, 2014; Sullivan, 2014). So, a turnout of over 84 per cent at the referendum represented somewhat of a triumph of engagement, and turnout at subsequent elections has also trended upwards from the pre-referendum levels, which is a legacy of the referendum peak.

The result of the referendum in September 2014, where 55 per cent voted No and 45 per cent voted Yes, suggests that the three in ten undecided voters at the beginning of the campaign broke fairly evenly between Yes and No. Studies conducted in the wake of the 2014 plebiscite provide plenty of clues to explain what motivated floating voters and the messages they responded to before casting their votes (see Shorthouse, 2014).

Among floating voters, those who ultimately voted Yes did so for a number of reasons, primarily related to a lack of trust in the UK government, the perceived negativity of the No campaign and the perception that a vote for independence would lead to positive change in society. Those who ended up voting No did so overwhelmingly because they felt the risk of independence was too great, although a small minority were won over by the promise of more powers being devolved to Scotland by the UK government. These findings are important, not only because they help understand the 2014 result but also because they offer significant clues to help campaigns in the event of a second referendum.

Who Are the Unconvinced Voters Now?

The traditional way of measuring and understanding the number of undecided voters in terms of constitutional preferences is to ask the binary Yes versus No question in an opinion poll and observe the number of respondents who answer that they are unsure of how they would vote.

While this allows understanding of the number of absolutely undecided voters and how they break down by a range of demographic and geographic factors, it is also limited and offers only a partial understanding. This is because the asking of a binary question does not allow the measurement of nuance in attitudes, which has two disadvantages. Firstly, it means that for those who answer either Yes or No to the binary question it is unclear how strongly held that opinion is or how likely the respondent might be to change their mind, while it also means that for those who are unsure, it is unclear if they are leaning in one direction or the other.

An alternative way to measure attitudes to independence that allows for a greater understanding of undecided voters is to enable polling respondents to express views on a scale from certain independence supporters through to certain supporters of the union.

While this technique was used in canvassing by both campaigns during 2014, it was not prominent in public polling. Its most notable usage in polling since the first referendum has been via the pro-independence think-tank Progress Scotland, which aims to understand the view of undecided voters and what is likely to be important to that group in the event of a second referendum. This is done by allowing respondents to answer a question such as: 'On a scale of nought to ten where nought means "I completely oppose Scotland becoming an independent country" and ten means "I completely support Scotland becoming an independent country" what number would you consider yourself to be?'

Analysis of this data is instructive in enabling a deeper understanding of undecided voters. To begin with, it illustrates that there are probably more undecided voters than polling of the binary Yes/No question suggests. In total, 23 per cent of voters place themselves between three and seven on the scale, meaning that nearly a quarter of voters do not have strong, fixed positions and are, to some extent, persuadable on the independence question. This means that when another referendum is called, around one million voters would be open-minded about the outcome. Analysis of the available data allows a greater understanding of this population, who and where they are, and what issues are likely to be important to them in a future campaign.

Polling analysis indicates the direction of travel for those who are undecided on the independence question. Around four in ten voted No in the 2014 vote, while around 35 per cent voted Yes and the remainder either chose not to vote or were too young to vote in 2014. The marginally greater movement away from the unionist No position in the period since the first independence referendum is consistent with the findings from polling on the binary Yes/No question since 2014 which shows movement towards Yes from the 45 per cent to 55 per cent result then.

As far as the demographic and geographic spread of undecided voters is concerned, much can be gauged from this research data. Women are more likely than men, by about 3:2, to be part of this cohort of undecided voters, reinforcing the broader sweep of polling evidence that the proportion of pro-union voters, more likely to be women in the 2014 referendum, has since fallen marginally. In terms of the age profile, the youngest voters, aged 16–24, are somewhat over-represented in the undecided cohort, compared to their representation in the population as a whole and will be a key group to win over in any future campaign. All older age groups are represented broadly in line with their presence in the population as a whole.

The geographic spread of the undecided electorate is both interesting and insightful for future campaigns. Essentially, undecided voters are concentrated in the central, urban centres of Scotland. Analysis by parliamentary region illustrates that around one-third of undecided voters live in the Glasgow and Lothian regions, significantly higher than the 27 per cent of Scots who live in those regions overall. Conversely, undecided voters are significantly underrepresented in the south of Scotland region, reinforcing the long-held finding that this remains the most pro-union area of the country.

Somewhat surprisingly, given what we know about the relationship between views on the constitutional issue and support for the different political parties, the profile of undecided voters covers the three main parties, with the SNP accounting for around 45 per cent of floating constitutional voters who state support for a party. More predictably, the vast majority of those voters are leaning towards support for independence (six and seven on the nought to ten scale) but remain open-minded. And although around one in five unconvinced voters support the Conservatives, the vast majority of that group are leaning towards the union (three and four on the nought to ten scale) as would be expected. Labour voters are significantly more likely than SNP and Conservative supporters to be at the mid-point of the nought to ten scale, reflecting less of an ideological outlook on the independence question among Labour voters.

What Do Unconvinced Voters Think About the Key Issues of a Future Referendum?

We know from studies conducted in the wake of the 2014 referendum that the three overwhelming key reasons that No voters gave for their decision were because they felt British and valued the union; believed there were unanswered questions about independence; and felt that Scotland would be worse off economically (Henderson, 2015). On the Yes side, the four key reasons given were to ensure that Scotland always got the government for which it votes; their disaffection with the 'Westminster system'; their belief that independence was the 'natural state' of nations like Scotland; and because they felt that an independent Scotland would be better off economically (though they were far smaller in number than those who felt an independent Scotland would be worse off economically). The other key issue that will affect the outcome of another referendum is Brexit, as polling has shown it has already had a significant impact on attitudes to independence and public services, in particular the NHS, which has grown in importance for voters as a result of the COVID pandemic.

Taking these issues together, it is likely that there will be three key themes that will dominate a second referendum: the impact of Brexit; governance (the level of government that makes key policy decisions); and Scotland's economic future. The outcome of another referendum is likely to rest on which campaign persuades the majority of the undecided cohort of voters on those key themes, and there is significant polling and research evidence to indicate the views of undecided voters on said themes. For example, given the demographic and geographic make-up of undecided voters, it is unsurprising that the majority are against Brexit and so this is likely to be of benefit to the pro-independence campaign, should this issue still be of key salience to undecided voters at the time of another referendum (Curtice, 2020).

This is reinforced by Progress Scotland research, which indicates the views of floating voters and the impact of Brexit on Scotland. Firstly, the proportion of undecided voters who think that Brexit will be bad for the Scottish economy in the long-term (more than four in ten) outweighs those who think it will bring economic benefits by nearly 2:1. Secondly, while it is true that the 45 per cent of undecided voters who report that Brexit has altered their opinions on independence contains those who voted No and Yes in 2014, there are significantly more who voted No and are since changing their minds, thereby benefitting the pro-independence campaign. In addition to these changing attitudes towards independence, around six in ten undecided voters think that Brexit makes independence more likely, compared to around one in ten who think the opposite. So, the issue of Brexit would appear to be one that works in the favour of independence support, as far as persuading undecided voters is concerned. The issue of governance, and voter views on which tier of government should be responsible for taking different policy decisions, was thrown into sharp focus by the COVID-19 pandemic and the lockdowns introduced in order to prevent its spread and protect health and social care services. For the first time in the devolution period, the Scottish Government and the first minister were making day-to-day decisions on immediate issues of life and death – impacting health, personal freedom, and the economy. Opinion research conducted throughout the period showed high levels of satisfaction in how the Scottish Government and First Minister handled the crisis, in contrast to views of the UK government and the Prime Minister. The impact was to push up support for independence.

Polling data on the governance issue among undecided voters reveals some contrasting opinions. The vast majority, around eight in ten, support the statement that 'control over all decisions affecting people in Scotland should be made by the Scottish Parliament/Government, regardless of which political party is in power'. This view is held regardless of whether the current undecided voter backed Yes or No in 2014. Similarly, the vast majority of floating voters support decisions about Scotland's relationship with the EU being taken by the Scottish Government. However, views on defence and foreign affairs are less clear cut. On this issue, a greater proportion agree than disagree with the status quo proposition that 'decisions over defence and foreign affairs affecting Scotland should continue to be made by the UK Parliament/Government.'

This suggests that, in principle, the issue of governance should play to the pro-independence campaign in a future referendum but those who argue in favour of the union are likely to find support on the specific issue of defence and foreign policy.

As we noted earlier, the key challenge that faced the Yes campaign in 2014 was persuading enough voters that an independent Scotland would thrive economically. While the period since has been marked with some increased support for independence, it is clear that the issue of the economy will continue to be a significant challenge to a future pro-independence campaign.

The potential prize for that campaign is clear in that the vast majority of floating voters report that they would vote in favour of independence if they were convinced that it would be good for the Scottish economy. In other words, the economy would appear to be a significant barrier to persuading the majority of floating voters.

It is, however, clear that the scale of this challenge is significant. Almost half of undecided voters report uncertainty about whether they think the Scottish economy would benefit in the long-term from independence, albeit that more undecided voters think that an independent Scotland would benefit compared to those who think it would not. The economic argument in relation to floating voters remains one that is a challenge for a future pro-independence campaign.

Conclusions

While it is unclear when, or indeed if, there will be a second referendum on the issue of independence, it is likely that neither side will enter the campaign with real confidence of the outcome. It is also clear that voters in Scotland are more open-minded towards the issue than the polls measuring binary Yes versus No attitudes would suggest. It is likely that between a fifth and a quarter of voters have not made their mind up on the issue, meaning that there would be significant uncertainty surrounding the outcome.

It is fair to say that a mixture of issues around governance, views of Scotland's economic future and the impact of Brexit are set to be the key issues that will be of greatest importance to undecided voters and, therefore, sway the outcome of a future referendum.

Research on the views of floating voters points to both the strengths and potential weaknesses of the respective campaigns. In order to maximise opportunities to persuade undecided voters, a pro-independence campaign in a future referendum should concentrate on the potential downsides of Brexit, issues of governance and having key decisions made by the Scottish Government and Scottish Parliament, and address the issue of the economy in an independent Scotland. Pro-union campaigners are likely to continue to benefit from voter uncertainty about the economy in an independent Scotland and should continue to emphasise the perceived benefits of the UK deciding policy on defence and foreign affairs.

References

Curtice, J. (2020), *Is Brexit Fuelling Support for Scottish Independence?*, Glasgow: What Scotland Thinks.

Hassan, G. (2014), *Caledonian Dreaming: The Quest for a Different Scotland*, Edinburgh: Luath Press.

Henderson, A. (2015), *Scottish Referendum Study*, Edinburgh: Centre on Constitutional Change.

Pike, J. (2015), *Project Fear: How An Unlikely Alliance Left A Kingdom United But A Country Divided*, London: Biteback Publishing.

Shorthouse, R. (2014), 'Key take-aways from the Better Together Campaign', *Speech by Better Together Head of Communications*, accessed at: https://www.youtube.com/watch?v=_UjKkVdiLtU

Sullivan W. (2014), *The Missing Scotland: Why Over A Million Scots Choose Not To Vote And What It Means For Our Democracy*, Edinburgh: Luath Press.

What Scotland Thinks (2021), *Opinion Polls*, accessed at: https://whatscotlandthinks.org/opinion-polls/

Section Two: The Legal and Political Process

CHAPTER 5

Unavoidable Challenges for the UK and Scottish Governments
Ciaran Martin

THE NEXT PHASE in the struggle for the future of Scotland is likely to begin with a prolonged game of constitutional chess between the UK and Scottish governments. There are two profound challenges affecting each side differently, existentially, and more or less in equal measure.

The first is the chasm between London and Edinburgh's respective interpretations of what Scotland's generally accepted right to self-determination means in practice; the second, obstacles to coherent presentation of their respective visions of independence and continuing union.

Underpinning both challenges is the sheer novelty of the proposal for Scottish independence. If Scotland ends up becoming an independent sovereign nation, the circumstances will be exceptional. Consensual secession from within an existing state is largely unknown in modern times. Most new states have been established in one of the following ways: violent rebellion from within part of an existing state; decolonisation (either following a violent campaign, one of peaceful agitation, or voluntary retreat from empire); reshaping of borders following major international conflict, or the collapse of a multinational non-democratic state like the Soviet Union or Yugoslavia. The Czechoslovak option where the existing state was, in effect, abolished is not available to Scotland (Crawford and Boyle, 2013). It is hard to think of any of the world's 193 countries that have come into being in the way Scotland plans to. Norway's separation from Sweden in 1905 provides perhaps the best, if now distant, comparators.

A Right to Secede, But No Way of Doing So

The UK has no rulebook for resolving the independence question. This distinguishes Britain from Canada, the only other Western democracy which accepts the right of its constituent parts to break away but since 2000 has had clear rules on how that can be done (Lajoie, 2013). This gives rise to the first major challenge: the absence of an agreed path for Scotland to decide on independence.

There is of course a direct precedent to draw on from the arrangements put in place for the 2014 vote; however, the Westminster government has emphatically rejected replicating this consensual approach, which poses a very significant challenge for the Scottish Government. The best illustration of this is the ultimately otiose debate over the legality of any referendum bill passed by the Holyrood Parliament, following Westminster's refusal of a request for the same Order-in-Council under Section 30 of the 1998 Scotland Act used to provide for the 2014 referendum.

There is much debate amongst legal scholars as to whether such legislation would be deemed lawful in the event of an inevitable court challenge from either a private citizen or the UK government, or an unlawful attempt to extend the powers of the Scottish Parliament (McHarg and McCorkindale, 2019; Tierney, 2017). The answer is unknowable until the courts opine, though the balance of opinion seems to predict defeat for the Scottish Government.

Ultimately it doesn't matter – this is a political issue, not a legal one. The importance attached to the issue of the legality of a referendum held without Westminster's agreement is mistaken because the goal of the SNP is independence, not holding a referendum on it. The form of independence sought, as already noted, is highly unusual: it is entirely dependent on the consent of the British state, and the British state has an inexhaustible list of options for withholding that consent.

Should the courts block Holyrood's referendum, there is no means of testing Scotland's consent, so the UK government faces no mandate for independence negotiations. Should, however, the Scottish Government win its court case, Westminster could change the law to clarify beyond doubt that Holyrood has no referendum power. Alternatively, unionist parties could boycott the referendum, alongside a UK government declaration that it would pay no heed to the outcome.

What then would the Scottish Government do? Its quest for lawful, democratic, parliamentary means of pursuing independence would be at an end. It would be patently unlawful and unconstitutional for Scotland to declare independence unilaterally and few countries, if any, would recognise it. Scotland would face the same rejection from the international community as that experienced by the aspirant Irish republic of 1919. The notion that the US, or a single European nation, would recognise secession from the UK in the face of objections from its government is even more preposterous than it was a century ago – a state that is not recognised by other states is not a state at all.

The hard truth for the Scottish Government is that without the acquiescence of the British government, the entire basis of its plans for independence collapses. Therefore, a dispassionate analysis devoid of any wider political or democratic context would appear to hand all the advantage to London and its objective of maintaining the union. Indeed, political stubbornness enforced by unmistakable legal supremacy might well prove to be a successful short-term strategy for a single administration to get through its time in office without losing the union. The bald cynicism behind this way of thinking was set out with striking candour by the former Chancellor George Osborne, architect of the UK government's approach to 2014 (Osborne, 2021).

However, the politics of stubborn refusal carry profound risks for the British state because they ignore what the British Union is and what has sustained it over time. The reason for the genuinely exceptional position of the UK is because of the history of the Anglo–Scottish union as a partnership between nations, sustained in the democratic era by the consent not just of the British people as a whole but the constituent parts of it separately. From the moment of union, whilst a distinctively British set of shared interests and sense of Britishness emerged and grew, this was never at the expense of either separate Scottish institutions in key areas, or Scotland's sense of national identity (Devine, 2012). Indeed from the mid-17th century onwards, one can discern the 'unionism nationalism' described by Graeme Morton that is, politics based on getting the best deal for Scotland within the UK and as such acknowledging Scotland's national distinctiveness, as well as the implicitly accepted need for the union to continue to secure the support of its constituent parts (Morton, 1999).

This implicitly accepted Union of consent became more explicit over the course of the 20th century. Before the First World War, the UK was on the brink of civil war over what would now be called modest devolution for Ireland – the union with that island being one unquestionably not based on consent. Scotland's evident contentment within the union in the course of the preceding century and a half meant that the question of its consent barely arose; however, since the departure of most of Ireland over a century ago, the right of Scotland, Wales or Northern Ireland to leave the UK, in principle, has become more and more accepted. The concept of self-determination based on consent has twice been put into law: permanently for Northern Ireland in the 1998 Agreement, enshrined in an international treaty; temporarily for Scotland in the 2012 Edinburgh Agreement and subsequent referendum legislation. It has been articulated by successive prominent British political leaders, most strikingly by arch unionist Margaret Thatcher in her memoirs (Thatcher, 1993).

It is this Union of consent that the UK government is on the brink of ending. Before the 2021 election its position was revealed, not in policy papers but in a series of seemingly ad hoc statements by senior ministers. The net impact of those statements was to rule out any lawful or democratic path to a referendum on independence for an unspecified period, stretching into decades regardless of any and all election results. As such, whilst paying lip service to the principle of Scotland's right to choose independence but simultaneously blocking any and all possible paths to it, the UK government was, in effect, on the cusp of ending the union of consent and changing it into a union enforced by law (Martin, 2021).

Should it choose to continue to maintain a legal blockade on Scotland's right to a referendum on independence indefinitely, the UK government would create an obvious and, in the short term, insurmountable obstacle for the Scottish Government. It also would create a more subtle, but no less existential, problem for itself in the long term. A change in the union from one based on consent to one based on law is not something Scotland has agreed to, nor is likely to. As such, a prolonged period of obstruction could risk increasing nationalist sentiment. In the long run, this could shift the national mood in Scotland towards independence. Likely court proceedings over a referendum bill provide an obvious example where such sentiment could be stoked – a finding against Holyrood could emerge in language that makes it plain that Scotland does not enjoy 'nationhood' in any meaningful sense. For example, the case in the High Court in Belfast, where the court held that part of the Act of Union had, in effect, been repealed by the enactment of the Northern Ireland protocol, demonstrated that powerful political arguments could emerge from court defeats. Ultimately, moving the union from one of consent to one of law could destroy the consent needed for the union to be sustained.

There are signs that the UK government is beginning to realise this risk: remarks ruling out a referendum for the decades have noticeably stopped emanating from ministerial lips. There appears to be a sense that this political issue, ultimately, needs to be decided in the polling booth but when and how remains unagreed.

The near-perfect split in popular votes cast between nationalist and unionist parties in the 2021 election provided neither side with an incentive to push forward at speed. Ultimately, both sides will want to move their numbers away from that 50:50 split and towards something resembling the 'settled will' of the Scottish people before testing it. That means both governments will in effect be leading political campaigns that set out their version of the future.

What Does Independence Mean? And What Does 'Continuing Union' Mean?

Here, and in any future referendum campaign, problems arise for both sides. For the Scottish Government, the challenge is once again obvious and fundamental: providing answers to the toughest questions on post-independence arrangements that hindered them in the 2014 debate, such as currency, EU membership, fiscal sustainability, national defence, and so on. The currency question remains. Brexit, and the form it took, gives rise to even more fundamental questions about the nature of a land border with England.

Setting out credible plans for tackling any of these issues is a considerable challenge, though one any movement serious about creating a credible state must meet. The bigger intellectual and practical problem for Scottish nationalism is that many of the toughest questions about the consequences of independence are unanswerable in advance of the referendum. That is because the arrangements for most of the big questions facing an independent Scotland require agreement with someone else – the remaining UK, the EU, or NATO for example.

None of those negotiations would start until after Scotland voted to Leave, and some of the most crucial wouldn't start until after independence took effect. It is highly likely, for example, that talks on EU accession would not begin until independence has been achieved (the same would apply to NATO). This would mean that the bilateral independence negotiations with the UK would make cross-border arrangements that might then change as and when Scotland joined the EU.

The nationalist strategy in 2014 was to assert that the negotiations with the UK government would be smooth and productive, as it was in the interests of the remainder of the union to reach an amicable, smooth deal with as little change and disruption as possible. If the history of the union has been one of 'unionist nationalism', this is also true of the Yes campaign's 2014 pitch, most noticeable in Alex Salmond's famous 'six union' speech, where he set out five unions Scotland would be staying in (monarchical, defence, European, social, and currency), as well as the political one it would be leaving (Kidd, 2021).

It didn't work, noticeably over currency. But such an approach *did* work for Brexiteers in 2016; however, the subsequent period proved a manifesto that assumes the acquiescence, generosity and goodwill of the partner one has just chosen to leave provides a terrible basis for governing. German carmakers, it turned out, did not prioritise the UK over the integrity of the single market, and the EU was not in the mood to do the quickest, easiest trade deal in history – nor was the US for that matter.

It is possible that a UK government would show the sort of generosity that it showed to John Jay in negotiating the Treaty of Paris in 1783 or to the Irish Free State in the 1920s, based on the self-interest of having a successful and friendly ally. But a prospectus for Scottish independence that presumed such generosity would be a dishonest and unsound one. In particular, while it is likely that constructive negotiations would begin over areas like defence cooperation (because of the obvious shared interest and the pragmatic attitude of military and security chiefs), there is every chance that a humiliated English polity would be in an ungenerous mood over border arrangements with Scotland, a country on which it is not heavily dependent economically.

In 2014, unionism successfully weaponised uncertainty as an argument against independence. This is likely to be a feature of any future campaign. Already, there are frequent demands for facts and more information about the future from unionists. This is a powerful tactic in a political campaign. Advocates of independence will need to find ways of convincing sceptics that they can competently meet the challenges of independence without relying on implausible claims about matters outside their control, and specifically the goodwill and agreement of others that they cannot guarantee.

However, and again less visibly but no less powerfully, unionism faces a far greater challenge selling the continuing union than it did in 2014. Since the last referendum, a narrow English and Welsh majority, confirmed by an England-based Commons majority in the second of two subsequent elections, has entirely remade the British state in the face of explicit and widespread opposition from within Scotland. Part of this stridently British nationalist project has been the relegation of the national ambiguities and complexities within the UK in favour of a traditional, Diceyan and highly contestable notion of 'sovereignty' (Keating, 2021). It is embodied in, amongst other things, a deep governing hostility to devolution.

This marks a very significant difference to the situation in 2014, where all three UK-wide unionist parties could credibly sell the late 20th century devolution settlement – substantial and increased autonomy for Scotland within the UK – as the best of both worlds. That is no longer credible when even the profoundly unionist Labour First Minister of Wales Mark Drakeford speaks of a government 'hostile to devolution'.

Pro-devolution, 'progressive' unionism reached its emotional and cultural high point in the 2012 Olympics and has gone rapidly downhill from there (Andrews, 2021). Unlike in 2014, a further extension of the constitutional settlement via more powers, including a move to a fully federal UK, appears unworkable and undeliverable (Martin, 2021). In the meantime, the governing Conservatives appear more and more willing to pursue what has been widely termed as 'muscular unionism'. This sees devolution itself, not the profound divergence of political choices between Scotland and England, as the root of the crisis in the union and seeks to contain and reverse it. The Internal Market Act is its signature achievement so far, with its provisions to set aside the regulations of the devolved administrations where

England regulates differently and, for the first time in the union's history, consciously play down the national identity of Scotland within the UK (Weatherill, 2021).

If successfully implemented, muscular unionism would extinguish Scottish nationalism in a way that devolution is never likely to; however the considerable problem is that it seems to be hugely unattractive to the Scottish electorate. Whatever the settled will of the Scottish people is, it is not muscular unionism. Paradoxically, this provides an opportunity for the Scottish Government and the wider independence movement that was not available in 2014, as muscular unionism seems to be the revealed preference, if not yet always the governing approach, of the UK government. In the next phase of the debate on the future of Scotland, expect more attention to focus not just on what the Scottish Government thinks independence would mean, but also what sort of union Scotland is being encouraged to stay in by the UK government. The best of both worlds may no longer be on offer.

References

Andrews, L. (2021), 'The Forward March of Devolution Halted', *Political Quarterly*, accessed at: https://onlinelibrary.wiley.com/doi/epdf/10.1111/1467-923X.13044

Crawford, J. and Boyle, A. (2013), *Referendum on the independence of Scotland: international law aspects,* London: The Stationery Office, accessed at: https://assets.publishing.service.gov.uk/government/uploads/system/uploads/attachment_data/file/79408/Annex_A.pdf

Devine, T.M. (2012), *The Scottish Nation*, London: Penguin, 3rd edn.

Keating, M. (2021), *State and Nation in the United Kingdom. The Fractured Union*, Oxford: Oxford University Press.

Kidd, C. (2021), 'New Unions for Old', *London Review of Books*, 4 March, accessed at: https://www.lrb.co.uk/the-paper/v43/no5/colin-kidd/new-unions-for-old

Lajoie, A. (2013), *The Clarity Act in Context*, in Gagnon, A. G. (ed.), *Quebec: State and Society*, Toronto: University of Toronto Press.

McHarg, A. and McCorkindale, C. (2019), *Constitutional Pathways to a Second Scottish Independence Referendum*, London: UK Constitutional Law Association, accessed at: https://ukconstitutionallaw.org/2020/01/13/

chris-mccorkindale-and-aileen-mcharg-constitutional-pathways-to-a-second-scottish-independence-referendum/

Martin, C. (2021), *Resist, Reform or Re-run: Short and Long-Term Reflections on Scotland and independence referendums*, Oxford: Blavatnik School of Government, University of Oxford, accessed at: https://www.bsg.ox.ac.uk/research/publications/resist-reform-or-re-run-short-and-long-term-reflections-scotland-and

Morton, G. (1999), *Unionist Nationalism: Governing Urban Scotland, 1830-60*, East Linton: Tuckwell.

Osborne, G. (2021), 'Unleashing nationalism has made the future of the UK the central issue', *Evening Standard*, 19 January, accessed at: https://www.standard.co.uk/comment/nationalism-union-brexit-b900299.html

Thatcher, M. (1993), *The Downing Street Years*, London: Harper Collins.

Tierney, S. (2017), *A second Scottish independence referendum without a s.30 order? A legal question that demands a political answer*, Edinburgh: Centre for Constitutional Change, University of Edinburgh, accessed at: https://ukconstitutionallaw.org/2017/03/13/stephen-tierney-a-second-independence-referendum-in-scotland-the-legal-issues/

Weatherill, S. (2021), *Will the United Kingdom Survive the Internal Market Act?*, London: UK in a Changing Europe, accessed at: https://ukandeu.ac.uk/wp-content/uploads/2021/05/Will-the-United-Kingdom-survive-the-United-Kingdom-Internal-Market-Act.pdf

CHAPTER 6

No Magic Bullets: Legal Issues in Achieving Independence and a Referendum
Andrew Tickell

DOES HOLYROOD HAVE the legislative competence to introduce an independence referendum on its own authority? This legal question has been bouncing around Scottish politics since before the Scotland Act first became law in 1998, shifting in and out of focus as the prospect of a first – then a second – referendum on Scotland's constitutional future has risen and receded. In 2012, the Edinburgh Agreement allowed both the Scottish and UK governments to sidestep this question, establishing a temporary constitutional platform for the first independence referendum without pre-committing to recognising any future polls (Tickell, 2016). The UK government's reluctance to sanction a second referendum and the election of a second pro-independence majority in Holyrood on clear manifesto commitments to legislate for a poll, has given this old question new life and new significance in 2022.

Independence and Legislative Competence

The legal answer to this opening question is not rooted in any antique features of the Act of Union, or political claims about the popular sovereignty of Scots, or even the application and implications of self-determination under international law. From the narrow perspective of domestic law, which will be applied by the courts if a referendum bill is subject to legal challenge, the question is essentially one of statutory interpretation. The Scotland Act 1998 established the Scottish Parliament. It did so using a 'reserved powers' model: rather than enumerating what Holyrood *can* do, the 1998 Act instead lists everything Holyrood *cannot* do. In Schedule 4, there is a list of statutes MSPs cannot repeal or amend, and in Schedule 5, a longer list of 'reserved matters' is set out, covering everything from the control of nuclear and biological weapons, to the date of Easter. The 'Union of the Kingdoms of Scotland and England' is one of the 'aspects of the constitution' reserved under Schedule 5. Referendums, by contrast, are not. MSPs exercised their legislative competence in this field to pass the Referendums (Scotland) Act in 2020, which sets out standard franchise and campaign rules for any future referendum passed by Holyrood.

Amongst other restrictions, the Scotland Act provides that if provisions of a bill 'relate to a reserved matter,' they are 'not law' (1998 Act, s 29(1) and (2)(b)). In determining whether or not a bill 'relates to a reserved matter,' judges are directed to consider its 'purpose and effect in all the circumstances' (1998 Act, s 29(3)). The legislation simultaneously requires the court to read provisions of any Holyrood legislation subject to legal challenge 'as narrowly as is required for it to be within competence, if such a reading is possible' (1998 Act, s 101(2)).

The concept of 'legislative competence' has a few guardrails written into the Scotland Act. A minister or MSP introducing a new bill must 'state their view' that the proposals fall within the Parliament's competence (1998 Act, s 31(1)). The Presiding Officer must also decide whether they believe the bill complies with the limitations written into the Scotland Act on the basis of independent legal advice (1998 Act, s 31(2)). No legal consequences flow from the Presiding Officer's adverse opinion, though an adverse statement is likely to sound politically in the debate on the bill. The Scotland Act gives both UK and Scottish law officers the opportunity to refer a bill to the Supreme Court before it receives royal assent where they believe there is a question about its competence. This power has been used on three occasions, all since 2016. The Lord Advocate, the Advocate General for Scotland and Attorney General have a window of four weeks to make the Supreme Court referral, failing which the legislation progresses to royal assent (1998 Act, s 33(1) and (2)). Referral interrupts this process, preventing a bill from becoming law unless and until its provisions are upheld by the UK Supreme Court.

After a bill receives royal assent, anyone with a 'sufficient interest' is entitled to seek judicial review of Acts of the Scottish Parliament in the Court of Session (*AXA v Lord Advocate*, 2011). While the UK Supreme Court is the ultimate arbiter of Holyrood's powers, this kind of legal challenge takes considerably more time to resolve than a direct referral under section 33, and will usually involve a judgement of both the Outer and Inner Houses of the Court of Session before the Supreme Court can consider the controversy. During the period of such a challenge, the courts generally suspend the implementation of the act until it has been determined to be *intra vires*. In a practical sense, this means that a referendum ordinated by the Scottish Parliament will not take place until any live legal challenges are resolved.

Pulling these strands together, would an independence referendum bill survive scrutiny? Does it 'relate to reserved matters'? What would its 'purpose and effect' be in all the circumstances? There are different and credible ways of describing this. Take the purpose of an independence referendum bill first. What is it for? Given the Scottish Government's political commitments, unionists tend to present the legal purpose of any independence bill as the destruction of Britain, and credibly so. But why look at it this way? For example, before the 2014 poll, every MSP in Holyrood supported the legislation setting up the legal framework for the referendum, whether they intended to campaign Yes or No. Would it make sense to say that Ruth Davidson's 'object and purpose' in voting for these referendum bills was to deliver Scottish independence? Do you really think Johann Lamont was endorsing separatist principles by agreeing that a referendum on our constitutional future should take place?

Similar observations obtain in considering the legal effect of a referendum bill. The case against Holyrood having the power to ask the question largely assumes that such a referendum would result in a Yes vote and, therefore, break up Britain. But why should this be assumed at all? Go back to 2014 again – what was the legal effect of the 2014 referendum? The public were consulted, a majority view was expressed, and a few campaigners found themselves fined for breaching campaign finance rules. But beyond this, what did the first referendum actually change? What rights did it create or eliminate? What rules of law did it rewrite? Like Brexit, the first independence referendum was not binding in any legal sense, though both had profound political effects.

Even if 2014 had produced a pro-independence majority, additional Westminster legislation would have been required to bring the union to an end and free Holyrood from the constraints of the

Scotland Act. Looked at this way, the legal effect of legislation enabling a referendum is extremely limited. These are the kind of arguments we can expect to be aired in any legal challenge to a referendum bill that is passed by the Scottish Parliament without the UK government's agreement. Whether you hold your brief for the UK government or the Scottish Government, both have a stateable case.

All of this could be avoided if the UK government followed the precedent of 2012 and made an order under section 30 of the Scotland Act to put Holyrood's legislative competence beyond doubt. Section 30 is perhaps the most misunderstood provision of public law in Scotland. Ewick and Silbey (1998) use the concept of 'legal consciousness' to describe the bundle of ideas and understandings that constitute how people understand, interpret, and experience the law, legal processes, and legal institutions. This 'legal consciousness' is not the technical knowledge of professional actors, but rather it aims to capture non-expert attitudes and perceptions of law and legal institutions and explain how these are socially generated, sustained, and reproduced.

Sometimes, social ideas about law are inaccurate. Legal consciousness studies concede they may be technically incorrect but often in interesting – and more importantly, socially significant – ways. Whether the interpretation of the Scotland Act 1998 is correct or not, if a particular understanding of constitutional law gains consistent social purchase, shaping perceptions, debates and the field of actions which seem open to political actors, then that constitutional (mis)understanding is likely to exert force in our social and political life. Scottish constitutional law furnishes a good example of the operation of this kind of constitutional consciousness in section 30 of the Scotland Act, and social perceptions of what it is about.

Ron Davies famously said devolution should be understood as a 'process, not an event.' This logic is reflected in the substance of the Scotland Act itself. Since 1998, a series of changes have been made by the Scotland Act of 2012 and of 2016, but most recently and most dramatically by the European Union (Withdrawal) Act 2018. Primary legislation in Westminster is often an unwieldy and time-consuming way to adjust the limits of Holyrood's legislative competence. Reflecting this, section 30 of the Scotland Act incorporated a legal mechanism through which the Government in Westminster could change what is and is not reserved using Orders in Council. These are effectively statutory instruments, formally made by the Queen on the advice of the Privy Council, and represent a way for the Government to alter the devolution framework without asking MPs to vote on a bill. Section 30 of the Scotland Act contains no mention of referendums, or independence; however, Section 30 was used after the Edinburgh Agreement temporarily to put, beyond doubt, that the Scottish Parliament did have the time-limited and conditional legal authority to legislate for the first independence referendum, tweaking Schedule 5's list of reserved matters. These amendments to Schedule 5 were repealed by Westminster in 2016 (Scotland Act 2016, s 10(5)).

Crowdfunder Challenges

Considered from a wider social and political perspective, however, this technical account of what section 30 of the Scotland Act is about jars with dominant social and political perceptions and representation of the idea of a Section 30 Order. In Scottish political discourse – whether pro or anti-independence – 'requesting a Section 30 Order' has become synonymous with being granted permission by the UK government to conduct an independence referendum. Similar framings regularly appear on the pages of Scottish newspapers and from the mouths of Scottish broadcasters. In the wider constitutional consciousness, section 30 has evolved from a technical provision allowing changes to devolution without primary legislation into a constitutionally-specific mechanism through which permission for independence referendums can be granted or refused. This (mis)understanding of the law at once reinforces the notion that the UK government inevitably has a veto power over independence referendums, but also positions the Scottish Government in what can appear to be a rather supplicatory position. This impression works for – and against – the UK government's position politically.

The strong purchase of this second, social understanding of section 30 is best demonstrated by considering the case of *Keatings v Advocate General for Scotland,* This was the subject of three decisions by the Court of Session in 2020 and 2021, which ultimately concluded that the case was 'abstract, hypothetical and premature.' Originally pitched by organiser Martin Keatings as '*The Scottish People v the UK Government on Indyref2,*' the legal action was ultimately badged on social media as the 'People's Action on Section 30.'

In the initial pitch for funds – which attracted £43,658 – Keatings framed the action as a mechanism to compel the UK government to make an order under section 30 'should they fail to acquiesce to a formal request by the Scottish Government.' Legally, this approach was entirely misconceived, rooted in the social rather than technical understanding of what section 30 of the 1998 Act was about.

The cause of action evolved significantly in the light of a legal opinion from Aidan O'Neill QC. In a second Crowdfunder – which pulled in over £225,000 – the case evolved from a legal challenge to the UK government's refusal to amend Schedule 5. This was to an ordinary action seeking a declarator that a future hypothetical bill providing for an independence referendum would be within Holyrood's legislative competence under the Scotland Act, when a hypothetical bill was introduced and voted on by MSPs. Although the legal action kept the reference to section 30 in its socials and persistent pitches for more funding, in legal terms, the case now had nothing to do with this section of the Scotland Act. It was prematurely arguing the more fundamental point that an independence referendum bill might be within competence – the very point the Scottish Government is likely to find itself defending if it introduces a referendum bill this parliamentary session.

The powerful appeal of Keatings' case is reflected in the volume of money ingathered to fund what was a highly speculative, and highly costly, piece of litigation. Parallel research into the scale of online crowdfunding in Scotland suggests the People's Action on Section 30 has comfortably outstripped every other legal action in Scottish history, in terms of the amount of cash crowdfunded and fruitlessly spent on it. This financial and political commitment to a case that was technically doomed from the outset is only explicable by understanding the legally misconceived but deeply embedded social framing of section 30 in the constitutional consciousness of some pro-independence activists. Section 30 has come to represent a locus for their frustration with the UK government, but also for hostility to the Scottish Government's commitment to an agreed referendum process with UK government recognition.

In court, the crowdfunders secured the kind of legal representations they had paid for: Aidan O'Neill's submissions – in echo of his performance in *Regina v Miller* in 2019 – were gingered up with extensive references to a distinctive Scottish constitutional tradition, the concept of popular sovereignty, and reference to the Declaration of Arbroath and medieval and renaissance tracts. While such arguments seemed to be what his clients wanted to hear, they were not winning ones and they were dismissed by the court as irrelevant to the narrower legal issues before them.

Plan B Politics

Hostility to section 30 – accompanied by an assertion that it will obviously be refused by the UK government in all circumstances – is an *idée fixe* for those pro-independence activists, politicians and writers demanding some kind of 'Plan B.' It is striking that the main proponents of a 'Plan B' – inside the SNP, and subsequently in Alba – have struggled to identify, never mind articulate, how precisely this route towards an independence referendum differs from the Scottish Government's.

Perhaps an instructive place to begin the search for Plan B is the Alba manifesto for the 2021 election. Untrammelled by the SNP government's preference for the 'gold standard' section 30 route, if there was a clear, legal and politically effective route towards a referendum beyond this, it would be expected that the 'only party serious about Scottish independence' would set this out in some detail in their founding statement of political purpose for the Parliament. In the event, the Alba manifesto did not do so. In his foreword, Alex Salmond claimed this was 'the one manifesto which is taking Scottish independence seriously with a proper plan on how to deliver independence for Scotland through a referendum (or another agreed democratic test)' (Alba, 2021: 3). Although allowing that 'the Scottish negotiating position should include, but not be restricted to, a formal demand for a Section 30 Order,' Alba's alternative strategies to deliver a referendum included the following:

If a Section 30 Order is refused, then the Scottish Government must pass a referendum bill with urgency and be ready to fight it through the courts if need be. A range of other tactics could be employed including diplomatic pressure and international legal action, and the mobilisation of the Scottish people through popular and peaceful demonstration and direct action.

Beyond the first commitment – which also found its way into the SNP's manifesto (SNP, 2021: 12) – the range of other tactics is vague, gestural, and non-specific. The phrase 'international legal action' suggests some kind of litigation in international courts. No legal route to any such court action exists. The International Court of Justice in The Hague adjudicates interstate disputes, and is not a forum open to individuals or non-state regional governments. The UK is no longer an EU member state, so the European Court of Justice has no locus to consider a case, even if there was anything in EU law which concerned itself with questions of self-determination. (There is not.) While the UK is subject to the jurisdiction of the European Court of Human Rights, self-determination is not one of the rights the European Convention on Human Rights protects.

The 'mobilisation of the Scottish people through popular and peaceful demonstration and direct action' is not exactly a detailed blueprint towards legal recognition. Considering the unrestrained vehemence with which its senior figures have attacked their former party's referendum strategy, one might have expected something more concrete. Despite all of the heat the issue has generated – and the instrumental role it has played in the public rhetoric and justification for the creation of and defections to Alba by some SNP politicians and members – when we boil off all the rhetoric, it amounts to disputes over preferred timetables for action, performative impatience, and 'indier than thou' squabbling based on the misplaced idea that making compromises with reality somehow demonstrates a lack of real commitment to realising Scottish self-government.

Plan B – like Plan A – is predicated on UK government recognition that whatever tactic, election result, or campaign, is taken as a mandate for a second referendum or independence. If the UK government is not prepared to recognise the election of a democratic majority in the Scottish Parliament on a clear manifesto commitment to deliver a referendum as a democratic basis to recognise a referendum, it is not obvious why pro-independence politicians presenting a Holyrood or Westminster election as 'plebiscitary' is any more likely to command the assent of the UK government, stir the majority of unionist MPs in Westminster into activity or, for that matter, be any more likely to result in the 'mobilisation of the Scottish people through popular and peaceful demonstration' than a Holyrood election mandate ignored. Beyond Scottish politics taking a revolutionary turn, nobody has turned up the legal skeleton key which can turn this constitutional deadlock and let a second referendum out of the box the UK government hope to keep it in. That is because there isn't one. People asserting otherwise are either kidding themselves on, or kidding you on.

There is no magic bullet for the Scottish Government to fire. The best proof of this is the fact that the pro-independence politicians and activists who have most been agitating for the Scottish Government to fire one – when left to their own devices – seem to have misplaced both ammunition and powder. Plan B is Plan A. If Plan A does not deliver a referendum, Plan B won't either. If you want to blame anyone for that, then you can lay your grief at the door of the UK government's undemocratic sensibilities, but also the Scottish people's lack of responsiveness to this attempt to stymie the exercise of their right to self-determination and popular sovereignty. Ultimately, it is a question of political rather than legal pressure. Unspecific demands for practically underdeveloped forms of 'radicalism' and 'boldness' are the bane of Scottish politics – whether it is conservative, socialist, centrist, or pro-independence in orientation. If only wishing made it so.

This legal impasse represents a real predicament for supporters of Scottish independence, but it is also a critical moment of choice for the UK government. For decades, the notion that the Scottish people have a right to self-determination has been recognised by the UK's political institutions. By adopting a 'no, not now, never' policy, the UK government must be conscious that it is at risk of increasing – rather than decreasing – the internal pressure pushing at the UK's territorial seams. Stopping up every constitutional relief valve will not release the internal pressure that has built around Scotland's constitutional future. The idea that these forces will harmlessly dissipate if only the UK government ignores them intensely enough seems hopelessly optimistic. Failing to engage with the legal, constitutional and democratic case for independence is guaranteed to shape not only perceptions of the UK government in Scotland, but also to condition the attitudes and outlooks of pro-independence activists and politicians. Negotiate a referendum and participate in a campaign, and you may lose the argument. But what happens when you leave your political opponents with nowhere to go?

References

AXA v Lord Advocate [2011] UKSC 4.

European Union (Withdrawal) Act 2018.

Ewick, P. and Silbey, S. (1998), *The Common Place of Law: Stories From Everyday Life*, Chicago: University of Chicago Press.

Keatings v the Advocate General for Scotland [2021] CSIH 25.

R v Miller 2019 UKSC 41.

Scotland Act 1998.

Scotland Act 2012.

Scotland Act 2016.

Tickell, A. (2016), 'The technical Jekyll & the political Hyde: the constitutional law and politics of Scotland's independence 'neverendum" in McHarg, A., Mullen, T., Page, A. and Walker, N. (eds) *The Scottish Independence Referendum: Constitutional and Political Implications*, Oxford: Oxford University Press, 325-346.

CHAPTER 7

Independence in the Age of Risk:
Transitioning to Independence
Sionald Douglas-Scott

IN 'SCOTLAND'S RIGHT to Choose' (Scottish Government, 2019) the Scottish Government sought to make a principled argument for a second independence referendum, based on the sovereign right of the Scottish people to determine their own future, a material change of circumstances since the 2014 referendum (namely Brexit), the mandate derived from election victories in Holyrood and Westminster, as well as a majority vote for a referendum bill in the Scottish Parliament on 28th March 2017.

What would have to happen for Scotland to transition to independence after a decision was taken? There would need to be negotiations in the period between the decision for independence and the actual date of its inception. Clearly many issues would have to be resolved; legislation, created by both the Scottish Parliament and Westminster, would be necessary to put the agreement into place. If the decision for independence was accepted as legitimate by the UK government (as it seems would have been the case in 2014, after the adoption of the 2012 Edinburgh Agreement and Section 30 order) then there should be no insurmountable barriers to independence. After all, UK law contains no such provisions as in Article two of the Spanish Constitution that mandates the 'indissoluble unity of the Spanish nation.'

Of course, Brexit does complicate matters. Although Brexit demonstrated it was possible for one state to exit a union, it was not obvious exactly what a vote for Brexit was for, and so the nature of the Brexit mandate was unclear. The UK government was evasive in the specifics of its goals and the EU was able to set the agenda; Scotland should learn from this, and indeed, 'Scotland's Right to Choose' states that, 'The experience of the EU referendum has demonstrated some of the risks involved in inviting a vote on a significant constitutional proposition without setting out in advance the consequences of a vote for change.' Annex B of this document contains legal amendments to UK legislation that are considered necessary to implement a vote for Scottish independence. It is also assumed that the Scottish Government would produce a document similar in purpose to 'Scotland's Future' (Scottish Government, 2013), which provided voters with an idea of the intended shape of an independent Scotland.

Negotiations

Although some matters – for example, much of the legal system, education, and health – are already within Scotland's authority, the Anglo-Scottish Union is over 300 years old, and would be complex to disentangle. A preliminary issue would be who should do the negotiating and what process should govern negotiations. Both the Scottish and UK governments would undoubtedly claim to be primary negotiators but others – backbencher MSPs and MPs, NGOs and members of civil society – would likely assert a right to participate or be consulted. To appreciate that this matter is not straightforward, we might consider the Miller litigation in the context of Brexit, where the UK government found that it could not commence Brexit negotiations with the EU, in spite of its royal prerogative to conduct foreign affairs, because the Westminster Parliament must first consent. Another complicating factor would be the likely need for Westminster legislation to authorise the Scottish Government to conduct negotiations on what would usually be matters reserved to the UK government.

A further question concerns the length of negotiations. In 2014, the Scottish Government suggested 18 months. This was a rather short time frame – not impossible, but somewhat dependant on good will between parties. Since then, Brexit has provided a lesson in how *not* to negotiate, and how matters between friendly states can deteriorate into an unamicable divorce. The Brexit negotiations took over three years to achieve a 'deal' that covered only some issues, namely the UK's financial obligations, the rights of EU citizens, the situation of Northern Ireland, and transitional arrangements. In contrast, the Scottish Government, in 'Scotland's Future' cited German reunification in 1990, and independence for the Czech and Slovak Republics in 1993, as evidence 'that after a democratically agreed and accepted expression of political will, countries can make significant constitutional changes happen in months rather than years.' This might be the ideal, but swift negotiations are not always favourable. The Anglo-Irish Treaty, which led to the creation of the Irish Free State in 1922, was negotiated very quickly (after a war of independence) and perhaps under coercion, producing some requirements deemed unattractive for Ireland (swearing allegiance to the Crown, membership of the Commonwealth and acknowledgement of the Privy Council in London as highest court). However, a longer time frame could mean negotiations drag on – creating uncertainty and, for some, the perception of democracy delayed.

Issues

Disengaging Scotland from the UK would not be simple. For the 2014 referendum, both the Scottish and UK governments set out many of the relevant issues in publications, although they often disagreed with each other.

We can divide the principal issues into several key groups: international recognition of Scotland as an independent state; defence and foreign policy; Scottish citizenship; and the economy.

International recognition of Scotland as an independent state would be important – otherwise, Scottish independence would fail to function. Defence and foreign policy would concern memberships of international organisations such as NATO, the UN and, possibly in the future, the EU. And Scottish passports would have to be issued as part of the establishment of new rules of Scottish citizenship.

The economy would be of upmost concern in many minds, including what currency an independent Scotland would use. In 2014, this was the subject of great controversy, especially after the UK insisted that an independent Scotland could not continue using the pound sterling, so it would be important to have greater clarity on this matter. There is also the issue of how the UK national debt be divided, and the determination of the ownership of North Sea oil and gas reserves, as well as the structuring of taxation and financial regulation.

There are countless other crucial issues – agriculture and fisheries; security and intelligence; broadcasting; pensions; education; the environment; immigration; health; policing and law and order – where not already within Scottish authority. If Scotland were to retain the monarchy, this should not provide legal complications, given many other independent countries also have the Queen as Head of State.

International Matters and Recognition of Scotland as an Independent State

An initial question is whether the UK itself would cease to exist after Scottish independence. The UK did not exist before the union of Scotland and England in 1707, which was effected by the Treaty of Union and legislation of the Scottish and English Parliaments. Some states, such as Czechoslovakia, have dissolved when separation occurred. The Scottish Government did not take a conclusive view on this prior to the 2014 referendum; however, the weight of opinion is that if Scotland was independent then the rest of the UK would continue in the role of the former UK, and Scottish independence would be treated as secession of Scotland to form a new or successor state (Boyle and Crawford, 2012).

If Scotland was the successor and the remaining UK the continuing state, then certain matters follow. The remaining UK, as continuing state, would retain its existing treaty obligations and memberships of international organisations (such as NATO and the UN, including the permanent seat on its Security Council) and all UK public institutions (such as the Bank of England, the BBC and the Westminster Parliament). Scotland should then become a member of international organisations in its own right. Whether Scotland would be admitted would depend on its international recognition, but assuming it was, membership conditions should not be too arduous in most cases. An independent Scotland would be a small state and NATO membership would offer a defensive umbrella. The siting of the UK nuclear deterrent is controversial – suffice to say, an unwillingness to host nuclear weapons is no barrier to NATO membership.

Membership of the EU (something the current Scottish Government aspires to) would be more complicated; however, as Scotland would not immediately be readmitted to the EU, neither the UK nor Scotland would be EU members during independence negotiations.

Therefore, Scotland would not manifest an EU border to England, and issues of customs duties, quotas and common standards for goods would not arise. There is no good reason why Scotland would not remain a member of the Common Travel Area (currently comprising the UK, Ireland, the Channel Islands, and Isle of Man) which notably provides for free movement of persons within the area.

Overall, if the UK were willing to recognise Scotland's independence, then most issues would be far easier. Why should third countries have a problem recognising Scotland as an independent state if its closest neighbours were willing to do so?

However, if the UK contested Scotland's independence, what options would Scotland have? Some countries, such as Kosovo, have made unilateral declarations of independence (UDI). The danger of UDI is that it often lacks international recognition. Such declarations are only usually accepted under international law if the seceding territory was oppressed by the rest of the state, and it is unlikely Scotland could make this claim. Otherwise, international law neither finds such a status to be illegal, nor explicitly recognises it (ICJ 2010). Although the Canadian Supreme Court, in its well-known 1995 'Quebec Secession Reference', stated that, in the absence of a right to secede under international law, internal constitutional law posited a duty on domestic actors to negotiate with the independence seeking party, this judgement is not binding in the UK.

Debts, Assets, Liabilities

If Scotland is the successor and the rest of the UK the continuing state, then some rules for other issues fall into place. The apportionment of debts and liabilities, which must be divided equitably between successor and continuator states, is important, as it is required by customary international law (and the 1983 Vienna Convention on Succession to State Property, Archives and Debts, not yet ratified by the UK). Under law, fixed assets (such as government buildings) are automatically property of the state where they are located, but movables (such as computers, military equipment) must be equitably divided through negotiations.

However, where no clear legal principles exist, opinions differ as to how assets and liabilities should be divided, and use of one principle rather than another (for example, whether division should be by historic share, GDP or population) can make a difference – notably,

Scotland's share of English debt at the time of the Acts of Union, taking the form of 'the equivalent,' proved very complex and controversial.

Scotland might pay its full share of debt at independence, but this sum (estimated around £102 billion in 2014) would be difficult to raise; alternatively, Scotland might make payments as and when they fell due. Division of debts and assets would not be straightforward but would be by no means impossible.

Constitution Making

The UK is one of a tiny handful of countries not to possess a codified constitution, instead choosing to privilege parliamentary sovereignty as its fundamental principle. An independent Scotland would not follow this example – it would have its own constitution, just as former British colonies opted for written constitutions after independence. To an extent, constitutions are presentations of a nation's identity, and popular sovereignty would certainly supplant parliamentary sovereignty in a new Scottish constitution. A Scottish constitution might also make other important changes in governance, such as stipulating that the Scottish Parliament have a second Chamber, that Scotland have a constitutional court, or opt for an entrenched bill of rights.

But the timeline for a new Scottish constitution could be unclear. Clearly, in voting for independence, voters need an idea of the state they are voting for, and a codified constitution could help to articulate this. The drawback of drafting a new constitution post-independence is that it may take a while for a new constitution to come into being, as in Pakistan, or end up being dropped altogether, as in Israel. Therefore, some argue for pre-independence constitution drafting, so it can function fully from Independence Day. This occurred in some former British colonies, but the disadvantage was that such constitutions were usually drafted with considerable input from the UK, often at conventions in Lancaster House, London. Indeed, a constitution drafted prior to independence might be thought to lack what has been described as autochthony – namely, self-sufficiency; denoting a clean break from the UK.

In 2014, the Scottish Government presented a draft interim constitution to operate from Independence Day until a new constitution could be properly agreed by a constitutional convention post-independence, which was probably the best solution to the issue of timing.

Concretising Independence Through Legislation

If agreement is reached, it will need legal implementation. First, this would require an international agreement between the remaining UK and Scotland, entering into force after Scotland's independence, to ensure future fulfilment of obligations between what would become two independent states. This should include some arbitration mechanism perceived as sufficiently neutral (a matter that became contested during Brexit). In the case of Irish independence, the 1921 Anglo-Irish Treaty was approved and given effect in legislation in both Westminster and the Dáil.

Scotland would need the authority to legislate the necessary measures. Preferably, competences would be transferred early on to allow Scotland to prepare for independence. This would require a transfer of powers to enact any enabling legislation for a withdrawal deal, a transfer of powers to terminate Scotland's status as part of the union, and continuity legislation.

The UK (Westminster) would need to adopt legislation to transfer power to the Scottish Parliament, and end the UK Parliament's jurisdiction over Scotland, adopt legislation to enact the results of negotiations, and repeal the Act of Union of the English Parliament (although perhaps unnecessary as the 1800 Act of Union with Ireland was not repealed).

All of this legislation in both parliaments would take time and ultimately delay independence. Additionally, much depends on the political climate. The EU Withdrawal Agreement Act 2019 was adopted very quickly, with a large government majority; the EU Withdrawal Act 2018 took much longer given the constraints of a minority government. The Scotland Act 1998 took 11 months to pass, even with a large government majority.

Continuity legislation

Scottish legislation – either the interim constitution, or separate legislation – should also provide for all law (including laws in areas currently reserved to the UK) to continue after independence, unless amended or repealed. Continuity of legislation is crucial, otherwise there would be considerable gaps in Scotland's laws on independence. The UK faced a similar problem with Brexit, and the EU Withdrawal Act 2018 retains EU law in the UK until repealed or amended. It also empowers UK government ministers, enabling them to repeal even statute law, which is not terribly democratic. Scotland should consider who might be empowered to amend retained legislation, especially if an aim of independence is to create a state enriching popular sovereignty.

Conclusions

Although some issues could be testing, a negotiated independence should not be impossible. There are many precedents of small states breaking away from larger ones – Norway from Sweden in 1905, dissolution of the Austro-Hungarian Empire after 1918, and Czechoslovakia in 1993. Why should Scotland be any different? It is ridiculous to argue that an advanced democratic state such as Scotland could not manage independence. Indeed, Brexit has demonstrated that secession from a larger union is possible, although its economic success has yet to be proven.

However, Scotland's transition to independence would be complicated if the UK did not cooperate. In such circumstances, international recognition becomes harder to achieve – including EU membership. Other issues, such as asset division and choice of currency become fraught, tinged with the emotions of a messy divorce.

The Scottish Government has stated that it is committed to 'an agreed, legal process [...] which will be accepted as legitimate in Scotland, the UK as a whole, and by the international community' ('Scotland's Right to Choose', 2019) and this echoes statements made by other advocates of independence, such as Neil MacCormick. But, as Ciaran Martin recently argued, the present UK government seeks to make a legal bid for Scottish independence impossible (Martin, 2021). And yet, there is no principled reason why the conditions of 2014 should not be replicated and another 'Edinburgh Agreement' issued.

In such a situation, it might seem tempting to turn to the courts for support. But courts can be unpredictable – even if a draft independence bill were to find its way to the UK Supreme Court, the outcome would not be certain. It is possible that the Supreme Court might uphold the validity of a referendum bill based on a narrow reading of its purpose. Central governments have not always fared well in the courts and the UK government was castigated for ignoring Parliament in the first Miller case, and for its unlawful prorogation in Miller/Cherry.

In these cases, the Supreme Court upheld the powers of Parliament against a UK government riding roughshod over it. But this was the UK Parliament, whose sovereignty the Supreme Court stressed, not the Scottish Parliament. The Canadian Supreme Court, in asserting (a theoretical) need to negotiate independence in 'Quebec Secession', took the Canadian government by surprise. On the other hand, the refusal of the Court of Session to rule on the legality of an independence referendum was a disappointment for some. Time will tell, and the UK Supreme Court's decision on the validity of two recent Scottish Parliament bills (one incorporating the UN Rights of the Child) may offer some guidance on how the Supreme Court interprets the Scottish Parliament's powers. But in any case, courts are not necessarily the best forums for such controversial and fiercely contested issues. The US Supreme Court decision of *Bush v Gore*, which determined the outcome of the 2000 presidential election, is still regretted by many.

In contrast, if a clear majority opt for independence in Scotland, political arguments for the legitimacy of independence become harder and harder for a UK government to rebut. In Ireland, an overwhelming vote for Sinn Fein MPs in the 1918 election clearly made the democratic case for independence (even if there were also violent clashes in Ireland, which thankfully have never taken place in Scotland). And if the democratic case can be made, it becomes very hard to identify overwhelming reasons, legal or otherwise, to defeat a transition to independence.

References

Boyle, A. and Crawford, J. (2012), *Annex A Opinion: Referendum on the Independence of Scotland – International Law Aspects*. HM Government.

Martin, C. (2021), 'Resist, Reform Or Re-Run?', Oxford: Blavatnik School of Government.

Scottish Government (2013), *Scotland's Future. Your guide to an independent Scotland.* https://www.gov.scot/publications/scotlands-future/

Scottish Government (2019), *Scotland's Right to Choose: Putting Scotland's future in Scotland's hands.* https://www.gov.scot/publications/scotlands-right-choose-putting- scotlands-future-scotlands-hands/

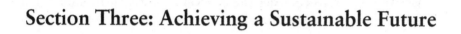

Section Three: Achieving a Sustainable Future

CHAPTER 8

Returning Economic Power to the People
Roz Foyer

IT IS IMPERATIVE to consider the economic issues surrounding and interweaving the constitutional debate on Scotland's future, not in order to take a position on that choice but, rather, to establish what priorities would genuinely serve the interests of working people and communities, and how they should take centre stage in any such decision. As a preliminary to that, the Scottish Trades Union Congress (STUC) has recently reaffirmed its long-held support for Scottish self-determination.

Sovereignty, as defined in the Scottish Claim of Right (1869), dictates that Scotland's constitutional future should be determined by the people who live there. Specifically, this means that the Scottish Parliament should have the power to call a referendum. In the absence of that power, a majority in the Parliament for a referendum coupled with public support for it should be respected by the Westminster Parliament by agreeing to a Section 30 order.

Of course, for the STUC, supporting the right to self-determination is an entirely different matter than taking a view on what the outcome of a referendum should be. Like the Scottish people more generally, trade union members are divided on the question of Yes or No. Equally, the STUC's support for a second referendum, if the aforementioned criteria are met, does not automatically suggest support for a re-run of the 2014 vote. The case for a third question proposing significantly increased powers for the Scottish Parliament is one that should, at the very least, be actively considered.

We know that there are significant groupings on both sides of the debate whose minds are unlikely to change. For many of these people, a sense of history, culture, and identity are the determining factors in any future vote. These views should be respected; however, our democratic future is ultimately likely to be determined by those of the electorate who will decide their position based upon an evaluation of whether an independent Scotland would be a better country to live in economically and socially. For trade unionists, this boils down to which option can best achieve a degree of prosperity through growth that is sustainable, significantly reduces inequality and is supported by a democratically owned economy.

Looking Back to Look Forward

In 2011, the SNP was re-elected with an 'unthinkable' overall majority. The key factor was the election of the Tories at Westminster in 2010 and the view of many that the Blair project had failed. The war in Iraq was also a galvanising factor for many on the left. Arguably, by 2011 we had reached 'peak neo-liberalism'. Though not the architects of neo-liberal economics, third way politicians such as Blair and Clinton entrenched the system. Multi-nationals and financial institutions grew more powerful on the back of de-regulation; asset wealth expanded year-on-year whilst wages as a proportion of GDP reduced. In 2009–2010 the chickens came home to roost with the financial crisis and following global recession.

The bailing out of the banks, followed by the imposition of austerity by governments around the world had a profound effect on electoral politics in Scotland and the subsequent referendum. The STUC's 'There is a Better Way' demonstration in September 2010 was its largest for a generation and six months later hundreds of thousands of people took to the streets of London for a similar Trades Union Congress (TUC) organised event. While many blamed Labour for the perceived economic mismanagement, the SNP government in Scotland successfully positioned itself as anti-austerity. Arguably, this was an easy position to adopt, given that the levers to pursue alternative fiscal policy sat with Westminster. Nevertheless, it was a position that dominated much of the debate during the referendum in the period that followed.

It would be wrong to say that the entire Scottish public supported alternatives to austerity, but clearly many on the left did. Anti-austerity positions and approaches also gained traction within Scotland's more working-class communities. Thus, the mainstream case for Yes at the start of the referendum was a vision of an independent Scotland able to pursue alternatives to austerity.

The vision was of a nation, within the EU, able to grow its economy in a comparable way to other smaller European nations. The argument was that Scotland would make spending choices based on a strong per capita GDP and reductions in spending areas, such as defence. In turn, this would enable us to strengthen social protections and support the services and jobs that were in the process of being decimated by austerity. Fears over the instability of the fledgling independent nation and concerns over currency were to be assuaged by keeping the pound and the UK central bank.

Because beginnings matter, the debate over initial fiscal conditions – relative per capita GDP and comparative levels of public spending in Scotland – was a dominant theme, alongside the question of whether the SNP's currency option would be viable, particularly as it relied in no small part on the future cooperation of the remaining UK.

Different Visions

Prior to 2010, the SNP case for independence had made little distinction between the 'Celtic Tiger' Irish model of growth and that of the Nordic countries. By the time the white paper on independence was published, and with EU enforced austerity in Ireland in full swing, the economic growth case for independence had swung more strongly to replicating the perceived successes of the Nordic model of a social economy and society. Though it should be noted that of the very few concrete tax proposals within the white paper, those that were set out were very 'un-Nordic' reductions in corporation tax and other business-friendly tax measures.

On the back of this position, and despite only ultimately achieving 45 per cent of the vote, the independence case grew in popularity during the campaign. True, there were other factors –including the very poor Better Together campaign; however, most would accept that the centre-left positioning had a positive impact for the Yes campaign.

But that was then and this is now. The context for the independence debate has changed, and this started with Brexit – it is both the clearest democratic trigger for a second vote and a major economic disruptor. The SNP's Sustainable Growth Commission was created in its wake and is highly focused on the policies required for EU re-entry.

While maintaining the central thrust of the white paper on growth – that an independent Scotland would grow by dint of being an open, small nation economy – the Growth Commission is intensely focused on fiscal discipline. This focus is both to meet the borrowing criteria for re-entry to the European Union and to support 'sterlingisation' as an alternative to seeking agreement from the rest of the UK to formally retain the pound. These fiscal rules have become the Commission's most defining and most debated feature.

The rules create significant problems – reducing government spending as a proportion of GDP when GDP is not growing significantly is the definition of austerity. Thus, arguably, the current mainstream prospectus for independence from 2019 is at total odds with the one put forward in 2014. Put simply, whilst the Scottish public supports re-entry to the EU, they may be less keen on the policy measures required to do so.

If this were not a significant enough challenge, the Growth Commission finished its deliberations before the outbreak of COVID. Meanwhile, if hardly 'new' news, the imperative to meet the challenges of the climate crisis has rightly continued to climb up the political agenda. These two issues have shone a new light on the way the world economy works, its inherent inequalities, and the impact of globalisation and corporate power on national economies.

We are also in the middle of a significant shift in the way the international economy operates. The pandemic provoked an almost unprecedented period of government economic intervention across the globe. In the USA, President Joe Biden wrestled with a big fiscal stimulus to meet the challenges of COVID and climate change, as well as pushing for corporation tax reform to bear down on profit shifting by multi-nationals. The EU is looking very closely at its trade relationships with China, and major EU economies – such as Germany and France – also announced green stimulus packages which, if not as large per capita as the US, dwarfed those proposed by Westminster.

Whether this represented a sustained policy shift, or was merely the latest example of government bailing out the failing private sector – last seen in 2010 – remains to be seen; however, there is a real possibility that the nature of the EU and wider world trading environment will look very different by the time any future referendum is held. The impact of Russia's invasion of Ukraine is one of many newer factors redrawing the landscape here.

In Scotland, the related issues of COVID recovery and the need for a just transition to net-zero have shone a spotlight on the massive inequalities in our labour market, driven by precarious work and the decades-long breakdown in social protections.

COVID Recovery

In September 2020, the STUC published a 'People's Recovery' paper. The paper was written as we considered what is potentially the biggest economic crisis in living memory. The immediate cause of the crisis was COVID-19, but the virus drew its strength from a generation of injustices. Coronavirus may not technically discriminate on the lines of class, but its effects are clearly exacerbated by imbalances of income, wealth and power. *The Peoples Recovery* took specific issue with the Higgins Report and called for a far more wide-reaching response that would see collective empowerment at work, public intervention and ownership, and an industrial strategy for Scotland as the foundations of recovery.

The paper argued that 'Whilst the Scottish Government's [2020] Programme for Government offers the potential for fundamental reform in care and the introduction of a National Care Service, on topics such as rent controls, wealth taxes, public ownership, collective bargaining, and state support being conditional on fair work practices, it has little or nothing to say.'

The People's Recovery explicitly recognises that some of its policy proposals lie outwith the current powers of the Scottish Parliament. This includes areas such as some powers of taxation, energy policy, employment law, health and safety, and aspects of equality. Unsurprisingly, we consider tackling precarity and increasing wage equality through trade union freedom and collective bargaining to be central to an alternative approach. Imagining a Scottish economy more akin to the Nordic model requires acceptance of a more powerful trade union movement that is able, through collective bargaining, to have an upward and equalising effect on wages that, when allied to progressive use of regulatory and fiscal powers, could reverse the growing disparity between the proportion of GDP accruing to unearned asset wealth and that spent on wages. This becomes even more acute as the impact of COVID favours the asset wealthy over the wage poor.

It is, at best, unclear that the mainstream case for independence fully embraces what we trade unionists mean by increased trade union freedom, and with it the full extent of our ambition to rebalance power between workers and employers. Ultimately, change is effected through industrial power. Assertive unions take industrial action more frequently and demand collective and sectoral bargaining mechanisms that would be met with strong opposition from employers – particularly those doing business across trade borders – whether with the rest of the UK, Europe or across the world.

Lacking powers over employment law, the Scottish Government has promoted the concept of Fair Work. This has been generally supported by unions even if, thus far, the rhetoric has been louder than the impact. Government promotion of Fair Work and its potential positive impact for workers and on productivity can take the case for independence so far; however, it is yet to be seen whether the ambition exists for a deeper and more far-reaching shift in workplace relations – one that would signal rejection of the neo-liberal approach of managing labour markets to meet the demands of global capital.

There are some employment policy areas in which the SNP Government has signalled different policy approaches and ambitions. It has, for instance, signalled support for a four-day work week and provided limited seed funding to pilot this. Public sector pay awards have been somewhat better than in the remaining UK, though still falling far short of what is required to restore pay to pre-2010 levels. The Fair Work framework and Scottish Government response to the Feeley review on social care support the development of sectoral pay bargaining in the care sector. The Fair Work action plan also commits to improving sectoral bargaining in construction (particularly through public procurement) and to exploring sectoral bargaining in the chronically underpaid and insecure care and hospitality sectors. Given that in all such areas the Scottish Parliament has limited powers, the offer to the hundreds of thousands of workers in these sectors of a brighter, more secure employment future is surely a vision the proponents of independence should be presenting.

A Democratic Economy

The People's Recovery also argues for a fundamental rethink on democratic control of the economy. The last four decades have been marked by a retreat from public ownership and provision, in all but the delivery of services where market failure is most man ifest – health, education and some municipal services. Decades of political sloganeering established the principle of private good, public bad. All evidence to the contrary was ignored, long after impartial reporting had exposed the failure of energy, transport and infrastructure privatisation. Thus, from a trade union perspective, the failure of both the white paper on Scotland and the Growth Commission Report to make a clear and positive case for public ownership is a weakness.

Democratic ownership has remained consistently more popular with the general public than with policy makers. And despite the general shift towards privatisation across the globe, there are still examples of thriving public enterprises in key and foundational industrial sectors, such as transport, energy and construction. Scotrail has been run, for a large part of the past decade, by the Netherlands' state-owned Abellio; Norwegian state-owned Statoil is a major player in offshore oil, gas, and renewables; and Scotland has lost construction work to Navantia, which is staked by the Spanish government.

The current devolution does not preclude public ownership, nor the taking of government stakes in companies. We have the examples of Scotrail, BiFab and Fergusons to indicate that the Scottish Government is not opposed to public ownership per se; however, it is within the scope of those arguing for independence to make the case much more strongly for the future democratic ownership in key areas, such as energy where the case can be made that the current division of powers limits the scope for public ownership in extraction, generation and transmission. More generally, the case can be made that current limited fiscal powers prevent the levels of state borrowing required to develop meaningful public enterprises.

A Just Transition and an Industrial Strategy for Scotland

Such policy positions are also fundamental to developing a vision of an independent Scotland able to meet the challenges of climate change through a just transition that protects Scotland's workers and communities. This is hardly a new challenge, but as every year passes it becomes more acute and rightly climbs up the political agenda. Despite some coinciding themes, there remain two different views of what a just transition means: on the one hand the market, guided by governmental policy frameworks and incentives, will adjust to mini- mise the impacts on those left behind and create new jobs in emerg- ing industries; on the other, a much more fundamental reorientation of democratic and economic relationships is required. In both cases, Scotland is currently failing – despite suggestions to the contrary, as things stand, Scotland is not headed toward a green jobs future. 20 years after the onshore wind boom, almost none of the manufac- turing associated with wind turbines takes place in Scotland. As we approach a decade of peak offshore wind licensing, project develop- ment, and construction, Scotland has a balance of trade deficit in the low-carbon and renewable energy economy.

Equally, our transport networks fail to offer viable alterna- tives to car use and we suffer from poor housing and fuel poverty, particularly in the private rented sector. Given that between them, energy, transport and heat are the dominant greenhouse emissions sectors, we require a national plan to reduce emissions and create new, high-quality, unionised, green jobs. But there is a gulf between where we are and where we need to be. STUC commissioned research from Transition Economics identifies the potential to create 140,000 high-quality jobs over two years through investment in infrastructure and new technologies, public ownership of transport and retrofitting. The research, which evaluates jobs produced in terms of quality and environmental sustainability, contrasts this potential with policies continuing the status quo that would create just 30,000.

The Scottish Government, and other proponents of independ- ence, could reasonably argue that with current powers they lack the power to raise the considerable sums required for this level of investment. An alternative view, particularly if the Growth Commis- sion approach is adopted, is that the fiscal reality of independence would actually reduce, rather than increase, the capacity to borrow to invest.

A just transition to net-zero, driven by a (sorely missing) indus- trial strategy, should be a national mission. We need the roll-out of a massive programme of buildings retrofit delivered by the public sector through municipal programmes. We need to fund the public ownership of buses. We need a nationally owned energy company, and public construction company.

In none of these are areas has the SNP been silent. The programme for government and the subsequent deal with the Scottish Greens proposed a community bus fund – with enough ambition this could be used to fund local authorities to create publicly owned bus networks. The Government also proposes the creation of a national infrastructure body. This falls some way short of public ownership but could at least be used to enforce much-needed minimum standards and promote collective bargaining in the sector. The proposal for a nationally owned energy company has run aground, despite ongoing support for it among SNP members; however, more encouragingly, a publicly owned Scotrail is in the process of being delivered.

Although these policy positions fall short of meeting trade union ambitions, they do suggest that there is an appetite, at least in some quarters in the SNP, to address the industrial challenges we face through intervention. But the current vision for the post-independence economy seems to be less than the sum of the Scottish Government's policy components. As with its policies on work and the workplace, there is no unifying narrative that describes how such measures could constitute a fundamental shift in economic and democratic relations.

Some would argue that this is simply ideological – despite being attracted to certain public interventions for tactical reasons, there is no desire to move away from the neo-liberal economy (despite its social dimension, the EU is hardly a bulwark against neo-liberalism). Re-admittance to the EU does not necessarily sit comfortably with such far-reaching economic and industrial reform. Neither does the future currency challenge of 'sterlingisation' open up the capacity of an independent Scotland to finance such interventions.

Thus, we return to a major problem for proponents of independence. One thing that the Growth Commission report cannot be accused of is dishonesty – it is entirely clear that in its view the first years, probably most of the first decade of an independent Scotland, would be characterised by a degree of fiscal discipline that is synonymous with austerity. A Scotland desperately needing to invest in public services and with the opportunity to develop public ownership, would instead start life reducing such interventions. And whilst, in principle, a fully independent currency and the creation of a Scottish central bank might avoid such problems, there is a fair distance to go before people are persuaded as to the viability of that option.

Popular Economic Sovereignty

What, therefore, emerges is a more complex view of sovereignty, in which the powers of Scottish Parliament are only one dimension. It is perfectly possible that an independent Scotland or a Scotland with greater devolved powers might, through the choices it makes, do little or nothing to increase the economic sovereignty of the people. Popular economic sovereignty is the capacity of the people of Scotland to make independent decisions about their own economy, but it would alter the political economy of Scotland to put the people in a situation of such control. It could be a basis for popular economic intervention, economic democracy, local democracy and the anchoring of industry and capital in Scotland, but increasing economic sovereignty has political economic pre-conditions. From the standpoint of trade unions, the challenge for the independence movement – in fact, the challenge for everyone in this debate – is not just to win their case on powers, but to set out a vision for how real power can be returned to working people.

CHAPTER 9

Fiscal Dimensions of Scottish Independence
Graeme Blackett

WHAT IS MEANT by fiscal policy? Well, it encompasses three main areas. The first is taxes set and collected by the government: taxes on employment; property and wealth; profits; consumption; 'sin', or activities that cause environmental damage; and on tobacco, alcohol and gambling. The second encompasses decisions on government spending, which include the justice system, healthcare, education, defence, pensions and social security; the third is how tax and spending decisions are balanced and the resultant effect on the overall level of demand in the economy, in conjunction with monetary policy. In simple terms, the Government can choose to spend more than it raises in taxes during a recession to stimulate recovery, and it can do the opposite during an economic boom to avoid demand increasing faster than the capacity of the economy to grow.

The fiscal dimensions of the Scottish independence debate have tended to focus on the current fiscal position of Scotland as part of the UK. It is a debate that would seem to be the wrong way around to anyone unfamiliar with Scottish politics. Those against independence often argue that Scotland has a persistent fiscal deficit (where government spending is higher than taxation receipts collected) suggesting that Scotland cannot afford to be independent while there is a need to fill a black hole in the Government's accounts. It is a curious argument – if there was such a black hole, surely that would be an argument for doing things differently, rather than persisting with the arrangements that have led to this situation.

Fiscal Choices

The fiscal choices to be made in an independent Scotland would be of a different nature to those that face a devolved Scotland. Whilst both taxation powers and areas of responsibility have expanded since the modern Scottish Parliament was established in 1999, both taxation and spending decisions are taken in a context set by decisions made in Whitehall. For example, while powers to vary the rates of income tax have been devolved, the decisions taken in Scotland concern whether income tax rates should vary from those in the rest of the UK and, if so, how. This is a marginal decision – hardly a matter of great strategic weight.

Should Scotland become independent, there would be some short-term decisions to be made on how to address the fiscal position that it inherits. The full fiscal consequences of the COVID-19 pandemic will not be fully apparent for some time, but we can already assume that they will likely make any persistent structural fiscal deficit that Scotland has seem trivial, compared to the rest of the UK. Nevertheless, if the inherited position is an excessive fiscal deficit, this will require a strategy to reassure both the public and the financial markets that Scottish public finances will be managed sensibly and prudently.

If the inherited position is that government spending is higher than taxes collected, the assumption in Scottish political debate has often been that there would be a choice between cutting such spending or increasing taxes; however, this is a false dichotomy that confuses economics with arithmetic. The economy is a complex system and any change in fiscal policy can have unintended consequences. For example, if the government of a newly independent Scotland decided to implement drastic spending cuts or taxation increases, this would likely have a negative economic impact, resulting in lower taxation receipts and higher demands for spending; thus worsening rather than improving the government's fiscal balance. If an independent Scotland began with a fiscal deficit that caused debt to increase as a percentage of GDP over time, the only realistic solution would be to set out a clear strategy to reduce the deficit gradually, by ensuring that the growth in government spending was less than the growth rate in the economy. This is the approach recommended in the SNP's Sustainable Growth Commission report (Sustainable Growth Commission, 2018).

Some supporters of independence have argued that the Government of an independent Scotland could continue to run a fiscal deficit indefinitely if Scotland established its own currency; however, there is also an ethical argument against such an approach, since it implies consuming more now, at the expense of future generations. This could only be justified if the current generation was accumulating, rather than depleting, capital – physical, natural, human, and social – that would be required to generate economic output for future generations.

In an independent Scotland, far more fundamental choices would need to be made: on how much to tax and what to levy the taxes on; on what the role of government should be and how its budget should be determined and allocated; and on how best to create the macroeconomic stability that is a prerequisite for a successful economy.

Scotland's Journey from Dependency to Agency

It is an important shift from dependence to agency when people in Scotland have responsibility for fiscal decisions and their outcomes. The science of positive psychology has been widely understood to have discovered that agency is critical for happiness and wellbeing, individually and collectively. Agency is the belief that one can influence their life and change the world for better and consists of efficacy (the belief that one is capable of making a difference), optimism (the belief that efficacy will hold in the future) and imagination (the ability to consider a range of scenarios and situations where one has agency). There is also evidence in economic history that agency is associated with periods of the greatest human progress (Seligman, 2021). So, the very shift from dependency to agency would be expected to deliver gains to wellbeing in Scotland.

The role that governments around the world have played in the public health and economic response to the COVID-19 pandemic has highlighted how narrow the fiscal debate in Scotland has been. The role and scale of government in the economy has fundamentally changed, with actions taken including advising; ordering whole sectors of the economy to shut down; furlough schemes, which saw governments paying the majority of wages for more than a third of employees in the UK at the peak of lockdowns; huge increases in healthcare spending; and wide-ranging schemes to provide grants and loans to businesses. The action that will be necessary to avoid catastrophic climate change also expands the role of government and of global collaboration.

The strategic fiscal decisions that an independent Scotland would face will include considering how much tax the Government should raise; what the Government should tax, and to what extent they should tax it; what services and needs should be provided for collectively, and what should be left to individuals and families; what social protection should be provided; and what level of government expenditure will be required to fund services and social protection. In summary, what sort of society do we want to live in?

The approach taken by other advanced economies provides some useful context for considering these concerns. The government in the UK (including national, devolved, and local government) spends almost $16,500 per person per year (around £13,000) on all public services and social protection, which is close to the average of 32 advanced economies and 11 larger advanced economies (Table 1). This is equivalent to almost 39 per cent of economic output (GDP). Government expenditure in smaller advanced economies is, on average, a little more, both in cash terms and as a proportion of the economy.

Table 1: Government Expenditure Per Capita and as Share of GDP (2019).

	Government Expenditure	
	$ per capita	% GDP
UK	$16,487	38.9%
Advanced Economies (32)	$16,864	38.9%
Large Advanced Economies (11)	$16,300	38.4%
Small Advanced Economies (21)	$17,159	40.1%

Source: Calculations from International Monetary Fund, World Economic Outlook Database, April 2021.

However, these averages hide a range of models. In the Nordic countries, and some other small advanced European economies, government expenditure accounts for at least, if not more than, half of the economy (Table 2). The per capita spending on public services and social protection in these countries is significantly higher than in the UK. Whilst more spending doesn't guarantee better services, we should not be surprised if these countries have better public services and high-quality public infrastructures required for economic prosperity.

There are other countries that have adopted lower tax models, including New Zealand, Switzerland, Ireland, and Singapore (Table 2). It is noticeable that both Ireland and Switzerland have been able to maintain higher levels of per capita government spending than the UK (whilst New Zealand's is at a similar level), despite much lower levels of taxation. This has been possible because these countries have outperformed the UK economically and are, therefore, taxing a larger economy at a lower rate.

Table 2: Government Expenditure Per Capita and as Share of GDP (2019).

		Government Expenditure	
		$ per capita	% GDP
Higher Tax Countries	Finland	$26,018	53.4%
	Norway	$39,037	51.6%
	Denmark	$29,695	49.2%
	Austria	$24,327	48.4%
	Sweden	$24,831	48.3%
Lower Tax Countries	New Zealand	$16,367	38.3%
	Switzerland	$26,993	31.5%
	Ireland	$19,742	24.5%
	Singapore	$9,250	14.1%

Source: Calculations from International Monetary Fund, World Economic Outlook Database, April 2021.

The level of government expenditure that is appropriate is not something that can be considered without context. When examples of other countries are highlighted in political debate, it is often selectively and to demonstrate a particular point. As well as considering tax rates, it is also necessary to consider how well the economies have performed. One useful indicator of this is to consider total GDP per capita and how it splits between government expenditure and disposable income available for private expenditure (Figure 1).

This demonstrates that lower tax economies have much higher levels of disposable income for private expenditure than the UK. It also shows that whilst countries such as Finland, Austria, Denmark, Sweden, and Norway have high tax rates and government expenditure, they also have levels of disposal income as high as, and in some cases considerably greater than, the UK.

Figure 1 Government Expenditure Per Capita and GDP per Capita After Tax (2019).

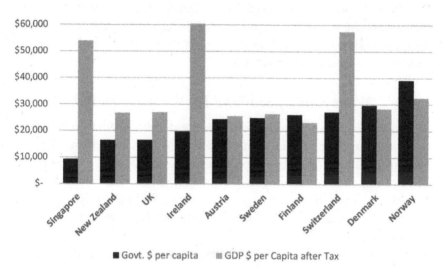

■ Govt. $ per capita   ■ GDP $ per Capita after Tax

Source: Calculations from International Monetary Fund, World Economic Outlook Database, April 2021.

Perhaps it is no accident that these countries are also amongst the highest-ranking for happiness and wellbeing (Sustainable Development Solutions Network, 2021). They benefit from well-funded public services and so can expect high-quality education, healthcare, infrastructure, and social protection, while still having after-tax disposable income to support private consumption.

This analysis does not take account of the distribution of income or taxes, although the Nordic countries and the other small, advanced economies have a combined high government expenditure. Successful economic systems also tend to have lower levels of inequality and score well in rankings of environmentally sustainable development.

Those countries that have decided higher taxes are desirable might be characterised as having a centre-left political consensus, and those with lower taxes a centre-right consensus; however, the decisions to be made are not that simple as the design of the system, as well as its principles, matters.

This is perhaps best demonstrated by healthcare provision in the US. A European style social provision of healthcare is considered as 'socialism' in US politics, and so a political consensus for collective provision of healthcare has not been possible. Instead, there is a market-based system, funded by insurance paid by individuals and employers, with the state funding some of the healthcare for the elderly and those not covered by insurance. But this system means that whilst the US government only funds half of healthcare expenditure, the high costs of this system means that it still spends more per capita on healthcare than the UK.

What Kind of Scotland Do We Want To Be?

So, how should an independent Scotland decide what sort of fiscal system to have? Given that there would be a shift from dependency to agency, a decision would be necessary. Even a decision to leave things broadly as they are requires a decision to be made. That would, however, be a surprising outcome, as independence would provide the opportunity to do things differently, based on the preferences of the people of Scotland.

To some extent, such decisions can be made in the political system, if voters have choices between parties with different visions of the kind of society they want, and different approaches to fiscal policy. This will include debates between those who believe that the Government should play a significant role in the economy, and those who believe it should have a limited scope so that the private sector can flourish. It will also be crucial to consider the characteristics and assets that Scotland has when designing the most appropriate economic model.

One way to balance all of these considerations would be to develop a framework that is outcome based – identifying the areas that are important for national and individual wellbeing, and the focus for designing, appraisal and evaluating policy. The Scottish Government's National Performance Framework (Scottish Government, 2018) and the UK government's guidance on wellbeing (HM Treasury and Social Impacts Taskforce, 2021) provide a basis for doing this. There is an opportunity for an independent Scotland to design and operate a fiscal policy that has increasing wellbeing as its purpose.

There are other aspects of fiscal policy that would need to be considered to ensure a sustainable future for an independent Scotland; however, many of these aspects are complex and will require a much more nuanced and sophisticated fiscal debate than is currently common in Scotland. Whilst that might seem unrealistic in the political arena, there are established alternative approaches for such consideration, including Citizens' Assemblies where voters are randomly selected and asked to participate in a process over time, to make recommendations based on deliberation.

The sorts of questions that could be addressed by such processes could include, should we use fiscal policy for redistribution, by taxing those that have more and redistributing to those who have less? Alternatively, should we try to develop a fiscal policy that seeks to incentivise some activities and discourage others, so that the outcomes mean there is less need for redistribution? Such questions require consideration of issues of efficiency, equality, and fairness, as well as what is the appropriate role for the Government.

The prospect of an independent Scotland should also provide some focus to consider doing things differently, since there would be little point in pursuing the idea if nothing was going to change. Should wealth or income be taxed and what should the balanced be between the two? This raises both efficiency and fairness questions. Whilst increasing tax for those with higher incomes and more wealth might seem attractive to many, would this result in capital leaving the country, to be invested elsewhere? Taxing wealth in this way does raise the question of whether it is fair to penalise those that have saved some of their income and accumulated assets.

What should the balance be between taxes on income (eg income tax and national insurance) and taxes on consumption (eg VAT and duties)? There has been a trend to increase the contribution that consumption taxes make to the public finances, and while this may discourage consumption, such a move is regressive. That is, it hits those with the lowest incomes the most, since they will generally spend most of their income, thus exacerbating inequality.

Fiscal policy is also relevant to the biggest challenge of our times – the existential threat posed by climate change. Avoiding the most catastrophic climate change will require significant investment from the public sector, a huge reallocation of private capital, and behaviour change. Fiscal policy can be a powerful tool, and it is difficult to see how the required changes can be made without carbon taxes. This would result in consumers facing higher costs for more carbon intensive goods and services (although this could be at least partially offset by lower relative prices for environmentally sustainable goods and services). As with any change, there will be winners and losers and it will be difficult to design a carbon tax system that is not regressive.

All of these strategic decisions are complex and there are no easy answers – they will require careful consideration and balancing of priorities and competing interests. It will be important to create a democratic system that can accommodate such complex deliberations, in order to seek consensus on the big decisions. One of the main lessons that can be taken from the most successful advanced economies is that they have sought, and largely achieved, a consensus on the type of society that they want to be.

An independent Scotland would mean a shift from dependence to agency and both psychology and economic history give us good reason to believe that this shift would make us wealthier and happier, since it requires us to engage with, and take responsibility for, the fiscal and other significant decisions that would need to be made.

References

HM Treasury and Social Impacts Taskforce (2021), *Wellbeing Guidance for Appraisal: Supplementary Green Book Guidance.*

International Monetary Fund (2021), *World Economic Outlook Database.*

RCSI MyHealth: Positive Psychology, Agency and Human Progress with Professor Martin Seligman (Lecture on 1 June 2021, available on RCSI MyHealth YouTube Channel)

Sustainable Development Solutions Network (2021), *World Happiness Report 2021.*

Scottish Government (2018), *National Performance Framework.*

Sustainable Growth Commission (2018), *Scotland – The New Case For Optimism: A Strategy for Inter-generational Economic Renaissance.*

World Bank (2021), *World Health Organisation Global Health Expenditure Database* (Data for 2018).

CHAPTER 10

Currency Options for an Independent Scotland
John Kay

A hail bawbee mine and aw tae mysel
Wi joy I'm like chowking if truth I maun tell
How best I micht spend it I cannae richt say
I'm fair in a muddle tae ken what tae dae

My First Bawbee, Archibald McKay

PROBABLY NO OTHER issue caused more confusion in the 2014 referendum campaign, or cast more doubt on the coherence of the plans of supporters of independence, than what currency an independent Scotland would use. There are three core options: the pound sterling, the euro, or a new Scottish currency that, for ease of reference, I will christen 'the bawbee'. For completeness, I note that there are hybrid possibilities: a bawbee pegged to either sterling or the euro, and perhaps initially operating alongside sterling. And some are excited by the possibilities of new digital currencies – a group of enthusiasts has already added 'Scotcoin' to the long list of newly-minted cryptocurrencies.

Today's financial world is remarkably different from the one that Innes Smith described in the lectures on Money and Banking that I attended at Edinburgh University in 1968. That world was overtaken by financial deregulation in the 1970s and 1980s which ended exchange controls, abolished restrictions on credit, replaced reserve requirements on banks by rules on capital adequacy, and allowed these banks to engage in a wide range of activities that the bank managers of an earlier era had not even imagined. New technologies made many of these activities possible. The theory of money and banking I learned as a student followed the traditional identification of three functions of money – unit of account, store of value, and medium of exchange.

Today you can make payments almost anywhere in the world in virtually any currency you choose. You can order a coffee in a Starbucks in Athens or Seoul and the payment will be debited in your preferred currency in the country where you choose to locate your account (Fintech is reducing the additional cost of cross-border retail transactions to nominal proportions.) Many Eastern Europeans, sceptical of their own country's government and judiciary, make contracts in dollars or euros which are enforceable under English law.

Until the 1980s, many countries worldwide, including the UK, maintained exchange controls so that resident individuals or companies needed government or central bank approval to deal in foreign currency. Today, with the growth of foreign travel, global trade and financial innovation, it is impracticable for financially-advanced democracies to implement such controls; thus the choice of currency is not just a matter for governments but a matter of the choices being made by households and businesses.

Governments and Currency

Governments have three roles in relation to currency. First, governments determine what is legal tender in their jurisdiction. To repay debt in legal tender is to settle it conclusively, but in the modern world, legal tender has no practical significance. There could be no better illustration than the curiosity that, by historical accident, the only legal tender in Scotland today is coins from the Royal Mint. If you want to annoy your bank, redeem your mortgage in legal tender. Reckon on about 1,000kg of pound coins per £100,000 outstanding or, if you really want to make trouble, 35,000 kg of pennies. You may find your lender prefers other means of payment even if they are not legal tender. And even your cabbie may take the same view.

Second, the Government must decide in which currency it will keep its own accounts, pay its employees and beneficiaries, and require payment of taxes (this choice does not necessarily have any implication for private actors). To illustrate with a ludicrous thought experiment, if the Scottish Government chose to adopt bitcoin or the Vietnamese dong for its own receipts and payments, then an exchange booth would immediately spring up in St Andrew's Square to enable bitcoin or dongs to be readily converted to and from some more practically useful medium of exchange. Neither Satoshi Nakamoto nor the State Bank of Vietnam need be consulted and the coffee shop in the square would no doubt continue to accept sterling and prefer plastic cards.

No one 'owns' the unit of account, so AstraZeneca and BP choose to present their reports in dollars; most physical commodities are traded in dollars. Foreign currency mortgages are common in Europe; private individuals and businesses in Scotland can compile their accounts and hold bank deposits in any currency they choose. The Scottish Government can choose any currency it likes as its unit of account, or it can use many different ones as AstraZeneca and BP do. No permission or agreement from any central authority is required for any of these things. In particular, neither households nor governments need the permission of the Bank of England to use sterling as the unit of account, or the bank's notes as a medium of exchange.

The bank receiving government payments in bitcoin or dongs would likely affect the conversion automatically, and the exchange booth would enjoy little custom. The likelihood of such immediate conversion means that the Scottish Government would need to adjust its payments in bitcoin or dongs to maintain the value of its payroll and pensions to the recipients, and to secure supplies of goods and services in the face of fluctuation in the exchange rate of the dong or the value of bitcoin.

Currency has substantial network effects. That is, the value of a facility increases when the number of people who use it increases. Particularly as medium of exchange, but also as unit of account, it is convenient to use the currency that is already locally the most popular. The desirability of aligning the preferred unit of account with trade and employment patterns leads to the concept of an optimum currency area, which identifies an economically integrated geographical area and minimises the need for adjustments to prices as a result of events elsewhere. That analysis justifies the concern of the EU with the close association of the single market in goods, the free movement of labour, and the shared currency. Now and for the foreseeable future, England's status as principal trading partner along with the existence of a Common Travel Area and labour market means that the UK is the optimum currency area for Scotland.

After independence, this might change. If Scotland were to rejoin the EU while the remaining UK stayed outside, labour markets, trade flows and other economic conditions might develop in such a way that Europe would be a more likely optimum currency area – although even now it is hard to argue that the entire eurozone represents an optimum currency area. Scotland would be required to acknowledge that the currency of the EU is the euro. But initially, Scotland would not even come close to meeting the Maastricht criteria for eurozone membership. It is likely that both Scotland and its EU partners could agree that adoption of the euro is no more than a far distant aspiration.

The third way in which governments can influence currency choices is to pass legislation to rewrite existing contracts in a new currency. For example, the European Commission issued regulations in 1997 and 1998, binding in all member states, which decreed that all contracts in French francs were converted at a rate of 6.56 FF to the euro and imposed similar conversion ratios for all eurozone members (Meyers and Levie, 1998). A Scottish Government could legislate that any reference to the pound should be construed as a reference to ten bawbees. But the differences are immediately apparent: the French transition applied to all agreements involving the French franc (virtually all agreements in French francs were made under European laws) and the external value of the French franc had been fixed relative to other potential eurozone currencies for several years. No one perceived any gain or loss as a result of the change, or saw any need to rearrange their business or financial affairs in anticipation.

None of these conditions would apply to the introduction of the bawbee by a Scottish Government. Self-evidently, most sterling contracts do not involve Scots residents or Scots law. So what would be the scope of the Scottish legislation? Whose pounds, exactly, would be translated into bawbees? As the Greek Government has learned, the logistics of joining a currency union are much easier than the logistics of leaving one.

Unless the change were purely semantic, it is inevitable that it would have some effect – positive or negative – on the value of existing loans, mortgages and bank deposits that were in some manner related to Scotland. The consequential gains and losses raise problems of equity, politics and law. While a reduction in the burden of

existing mortgages would undoubtedly be welcomed, a correspond-
ing reduction in the value of existing bank deposits and pensions
would not; if the bawbee represented an appreciation, mortgagees
would be upset, but depositors and pensioners delighted. The measure would invite claims of expropriation and challenge under the
European Convention on Human Rights, to which Scotland would
presumptively be a signatory.

Perhaps more seriously still, anticipation of such changes and
associated uncertainty would lead to pre-emptive action of a damaging and disruptive kind. Czechoslovakia experienced major disruption during the separation of its monetary union, even in the context
of a tightly-controlled financial system inherited from its recently
communist past. As the introduction of the bawbee approached,
loans secured against Scottish property would be hard to obtain;
the savings of Scots residents would be moved outside the potential
jurisdiction of Scots law (capital flight). The financially sophisticated
would gain at the expense of the rest of the population.

In the light of these considerations, it is essential any discussion
of currency options after independence make clear that a potential
Scottish Government would have no intention of changing the terms
of its own existing contracts, or of legislating to change the terms of
private contracts. This assurance should include – but not be con-
fined to – agreements governing savings and loans, employment and
pensions.

The bawbee would therefore be used only in agreements made
after its introduction. It is not apparent that businesses and households would have much desire to make such agreements in bawbees.
On Independence Day, almost every adult in Scotland would have
a fistful of pound notes and a sterling bank account; some would
change these to bawbees out of patriotic fervour, others might take
the opposite view. And many, uninterested in political statements,
might simply prefer the familiar to the new. Most transactions in
shops would, as now, be made using plastic cards; the tickets on the
shelves might be labelled in pounds or bawbees or – as in the eurozone for several years – in both.

Any transition to the bawbee would inevitably and sensibly be
gradual. The wag who said the Scottish currency should be called the
thistle – lovely to look at but not to hold – made a serious point. There
is a real possibility that a premature and ill-planned introduction of a

Scottish currency would be an embarrassing fiasco, ignored by most of the world and unappreciated by Scottish residents.

Monetary Freedom

An independent Scotland with its own currency would be able to determine its own monetary policy. It could also allow the value of its currency to float, in recognition of any particular character of Scotland's imports and exports and any particular pattern of growth or recession in the Scottish economy. It could derive seigniorage (profit made by a government by issuing currency) – banknotes represent interest-free borrowing, and the interest saving has value. And an independent Scotland could attempt to borrow in bawbees rather than an established internationally-traded currency.

However, it is important to note that while monetary policy is concerned with interest rates and the money supply, people often talk about 'money' without specifying what they mean by 'money'. There is no magic about money; it is simply transferable debt, and such debt may be issued by governments or private actors and specified in any unit of account. There are different statistical measures of money depending on the identity of the issuer and the term of the debt, ranging from narrow money, M_0, through M_1, M_2, and M_3 to the broadest measure M_4, which encompasses a wide range of money market instruments. These statistical measures are prepared for each currency in which the debt is denominated.

The most familiar and narrowest concept of money is the banknote. According to the Bank of England (2021c), the value of notes currently circulating in Scotland is probably around £7 billion, roughly equally divided between Bank of England notes and those of the Scottish banks. (Anomalously, Scottish banks are allowed to issue their own notes, which must, however, be fully backed by Bank of England notes.) This £7 billion figure should be compared with the Scottish national income of around £163 billion (National Statistics, 2021).

A comparison with overall Scottish Government debt is also relevant. Liability for existing UK Government debt would stay with the remaining UK Government. The division of assets and liabilities would be a complex and central issue in independence negotiations. It may be reasonable to assume that Scotland would begin independent life carrying, explicitly or implicitly, a pro-rata share of UK debt, which might be in the region of £180 billion. Scotland would also need to borrow to cover its budget deficit after independence, a figure which might initially be between £10 billion and £20 billion annually. This scale of borrowing should not be difficult to service if the new government showed ordinary fiscal prudence; however, it is likely that international lenders would choose to provide – and look to receive payment in – pounds, dollars or euros, rather than bawbees.

Issuance of notes and coins is therefore very small relative to the scale of government borrowing, yet very large relative to the practical need of the public for a medium of exchange. The value of sterling notes held outside the banking system is over £1000 per head of population, a startlingly high figure. Much of the public holding of cash probably relates to its use in criminal or money laundering activities, a conjecture supported by the still higher level of per capita cash circulating in euros and – especially – dollars (Rogoff, 2017). It is probably all to the good that the bawbee is unlikely to be of much interest to international criminal networks Cash was only used in about 20 per cent of UK transactions in 2019 (down from ~80 per cent in 1990) (Caswell et al., 2020). Since the pandemic the amount of cash withdrawn from ATMs has fallen by at least 30 per cent year-on-year. The shift to electronic money leads many to welcome 'the death of cash' – an end state already approached in countries such as Sweden.

Innes Smith taught his students to pay particular attention to M0, the monetary base. Banks were at that time required to hold interest-free reserves at the Bank of England equivalent to a fraction of their deposits (hence the reference still frequently made to 'fractional reserve banking'). The size of the monetary base – the total of the note issue and reserves held at the central bank – thus determined the scale of bank lending and deposits (M1) and control of this base was the essential tool of monetary policy. But these restrictions on banks have been removed and under the international Basel agreements, which an independent Scotland would be expected to follow, banks are now obliged instead to maintain regulatory capital – shareholder funds – based on their risk-weighted assets. Bank deposits are now the amounts bank customers choose to hold and reserves at the central bank, which bear interest, are now the amounts banks decide to place. For the avoidance of doubt, these deposits are debts of the commercial banks, and the reserves held at the central bank are effectively the debts of its owner – the Government. No magic here.

These reserves with the central bank are used to facilitate payments between banks – when I make a transfer from my Bank of Scotland account to your Royal Bank account, the resulting credit from BoS to RBS goes through the clearing system operated by the Bank of England. A Scottish central bank could operate a sterling clearing system in Edinburgh, but need not since one already exists in London (which all banks operating or likely to operate in Scotland have access to). If, however, these banks provided bawbee accounts, then it would be necessary for the new bank to establish a bawbee clearing house.

Initially, commercial bank reserves at the central bank were the modest amounts needed to lubricate the payments system, but they have grown explosively since the global financial crisis. This growth is mainly the result of quantitative easing – the policy under which central banks buy long-term government, and some commercial, debt. The effect is not just to fund current government debt through short-term borrowing from financial institutions but also to refinance existing debt on a similar basis. The Bank of England has acquired around £900 billion of assets in this manner.

This essay is not the place to assess the rationale or effectiveness of these measures, but it is appropriate to review the ability of a Scottish central bank to carry out quantitative easing. It is unlikely that there would be any considerable amount of either government or private long-term debt denominated in bawbees in the short or medium term. The Scottish Government could issue long-term debt and encourage the Scottish central bank to buy it with bawbees. The bank could even buy tangible assets – housing, offices, warehouses – but would need to persuade financial institutions or citizens to hold the short-term bawbee debt issued to pay for them. It is difficult to envisage much demand for such debt. The asset-holding patterns of Scots residents and institutions would be influenced little by the policies of the Scottish central bank but greatly by the policies of the Bank of England, the European Central Bank, and the US Federal Reserve. This financial interdependence remains a reality, whether Scotland is constitutionally independent or not.

M1 (narrow money) adds to M0 the current account balances maintained by households and businesses. A pro-rata share of the UK figure would indicate that Scots might maintain balances of around £200 billion (Bank of England, 2021a); however, conditions after independence would determine the nature and location of these balances. At present, all banks operating in Scotland are members of groups with the majority of their activities based outside Scotland. These banks might take deposits from Scottish resident individuals and businesses through branches – which may be virtual – or by establishing Scottish subsidiaries. These deposits might be of sterling, bawbees, or indeed dollars or euros and would be repayable in the currency of deposit and transferable in the currency of the depositor's choice. It is realistic to anticipate that a substantial fraction of this £200 billion of 'money' might be held outside Scotland and in currencies other than bawbees. This currency diversification is even more likely to be true of M3 or M4 (broad money), which includes other short-term assets such as Treasury bills and commercial paper. Like all measures of 'money', broad money holdings have increased substantially over the past decade as a result of quantitative easing.

Because money markets are global, and the international demand for bawbees likely to be limited, especially in the short term, both the scale and denomination of broad money held by Scots households and businesses would be a product of their decisions and international forces, rather than the actions of a Scottish central bank. The measure of broad money relevant to the Scottish economy would be much wider than bawbee M4 and much narrower than sterling M4.

Under retained EU law, the European Economic Area (EEA) principle that regulation of bank branches and liability for their deposit insurance lies with the home country but responsibility for subsidiaries with the host continues to apply. This rule would naturally remain as part of the Scottish independence settlement. Liability for such insurance falls – at least in the first instance – on other financial institutions.

A Scottish Government would sensibly require Scottish-based subsidiaries to maintain, at all times, sufficient collateral of high-quality assets, enabling their operations to be taken over by the Scottish central bank if their ability to meet obligations was in doubt. It would need to do so at little or no cost to the Scottish taxpayer. The Scottish central bank has neither resources nor obligation to act as 'lender of last resort'. (The concept of lender of last resort came into use in the 19th century to describe emergency liquidity assistance to solvent banks. By 2008 the meaning appeared to have been extended to include a duty to bail out failing international banks.) The Scottish Government does, however, have resources and obligation to protect the deposits of Scottish households and SMEs, and secure the continued functioning of the payments system in Scotland; therefore it could and should act accordingly.

Assessment

The opportunities and difficulties that currency questions would raise for an independent Scotland have both been greatly exaggerated. The debate is unduly influenced by an outdated Chartalist model in which coinage stands alongside flag, anthem and army as symbols of sovereignty, and by an understanding of money and banking derived from a bygone era. For better and worse, most decisions about currency, money and banking in an independent Scotland will not be made by a Scottish Government or central bank. They will be made by: individual businesses and households; international banks; foreign exchange markets controlled by no one at all; the Federal Reserve and the European central bank; and the influential central bank in Scotland's larger neighbour and principal trading partner.

Nevertheless, the circulation of ideas that are poorly thought through, even if they are not implemented, can damage the credibility of a future Scottish government and the reputation of a financial services sector, which is an essential contributor to the Scottish economy. It is not the case that an independent Scotland could be free of constraints on public expenditure because it could print its own money; nor is it plausible that the Sauchiehall Street branch of a London-based bank could supply its customers with dollars or euros or, with a few days' notice, Vietnamese dongs but would be unable to provide them with sterling. (Both arguments have been presented, evidently seriously, by protagonists in the currency debate.) But if people think these things might happen, they will take steps to protect themselves against them – actions which may be costly to them as individuals and detrimental to the Scottish economy. And while there may be good arguments against independence, the assertion that countries need to be big so that they can rescue 'too big to fail' banks is not one of them.

The recommendation of the Sustainable Growth Commission that an independent Scottish Government should continue to use sterling as its unit of account for the foreseeable future, with the consequence that its citizens would continue to use sterling as the medium of exchange (to the steadily diminishing extent that they use any currency in this way) is a prudent and feasible approach (Sustainable Growth Commission, 2018). Once an independent Scottish Government has established its credentials for fiscal responsibility with its own population and the international financial community, and once trading patterns have adapted to new constitutional arrangements, there would be an opportunity to review these arrangements. But in the short term, there is little to gain and much to lose from precipitate change – or the threat of it.

References

Bank of England. (2021a), 'Quarterly amounts outstanding of monetary financial institutions' sterling and all foreign currency M1 (UK estimate of EMU aggregate) liabilities to private and public sectors (in sterling millions) seasonally adjusted', *Bank of England.*

Bank of England. (2021b), 'Weekly amounts outstanding of Central Bank sterling reserve balance liabilities (in sterling millions) not seasonally adjusted', *Bank of England.*

Bank of England. (2021c), 'Weekly amounts outstanding of total sterling notes and coin in circulation, excluding backing assets for commercial banknote issue in Scotland and Northern Ireland (in sterling millions) not seasonally adjusted', *Bank of England.*

Caswell, E., et al. (2020), Cash in the time of COVID', *Bank of England Quarterly Bulletin.*

Meyers, J. and Levie, D. (1998), 'The Introduction of the Euro: Overview of the Legal Framework and Selected Legal Issues', *Columbia Journal of European Law* 4 (2), pp. 321-352.

National Statistics (2021), 'GDP Quarterly National Accounts, Scotland: 2020 Quarter 3 (July-September)', *National Statistics.*

Rogoff, K. S. (2017), *The Curse of Cash*, Princeton, NJ: Princeton University Press.

Sustainable Growth Commission (2018), 'Part C: The Monetary Policy and Financial Regulation Framework for an Independent Scotland', *Sustainable Growth Commission.*

Shaping a Wellbeing Economy for Scotland: Introducing a 'New Grammar' of Human Flourishing
Michael J. Roy and Karen Lorimer

A CENTRAL TENET of arguments for and against independence for Scotland is the ability, or otherwise, to plot a different economic course than the rest of the UK. There has been some evidence of feelings of genuine admiration at home and abroad – within progressive circles, at least – at signals that Scotland is ready to embrace what has become known as the 'wellbeing economy' model: an economy designed to work for people and the planet, rather than the other way around (Coscieme et al., 2019; Costanza et al., 2018; Trebeck and Williams, 2019). In the clamour to find new ideas and thinking to shape post-pandemic political economies – recognising the destructive qualities of neo-liberal capitalism in terms of ever-growing inequalities, the climate crisis, the rise of populism and extremism – the idea of repositioning a national polity and economy to focus on wellbeing has captured the imagination of politicians and policymakers across the globe. Not least, this is because of recognition that the impacts of the pandemic have been felt profoundly unequally, with poor and disabled people, ethnic minorities, and women all being disproportionately affected (Scottish Government, 2020).

Scotland has been at the forefront of advancing the wellbeing economy idea, particularly through the work of the Wellbeing Economy Alliance (WEAll) and the formation of the Wellbeing Economy Governments (WEGo) initiative alongside the governments of Iceland, New Zealand and, more recently, Wales and Finland. Since 2018, the core objective of the Scottish Government's National Performance Framework has been to ensure 'opportunities for all of Scotland to flourish through increased wellbeing' (Scottish Government, 2019). Nicola Sturgeon has taken a lead in reshaping conversations around the need for economic and social policies that emphasise wellbeing over a narrow focus on GDP (Gregory, 2019; Trebeck, 2020). In what might be seen as an unusual move for a politician, she gave a TED talk on the topic at a summit in July 2019, a recording of which has been viewed around 2.5 million times internationally to date:

> When we focus on wellbeing, we start a conversation that provokes profound and fundamental questions – what really matters to us in our lives. What do we value in the communities that we live in? what kind of country, what kind of society do we really want to be? (Sturgeon, 2019).

After the Scottish Parliamentary elections of 2021, in a slightly expanded role to Kate Forbes' portfolio as cabinet secretary for finance and the economy, 'wellbeing economy' was explicitly added to her brief.

But wellbeing is a notoriously slippery, contested subject (Roy, 2021). It is also, at least in some conceptualisations, highly subjective: what matters to you in terms of your wellbeing may not matter much to me, or at all (Sayer, 2011). So how do we ensure that the views of those that matter most in this context are best considered? We would argue that those who matter most in such considerations are those whose (health and) wellbeing have been most detrimentally affected by a toxic mixture of bad politics and poor economic and social policies over at least the last half a century or so (Walsh et al., 2016). The 'lost decade' of austerity has left significant swathes of the population particularly vulnerable to the deleterious impacts of the pandemic (Chakelian and Goodier, 2020) meaning that life is precarious for far too many. It is next to impossible for people to withstand profound shocks when they are unable to stock-up on food as their income is so low, or when their personal space is limited or non-existent.

There is therefore both a moral and an economic reason for focusing on those most adversely affected. By turning our attention to the worst off, focusing on unjust inequalities, and building policy from there, we help more people. In this chapter, we will cover some of the issues in trying to operationalise the wellbeing economy concept, particularly through the lens of one leading philosophy of

wellbeing: the capabilities approach. We will discuss some of the
challenges that policymakers are likely to face moving this agenda
from rhetoric into reality, and how and why these might matter to
debates on independence. First, we ask: where did the focus on wellbeing come from? And how has it developed since?

Wellbeing Within Scottish Policymaking

In a recent paper, Heins and Pautz outline the 'career' of the concept
of wellbeing within Scottish Government policymaking:

> even under dramatically different economic circum-
> stances [following the Global Financial Crisis] and with
> a changing view even within mainstream economics on
> what kind of growth may constitute societal progress,
> it took many years for wellbeing to become an explicit
> and central concept in Scottish politics (2021: 96).

Ironically, they explain, wellbeing only gained impetus when econ-
omists started to give it attention. They show how key civil society actors such as the Carnegie UK Trust, especially via their report
'More than GDP: Measuring what Matters' (Carnegie UK Trust,
2011) and Oxfam Scotland, particularly through their 'Humankind
Index' (Oxfam, 2012) brought significant influence and attention
on the topic to bear with key politicians and policymakers within
Scotland. Both of these followed hard on the heels of the report by
the Commission on the Measurement of Economic Performance and
Social Progress (Stiglitz et al., 2009). This had been commissioned
by the Sarkozy Presidency in France. It involved Nobel Laureates
Joseph Stiglitz, who later came to serve on the Scottish Government's
Council of Economic Advisers, and also Amartya Sen, most famous
for his 'capability approach' to wellbeing.

Several of the key individuals involved in the original Oxfam
work on the topic later went on to form the Wellbeing Economy
Alliance, and this collaborative network of individuals and organisations has been especially active and influential throughout the
pandemic. Among a range of popular briefing papers, they produced a series of ten 'principles' to 'build back better' (Büchs et
al., 2020) that echo many of the key principles of 'Green New
Deals' being pursued in both the US and Europe. Such ideas clearly

offer food for thought for those imagining what kind of Scotland we might wish to build, and what powers we would need to get there. But, setting questions of Scottish independence aside just for the present, there is a clear recognition that to make such rhetoric meaningful, action cannot be restricted to central government policymakers alone. It needs to be embraced and embedded at the level of local communities; however, attempts to deliver economic, social, and environmental justice regularly raise awkward questions. What do people residing in local communities want from such an approach? And, perhaps just as importantly, how should progress and success – or indeed failure – be measured? It is here that we feel that Sen's 'capability approach' could prove to be a useful framework to start to answer such questions, and it is to this that we next turn

The Capability Approach

The capability approach is a theoretical framework that entails two normative claims: first, the claim that the freedom to achieve well-being is of primary moral importance and, second, that well-being should be understood in terms of people's capabilities and functionings. Capabilities are the doings and beings that people can achieve if they so choose, such as being well-nourished, getting married, being educated, and travelling; functionings are capabilities that have been realised. (Robeyns and Byskov, 2020).

The capability approach provides a common language for framing some of the points we should consider: such as what aspirations a wellbeing economy should seek to achieve and, perhaps more importantly, how we measure progress and success. The capability approach is a multidimensional framework that focuses on people's real freedoms and opportunities to lead a life they have reason to value (Sen, 1985). As Nussbaum writes:

We ask not only about the person's satisfaction with what she does, but also about what she does, and what she is in a position to do (what her opportunities and liberties are). And we ask not just about the resources that are sitting around, but about how those do or do not go to work, enabling [the person] to function in a fully human way (2000:71).

It is an approach to wellbeing assessment and theorising about social justice that focuses less on what people do ('functionings') than what they are able to achieve ('capabilities') given a combination of personal abilities and the political, social and economic environment (Nussbaum, 2011). Amartya Sen's well-known example of the fasting priest compared to the starving man reveals the difference between functionings and capabilities – although each arguably has similar deficiencies in nutrition (functioning), their capabilities differ, with one of them able to eat. The framework is multidimensional in that it allows analysis to be more holistic than just focusing on health and employment (or income/economy) – we can look all issues in the eye. A shift towards a wellbeing economy will involve innovation and transformation, so we should consider whether using the same old tools will suffice. If we intend to reimagine a society that works for people and planet, we need to reimagine the questions we ask, since the unasked question is never answered.

Sen never specified a list of capabilities, instead they left it deliberately underspecified for people to operationalise in their own contexts. With no recipe or readymade tool, we have some work to do. But many have taken this path already, as we can see from the impact the framework has had on United Nations Development Programme (UNDP) indices (capabilities have influenced the Human Development Reports since 1990), as well as assessments of small-scale development projects (Alkire, 2005). The framework not only expanded the datasets that underpin the Human Development Reports, but we can see that it has shifted the questions that are asked.

Starting to build a wellbeing economy that is consistent with Sen's participatory approach, and employing best practice in democratic participation, involves a need for meaningful engagement between those responsible for building a wellbeing economy, and those whose cooperation would be required for its successful implementation. There is also a need to explore how a new 'grammar' of human flourishing and social justice – in relation to the wellbeing economy idea – is interpreted, understood, and embraced by actors involved in key areas of policy across Scotland. Certain initiatives are emblematic of the wellbeing economy approach, and so may lend themselves best to trialling new approaches, such as the 'Community

Wealth Building' initiative currently being developed in North Ayrshire and elsewhere in Scotland. This is a 'people-centred' approach to local economic development that 'redirects wealth back into the local economy, and places control and benefits into the hands of local people' (CLES, 2021).

There is also a need to improve public understanding of the wellbeing economy concept, particularly what it can bring in terms of individual and community freedoms, and how those connect to the wellbeing of people and the planet. When engaging with people, we could also ask about people's priorities and wishes, such as the preference for a function or capability (to do and be, or to *be able* to do and be). Such questions have been asked before, and views seem to vary once you go beyond basic needs (Lorgelly et al., 2015). For example, most people value having the capability to influence decisions, rather than actually doing so, but there is more variation in preferences for being *able* to enjoy the love, care and support of your family, and *actually* enjoying it. It would be good to develop a framework for evaluation that combines the strengths of the capability approach with meso-level (local authority) and macro-level (National Performance Framework) objectives, to be able to evaluate policies that aim to improve individual wellbeing and social justice.

Conclusion

The entire notion of wellbeing is profoundly political (Bache and Scott, 2018) and has to be dealt with carefully, not least because the imprecision and subjectivity of the concept can leave it open to co-option. As Atkinson (2020) explains, the dominant understanding of subjective wellbeing is often too narrow, and overly focused on individual agency, rather than on the collective. Individualistic approaches regularly serve to obfuscate the systemic factors in the social environment that drive poverty and inequality, for example. The notion of 'collective agency' and 'collective capability' (see Pelenc et al., 2015) and, in a similar vein, 'community wellbeing' (see Atkinson et al., 2017) have developed out of attempts to recognise that a concept such as wellbeing is largely dependent upon how we interact with others. At heart, then, is the key message: wellbeing is a matter of how we live well together, and independence offers us an unrivalled opportunity to examine how we do so in detail. If independence for Scotland is secured, then the powers handed to Holyrood will allow a new Scottish economy and polity to be shaped. This could, and we would argue should, be designed with wellbeing at its heart. After major shocks, it is natural for some to reside in the safety of the known, such as evaluating how well we are doing (as an economy, if not as a society) by 'doubling down' on the use of GDP. It will be a challenge to make alternatives convincing and compelling, but we will be judged in future generations by not only how successful the process was, but how inclusive – how just – it was. Before much longer too, we will likely have to address just how democratic Scotland *actually* is. Such conversations need to go far beyond the knotty perennial problem of the missing layer(s) of democracy in Scotland, or inequitable land ownership (which is not an insignificant driver of wellbeing in itself). We must explore the best ways of encouraging meaningful civic dialogue – between central and local government; between local government and communities; and between communities and individuals. There will be a need, too, to consider at what level decisions should be best made, with a view always to maximising the wellbeing of those most affected by such decisions. Finally, we must repeatedly keep in mind the question: what is independence *for*, if it is not the freedom for people to achieve the kind of life they wish to lead?

References

Alkire, S. (2005), *Valuing Freedoms: Sen's Capability Approach and Poverty Reduction*, Oxford: Oxford University Press.

Atkinson, S. (2020), 'The Toxic Effects of Subjective Wellbeing and Potential Tonics', *Social Science & Medicine*, available at: https://doi.org/10.1016/j.socscimed.2020.113098.

Atkinson, S., Bagnall, A.-M., Corcoran, R., South, J., Curtis, S., di Martino, S. and Pilkington, G. (2017), *What Is Community Wellbeing? Conceptual Review*, London: What Works Centre for Wellbeing.

Bache, I. and Scott, K. (2018), *The Politics of Wellbeing: Theory, Policy and Practice*, Springer, Cham, Switzerland.

Büchs, M., Baltruszewicz, M., Bohnenberger, K., Dyke, J., Elf, P., Fanning, A., Fritz, M., et al. (2020), 'Wellbeing Economics for the COVID-19 Recovery', Wellbeing Economy Alliance, available at: https://weall.org/wp-content/uploads/2020/05/

Wellbeing_Economics_for_the_COVID-19_recovery_10Principles.
    pdf.

Carnegie UK Trust (2011), *More Than GDP: Measuring What Mat-
    ters. Report of the Round Table on Measuring Economic Per-
    formance and Social Progress in Scotland*, Carnegie UK Trust/
    Sustainable Development Commission, Dunfermline, Fife,
    available at: https://www.carnegieuktrust.org.uk/publications/
    more-than-gdp-measuring-what-matters/.

Chakelian, A. and Goodier, M. (2020), 'Ten Years of Data Reveal How
    Austerity Weakened the UK's Pandemic Response', 1 July, available
    at: https://www.newstatesman.com/2020/07/ten-years-data-reveal-
    how-austerity-weakened-uk-s-pandemic-response.

CLES (2021), 'What is Community Wealth Building?', avail-
    able at: https://cles.org.uk/community-wealth-building/
    what-is-community-wealth-building/.

Coscieme, L., Sutton, P., Mortensen, L.F., Kubiszewski, I., Costanza,
    R., Trebeck, K., Pulselli, F.M., et al. (2019), 'Overcoming the Myths
    of Mainstream Economics to Enable a New Wellbeing Economy',
    Sustainability, Vol. 11 No. 16, p. 4374.

Costanza, R., Caniglia, B., Fioramonti, L., Kubiszewski, I., Lewis, H.,
    Lovins, L.H., McGlade, J., et al. (2018), 'Toward a Sustainable
    Wellbeing Economy', *The Solutions Journal*, Vol. 9 No. 2, p. 5.

Gregory, A. (2019), 'Governments Should Put Wellbeing of Citizens
    Ahead of GDP in Budget Priorities, Iceland PM Urges', available
    at: https://www.independent.co.uk/news/world/europe/iceland-
    gdp-wellbeing-budget-climate-change-new-zealand-arden-stur-
    geon-a9232626.html.

Heins, E. and Pautz, H. (2021), 'Social Wellbeing in Scotland – the
    'Career Network' of a Policy Concept', *International Journal of
    Wellbeing*, Vol. 11 No. 1, pp. 89–105.

Lorgelly, P.K., Lorimer, K., Fenwick, E.A.L., Briggs, A.H. and Anand, P.
    (2015), 'Operationalising the Capability Approach as an Outcome
    Measure in Public Health: The Development of the OCAP-18',
    Social Science & Medicine, Vol. 142, pp. 68–81.

Nussbaum, M.C. (2011), *Creating Capabilities: The Human Devel-
    opment Approach*, Cambridge, Mass.: Belknap Press of Harvard
    University Press.

Oxfam (2012), 'Oxfam Humankind Index: the New Measure of Scotland's Prosperity. Second Results', Oxfam, available at: https://oxfamilibrary.openrepository.com/bitstream/handle/10546/293743/rr-humankind-index-second-results-100613-en.pdf;jsessionid=6BAA2E0CCI021A4F7D77B7FAC7EF4C90?sequence=1.

Pelenc, J., Bazile, D. and Ceruti, C. (2015), 'Collective Capability and Collective Agency for Sustainability: A Case Study', *Ecological Economics*, Vol. 118, pp. 226–239.

Robeyns, I. and Byskov, M.F. (2020), 'The Capability Approach', in Zalta, E.N. (ed.), *The Stanford Encyclopedia of Philosophy*, Winter 2020., Metaphysics Research Lab, Stanford University, available at: https://plato.stanford.edu/archives/win2020/entries/capability-approach/.

Roy, M.J. (2021), 'Towards a 'Wellbeing Economy': What Can We Learn from Social Enterprise?', in Gidron, B. and Domaradzka, A. (eds), *The New Social and Impact Economy: An International Perspective*, Cham: Springer International Publishing, pp. 269–284.

Sayer, A. (2011), *Why Things Matter to People: Social Science, Values and Ethical Life*, Cambridge: Cambridge University Press.

Scottish Government (2019), *National Performance Framework*, available at: https://nationalperformance.gov.scot/.

Scottish Government (2020), *Scotland's Wellbeing: The Impact of COVID-19*, Edinburgh: Scottish Government, available at: https://nationalperformance.gov.scot/sites/default/files/documents/NPF_Impact_of_COVID-19_December_2020.pdf.

Sen, A. (1985), *Commodities and Capabilities*, Oxford: Oxford University Press.

Stiglitz, J.E., Sen, A. and Fitoussi, J.-P. (2009), *Report by the Commission on the Measurement of Economic Performance and Social Progress*, available at: https://ec.europa.eu/eurostat/documents/118025/118123/Fitoussi+Commission+report

Sturgeon, N. (2019), 'Why Governments Should Prioritise Wellbeing', July, available at: https://www.ted.com/talks/nicola_sturgeon_why_governments_should_prioritize_well_being.

Trebeck, K. (2020), 'Agenda: Working Towards an Economy That Is Focused on Wellbeing', *The Herald*,

available at: https://www.heraldscotland.com/opinion/18177452.
agenda-working-towards-economy-focused-wellbeing/.

Trebeck, K. and Williams, J. (2019), *The Economics of Arrival*, Bristol:
Policy Press.

Walsh, D., McCartney, G., Collins, C., Taulbut, M. and Batty, G.D.
(2016), 'History, Politics and Vulnerability: Explaining Excess
Mortality in Scotland and Glasgow', Glasgow Centre for Population Health, May, available at: http://www.gcph.co.uk/
assets/0000/5574/History_politics_and_vulnerability.pdf.

CHAPTER 12

Strengthening Scotland's Democracy
Susannah Fitzgerald

QUESTIONS OF DEMOCRACY and power have always been at the heart of the independence debate. The 'democratic deficit' – the sense that governments in Westminster, and the policies they implement, lack popular support in Scotland – is one of the independence movement's most powerful messages. In a poll held in the wake of the 2014 referendum, 74 per cent of Yes voters listed 'disaffection with Westminster politics' as one of the top issues in deciding how they voted – the highest level of support for any issue listed (*The Guardian*, 2014).

The potency of these concerns has ebbed and flowed in line with changes of government in the UK, but they have become particularly pertinent in the context of the past decade. Conservative grip has tightened on Westminster – ushering in austerity, Brexit, and now an onslaught of cronyism and misconduct amidst a global pandemic. With concerns now growing about hostility to devolution itself (*BBC News*, 2020), it is no wonder many in Scotland are looking for the exit door.

Yet, it is crucial that the independence movement, in its laser-focus on its final goal, does not forget why it began this quest for greater self-determination in the first place: the desire for a different type of politics. As the 20th century drew to a close, devolution meant Scotland looked to a new beginning. Henry McLeish, Chair of the group tasked with building a vision for Scotland's Parliament, wrote that it offered, 'the opportunity to put in place a new sort of democracy in Scotland, closer to the people and more in tune with Scottish needs' (CSG, 1998).

Devolution was intended to signal a rupture with the ways of working in Westminster: there were to be no leather benches from which to jeer and sneer, no places reserved for patronage or inheritance, and no convoluted procedures preserved for tradition rather than merit. Instead, Scotland's Parliament was to be based on four guiding principles: that power would be shared among the people, legislators, and the Executive; that the Government of Scotland would be accountable to the Parliament and the Parliament, in turn, accountable to the people of Scotland; that the Parliament would be accessible, open and responsive, involving people in its decisions as much as possible; and that the Parliament should promote equal opportunities for all (CSG, 1998).

But how well have we honoured these principles in the past two decades? As a country which may be asked to consider its constitutional future once again, we need to reflect on the state of our democracy and ensure that we are not replicating the same dynamics that led to disillusionment with Westminster in the first place. There are challenges for our democracy beyond independence, and we need to grapple with them sooner rather than later. One such challenge is the risk of undue influence over our politics, particularly the ways in which the shadowy world of lobbying operates.

What is Lobbying and Undue Influence?

Put simply, lobbying means, 'any activity carried out to influence a government or institution's policies and decisions in favour of a specific cause or outcome' (Transparency International). This can encompass a range of tactics, from shifting the terms of the debate and spinning the media through carefully crafted messaging, to sponsoring think tanks or other friendly groups to obscure your directing hand. At the other end of the scale, lobbying can be as simple as sending a letter or, if you are as well-connected as the likes of David Cameron, a text.

It is also essential to remember that lobbying can bring about positive outcomes as well as negative – just look at the success of Marcus Rashford's Free School Meal campaign. Lobbying therefore operates as a double-edged sword – it is both a necessary and important part of the democratic process, and one which can distort and undermine it. This distortion occurs when one group has excessive sway over policymaking, leading to private interests being prioritised over the public good. This risk of undue influence can be compounded by other factors. For example, decision-makers may have conflicts of interest which lead them to favour a particular outcome, they may have received donations from certain groups, or they may have their eye on a job in the private sector for when they leave office or public service.

We need to keep a check on how lobbying operates in Scotland for three reasons: to ensure that policies work for the public; to ensure that public money is spent judiciously; and to honour Holyrood's founding principles. With Scotland's Parliament legislating on a growing number of policy areas, so grows the scope for lobbying and the risks of undue influence around decisions – a dynamic that would only increase if Scotland were to become independent. Not least in the process of negotiations themselves, which would be subject to intense lobbying by those determined to shape the outcome of this process in their vision.

What Does Lobbying Look Like in Scotland?

The simple, and frustrating, answer is that we just do not know exactly how lobbying operates in Scotland; only a fraction of this information is captured by our lobbying register, where lobbyists record their activity. We are entirely in the dark about the amounts spent on lobbying in Scotland, we fail to capture how key groups of decision-makers are influenced, and evading lobbying regulations is as easy as sending an email, making a phone call, or turning off your camera on a Zoom call (SALT, 2020). This is particularly concerning during the pandemic, with research showing that phone calls jumped from just over one per cent of ministerial meetings in January 2020 to nearly 29 per cent in April 2020 (SALT, 2021).

One of the biggest risks of hidden lobbying is that it can unfairly skew policies without the public being able to identify how this has happened, with serious consequences for the wellbeing of our society, the fairness of our economy, or the health of our environment. Take, for example, the oil and gas industry, a sector that has had real significance for both Scotland's economy and narratives surrounding independence. It is also a sector where lobbying is extensive – Influence Map calculated that the five largest companies spent over $1 billion on branding and lobbying to ensure they could continue and even expand their fossil fuel operations in just the three years following the Paris Agreement (Influence Map, 2019).

One of these companies, Royal Dutch Shell, has previously boasted of its role in a controversial part of the Paris Agreement, despite rules against such things (Aronoff, 2018). Alongside Siccar Point Energy, Shell has also been behind the highly controversial and environmentally damaging Cambo oil field proposed for the North Sea, which they seem to be seeking to reinvigorate as a proposal after the Scottish Government moved towards questioning it. In Scotland, we know that Shell lobbied the former energy minister on 'the importance of balanced messaging in the lead up' to COP26 at an industry conference, described in turn by Will Dinan, as 'really code for ensuring that business-friendly policies are reflected in COP outcomes' (Edwards, 2021).

Another key concern is access to housing. In certain parts of the country, short-term lets for tourists have significantly reduced the available housing stock for local residents – in Edinburgh, this has reduced the number of homes available for long-term private rent by ten per cent (Tibbitt, 2019). Yet when policymakers in Holyrood sought to legislate for changes that could help manage this problem, Airbnb lobbied extensively to limit and delay these reforms. It used both its own representatives and external agencies, including an Edinburgh-based agency established by former Scottish Conservatives staff, one of whom was previously a MP and minister in the Scottish Office (Lo, 2019). Airbnb's lobbying efforts are not unique to Scotland either – research has shown that they fund deregulation campaigns in cities around the world that disguise the extent to which the platform is used by professional accommodation providers (Yates, 2021).

While policymakers defended their right to have these meetings, campaigners Living Rent stated that, 'dodgy deals behind closed doors and sweet-toothed lobbyists cannot conceal the fact that whole areas of our country are being gutted by these types of housing' (Lo, 2019). Outwith Scotland, the experience of similar groups shows they have reason to be concerned – Transparency International UK (2021) have shown that private renters are the only group who are regularly excluded from the housing policymaking process in Westminster, despite representing nearly a fifth of UK households. Yet, in both of these cases, our understanding of the full scope of this lobbying is limited by what researchers and journalists can dig up from the register and other sources. In the words of a Holyrood Committee, 'there is a body of communication and influencing being carried on that is not... being seen' (PAPLS, 2021).

What You Know or Who You Know?

While there is no implication of wrongdoing by officials or businesses in these circumstances, this gets at the crux of the issue facing Scotland. Scandals grab headlines, but they are not the entire story, There is a bigger question of who has a say and who does not; of who gets listened to and who is ignored in Scotland's politics. Alcohol Focus Scotland (AFS) succinctly outlined this issue:

Our concern about lobbying activity in Scotland is not restricted to, or even particularly focused on, possible impropriety in lobbying conduct. Far more problematic is the potential for large organisations, especially corporations, to gain privileged and disproportionate access to decision-makers in Parliament and government by virtue of fact that they are significantly better resourced (AFS, 2020).

There is not always, or even often, a parity of arms when it comes to lobbying, and there is a real risk that this asymmetry biases policies in favour of the well-connected and well-resourced. This becomes particularly pertinent when we look closer at who is carrying out lobbying in Scotland. One lobbying firm that provides an interesting case study, not least due to the attention it has drawn, is Charlotte Street Partners (CSP). One of its founding partners, a former SNP MSP and leading figure behind the SNP's Growth Commission, has strenuously denied that he is a corporate lobbyist on more than one occasion, on the basis that he does not meet with policymakers on behalf of clients (Hutcheon, 2018; Mackay, 2020). This is disingenuous, as lobbying incorporates more than just meetings with policymakers. Beyond this, it is clear that his colleagues regularly carry out exactly this type of lobbying. *The Herald* have reported that 'SNP insiders say CSP staff are regularly visitors at Westminster', records show that CSP attended a UK ministerial roundtable in 2017, and they have filed a number of returns in Scotland's lobbying register, including lobbying an MSP for Airbnb in 2020 (Gordon, 2016; Open Access UK; Lobbying Register). A previous claim that they 'won't ever speak on your behalf' has been removed from their website (Hassan, 2020; CSP).

It is also worth considering why there is such an aversion to the term 'corporate lobbyist', given that many who work as lobbyists do not consider it a 'pejorative term'. Negative connotations do arise, however, from lobbyists who act in a untransparent or inappropriate manner – accusations which CSP have left themselves exposed to. They publish no current client list that would help the public and policymakers understand on whose behalf they are working, and they were expelled from the Association for Scottish Public Affairs (ASPA), an industry body, for hiring a member of the House of Lords. ASPA stated that 'you can be a lobbyist or you can be a law maker, but you cannot be both' (Walker, 2021).

Unfortunately, they are not alone in the 'double jobbing' game. A former Scottish Conservatives leader and now peer accepted a position with a London-based lobbying firm that would have seen her paid £50,000 for 25 days' work a year while still a sitting MSP (*BBC News*, 2019). She agreed to 'step back' once questions were asked over whether she was placing personal gain or private interests before her constituents. Within the Scottish Government, efforts to understand possible conflicts of interest among more than 450 civil servants holding external roles were thwarted earlier this year when a Freedom of Information request was released in which almost every role was redacted (Matchett, 2021).

How Can We Make Decisions Accountable?

In setting out these concerns, the intention is not to demonise anyone, but to put forward a plea for honesty, transparency, and accountability about how policies and politics are influenced in Scotland. There is no silver bullet for managing undue influence, but other countries offer practical examples for how we can at least bring lobbying out of the shadows (SALT, 2020; SALT, 2021). Canada asks lobbyists to disclose all communications with policymakers, even when this is done indirectly, which allows us to focus on the lobbying itself rather than the medium through which it was made. In the US, lobbyists provide a 'good-faith estimate' of their spending on campaigns, helping the public, journalists, and researchers assess if big money is warping decisions. In Ireland, their register covers decision-makers right down to councillor level.

While a parliamentary review was supportive of changes that would close the loopholes in our register, responsibility has now shifted back to the Scottish Government to carry out further assessment (PAPLS, 2021) There is a real risk that these much-needed reforms could slip through the gap in the absence of political will. This would be a mistake.

The latest SSA Survey showed that the percentage of the population who trust the Scottish Government to make fair decisions declined by 12 per cent between 2015 and 2019 (Reid, Montagu, and Scholes, 2020). While public trust in the Scottish Government still significantly outweighs that of the UK government, it is crucial that we do not allow this to translate into complacency. While the reasons for this decline of trust are undoubtedly complex, better protecting the integrity of our policymaking process could go some way to addressing it.

Democracy is Not a Static Label

This is about the health of Scotland's democracy. Like a growing number of Scotland's population, I have grown up with devolution as a fact of life: I was born in 1995, when the Scottish Constitutional Convention issued their final report, and started school in 1999, a few weeks after the Scottish Parliament re-convened for the first time in nearly 300 years. On 18th September 2014, I cast my first ever vote. Scotland's own Parliament and the power to make policies with our own needs in mind is not something that my generation had to dream up, deliberate, or design – it is all we have ever known, and it is essential that we do not take it for granted.

As an adult, I spend my days as an anti-corruption campaigner, challenging the powerful to act with integrity. This experience has taught me that democracy is not a static label but something that we continuously make and evolve. Its health is a collective responsibility, and one which should not be abrogated for something as transient as party gain or wielded only with a political scalping in mind. The risk of undue influence is a question of power, not party politics; our democracy cannot only be for those with deep pockets and a full contact book, and this is something that politicians of all stripes should be able to rally around solving.

With the power of governance comes a responsibility to foster the type of politics we envisioned for this country: open, accessible, and accountable. While there have been welcome and innovative steps taken towards this, such as Citizens' Assemblies, we need to do more. Better understanding and managing the risks of undue influence is a critical part of this, but there is no shortage of ideas for rejuvenating Scotland's democracy – strengthened Parliamentary Committees, a new Constitutional Convention, or empowering local government, to name but a few (St Denny, 2019; Gray, 2020).

It is essential that the independence movement takes this issue seriously. If a narrow focus on independence is permitted to crowd out or de-prioritise the vital work needed to safeguard and strengthen our democracy, then it risks becoming a pyrrhic victory in which our politics is left more cynical, divided, and concentrated than before. This work should not be seen as a peripheral concern or distraction from its end goal. Instead, it is an integral part of bringing it to fruition, critical to both the integrity of the independence project itself and its ability to win over the unconvinced.

References

AFS (Alcohol Focus Scotland) (2020), *Consultation Submission to PAPLS Committee Review of the Lobbying (Scotland) Act 2016*, accessed at: https://yourviews.parliament.scot/papls/lobbying-act-review/consultation/view_respondent?uuId=687965174

Aronoff, K. (2018), 'Shell Oil Executive boasts that his company influenced the Paris Agreement', *The Intercept*. Accessed at: https://theintercept.com/2018/12/08/shell-oil-executive-boasts-that-his-company-influenced-the-paris-agreement/

BBC News (2019), 'Ruth Davidson backs down on plan to take job with lobbying firm', accessed at: https://www.bbc.co.uk/news/uk-scotland-scotland-politics-50222755

BBC News (2020), 'Boris Johnson 'called Scottish devolution disaster"', accessed at: https://www.bbc.co.uk/news/uk-politics-54965585

Charlotte Street Partners (CSP), *Services*, accessed at: https://www.charlottestreetpartners.com/services/

Consultative Steering Group (CSG) on the Scottish Parliament (1998), *Shaping Scotland's Parliament*, London: The Scottish Office.

Edwards, R. (2021) 'Oil firms under fire for lobbying on COP26 summit', *The Ferret*, accessed at: https://theferret.scot/oil-firms-lobbying-cop26-climate-summit/

Gordon, T. (2016) 'SNP growth commission hit by lobbying row', *The Herald*, accessed at: https://www.heraldscotland.com/news/14722014.snp-growth-commission-hit-lobbying-row/

Gray, M. (2020), 'People and Politics: Reshaping how we debate, discuss, and listen' in Hassan, G. and Barrow, S. (eds), *Scotland after the Virus*, Edinburgh: Luath Press.

Hassan, G. (2020), 'The UK is increasingly run by corporate insiders. And Scotland is, too', *openDemocracy*, accessed on at: https://www.opendemocracy.net/en/opendemocracyuk/ uk-increasingly-run-corporate-insiders-and-scotland-too/

Hutcheon, P. (2018), 'SNP Growth Commission chair Andrew Wilson: I am not a corporate lobbyist', *The Herald*, accessed at: https:// www.heraldscotland.com/news/16325587.snp-growth-commission-chair-andrew-wilson-not-corporate-lobbyist/

Influence Map (2019), 'Big Oil's Real Agenda on Climate Change', accessed at: https://influencemap.org/report/How-Big-Oil-Continues-to-Oppose-the-Paris-Agreement-38212275958aa-21196dae3b76220bddc

Lo, J. (2019), 'Airbnb lobbying revealed as SNP and Tories water down regulation', *The Ferret*, accessed at: https://theferret.scot/ airbnb-lobbying-snp-tories-regulation/

Lobbying Register, 'Return 23546', *Scottish Parliament Lobbying Register*. accessed at: https://www.lobbying.scot/SPS/ InformationReturn/SearchInformationReturnDetail/23546

Mackay, N. (2020), 'The Big Read: SNP target 2026 in 'roadmap for independence' from party's top strategist Andrew Wilson', *The Herald*, accessed at: https://www.heraldscotland.com/ news/18802847.big-read-snp-target-2026-roadmap-independence-partys-top-strategist-andrew-wilson/

Matchett, C. (2021), "Utterly useless': Hundreds of Scottish civil service external roles in response to second job concerns', *The Scotsman*, accessed at: https://www.scotsman.com/news/politics/ utterly-useless-hundreds-of-scottish-civil-service-external-roles-re-dacted-in-response-to-second-jobs-concerns-3270686

Mcilkenny, S. (2021), 'Calls for probe into SNP minister's meeting with Greensill', *The Herald.*, accessed at: https://www.heraldscotland. com/news/19225128.calls-probe-snp-ministers-meeting-greensill/

Open Access UK, 'Rt Hon Elizabeth Truss MP – 07/09/2017 – Scottish Council for Development and Industry Roundtable', accessed on 28/07/21 at: https://openaccess.transparency.org. uk/?meeting=38157

Public Audit and Post-Legislative Scrutiny Committee (2021), *Post-legislative scrutiny: The Lobbying (Scotland) Act 2016*. Scotland: Scottish Parliamentary Corporate Body, accessed

at: https://digitalpublications.parliament.scot/Commit-
tees/Report/PAPLS/2021/3/22/79252553-8fd1-49af-acc0-
66899fb52338#3618ec20-8175-47d2-af4c-8aed86688816.dita

Reid, S., Montagu, I. and Scholes, A. (2020), *Scottish Social Attitudes
2019: Attitudes to government and political engagement*, Scotland:
Scottish Government.

SALT (Scottish Alliance for Lobbying Transparency) (2020), *Consultation Submission to PAPLS Committee Review of the
Lobbying (Scotland) Act 2016*, accessed at: https://yourviews.
parliament.scot/papls/lobbying-act-review/consultation/
view_respondent?uuId=553302572

SALT (Scottish Alliance for Lobbying Transparency) (2021),
*Consultation Submission to PAPLS Committee Draft
Report*, accessed at: https://archive2021.parliament.
scot/S5_Public_Audit/General per cent20Documents/
Scottish_Alliance_for_Lobbying_Transparency_(SALT)_v2.pdf

St Denny, E. (2019), 'The Scottish Parliament and 'new politics' at
twenty' in Hassan, G. (ed.), *The Story of the Scottish Parliament:
The First Two Decades Explained*, Edinburgh: Edinburgh University Press.

The Guardian (2014), 'Scottish independence: poll reveals who
voted, how and why', accessed at: https://www.theguardian.com/
politics/2014/sep/20/scottish-independence-lord-ashcroft-poll

Tibbitt, A. (2019), 'Exposed: Airbnb lobbying to stop laws on lets', *The
Ferret*, accessed at: https://theferret.scot/airbnb-lobbying-law-lets/

Transparency International, *Corruptionary A-Z*, accessed at: https://
www.transparency.org/en/corruptionary/lobbying

Transparency International UK (2021), *House of Cards: Exploring
Access and Influence in UK Housing Policy*, accessed at: https://
www.transparency.org.uk/house-of-cards-UK-housing-policy-influ-
ence-Conservative-party-donations-lobbying https://www.transpar-
ency.org.uk/sites/default/files/pdf/publications/House per cent20of
per cent20Cards per cent20- per cent20Transparency per cent20In-
ternational per cent20UK per cent20 per cent28web per cent29.pdf

Walker, P.A. (2021), 'Trade body bans Charlotte Street Partners over
Lord Duncan hire', *Insider.co.uk*, accessed at: https://www.insider.
co.uk/news/trade-body-bans-charlotte-street-23340011

Yates, L. (2021), 'The Airbnb 'Movement' for Deregulation: How platform-sponsored grassroots lobbying is changing politics', Manchester: University of Manchester and Ethical Consumer, accessed at: https://research.ethicalconsumer.org/sites/default/files/inline-files/Yates per cent202021 per cent20- per cent20The per cent20Airbnb per cent20Movement per cent20for per cent20De-regulation per cent20report.pdf

CHAPTER 13

Scotland's Sustainable and Post-Fossil Fuel Future

Iain Black

THIS CHAPTER WILL address challenges facing arguments for independence based on how Scotland can, and indeed is, transitioning to a sustainable, post-fossil fuel future, while also addressing broader themes as to what type of country we want ours to become. My proposition is that only with the full powers of statehood can we take the action required to address the climate crisis. Further, demonstrating progress in the immediate and short term against this 'wicked problem', so the argument develops, will act to reassure voters as to what Scotland could achieve when unbridled from a recalcitrant UK state.

These important arguments are at considerable risk of being undermined. The danger comes, in part, from the solutions, including technologies, chosen to deliver our emissions reductions and structure our just transitions. More fundamentally, it comes from the established interests invited to deliver and control these solutions and the continued power this grants them over the current and new Scottish state. This is a stark manifestation of the current Scottish Government's observed reluctance hitherto to replace or reform established institutions in order to achieve its goals. It continues to seek to address the consequence of structural inequalities by maintaining the power and pre-eminence of the very structures causing the problems.

Scotland's post-fossil fuel future is increasingly being gambled on hydrogen, carbon capture utilisation and storage (CCUS) and offsetting. Yet any technology, however transformational, serves the goals of its owners and the system within which it works, and these are the solutions of the fossil fuel industry and global GDP-growth-based capitalism. Our fossil fuel free future is to be delivered by the same actors and owners of financial capital working toward the same system's goal, one which is widely recognised to be causing the ecological and social sustainability crises.

Our climate crisis responses and our future independence are therefore being re-tied to fossil fuels and fossil fuel companies through technologies yet to show anywhere near the scale of success required of them. This path puts Scotland's ability to meet its greenhouse gas reduction commitments at grave risk.

To reform a broken system the most powerful leverage point is to change its goal, institutions and structures. The full implementation of such plans ultimately requires powers we do not have, but there is much we can achieve by maximising the use of existing powers. Ultimately, the weakness and incompetence of the UK state may mean the route we are now on may just take us to independence, but not to a Just Transition and not to a Just Independence.

It's Scotland's Air, Land and Water

Building a greener Scotland has become as synonymous with the case for independence as control of 'our' oil was in the 1970s. Indeed a Greener Scotland is now, along with Equality, Fairness and Prosperity, one of the pillars of Scotland's civic nationalism. To take fast enough, deep enough and (the hard one) successful enough action on the climate (and interrelated) emergencies, independence supporters can, with significant justification, claim that Scotland cannot remain shackled to the UK. The UK is wedded to a discredited growth-based economic model. This will always default to protecting profit over the planet, and is therefore unwilling and incapable of appropriate climate action. Brexit strengthens this contention, with some voters for the first time considering a future inside the UK without the guiding hand of an EU more committed to environmental and social sustainability.

So is Scotland capable of reaching net zero by 2045 and are the full powers of independence needed to achieve it? Answering this question requires an examination of our nation's resources and assets, a case made for the repatriation of missing powers, and an explanation concerning which policies this would allow us to pursue and how we could pay for them. Crucially, how much more carbon dioxide could we remove, how much more quickly, and how sure would we be to succeed? We also need to examine critically our past record and current plans in order to see if they support the contention that we can be trusted with powers old and new.

Big Enough, Rich Enough?

We must start by considering Scotland's structural capacities and limitations as an independent country. Can a medium-sized, high GDP per capita, northern-situated European state successfully address the climate emergency? Does it have the energy resources, land, human, social and economic capital required? The clear evidence is that, yes, we have what is required for an appropriate decarbonisation pathway achieved through a just transition, ensuring that workers and communities are not left behind in the creation of a climate resilient society.

From here, the focus moves to the cooperation and alliances made possible through statehood. To reduce emissions fairly, we have to solve intensely difficult problems around industrial energy provision, decarbonising transport, retrofitting housing stock and producing food sustainably. This is easier to achieve through collaborative international partnerships, sharing knowledge, finance and a common future.

As an independent state able to choose its alliances (EU, EEA or EFTA) Scotland can more readily benefit from global efforts and better share its successes and learnings. It can also enjoy a full voice in deciding the direction of a shared future, rather than being hitched to an increasingly isolationist UK.

Scotland's Powers in Scotland's Hands

Building the case for the repatriation of powers requires us to understand that what is gained by independence is more complex than adding devolved powers to those reserved to Westminster. Simply put, one plus two can equal more than three, as complete oversight brings the opportunity for greater consistency and focus in policymaking. But having powers is not the same as using them well. Accepting that dangers exist from wielding some powers while others rest elsewhere, and that some will be given up as the price of participation in supranational organisations, adds to the complexity of analysing what can be achieved with full statehood.

The superior relative record of the Scottish Government in reducing carbon emissions, together with Westminster's poor job of delivery on reserved matters, provides a strong *prima facie* case for repatriating UK-controlled powers. Rather than assume this democratic and managerial case is undeniable, it would be wise to examine which currently reserved powers are central to the fight against climate change, and to integrate their repatriation into an engaging vision of post-fossil fuel Scotland.

As set out under Schedule 5 of the Scotland Act 1998 (2012 and 2016) there are 98 categories of 'reservations' controlled by the UK Parliament. The general reservations – particularly international relations, international development and regulation of international trade – are essential for forming, maintaining and influencing alliances and collaborations vital for delivering a just transition and a climate justice agenda.

Of the specific reservations, finance, economic, energy and transport powers have the most powerful and direct impacts on whether, and how, Scotland can achieve net zero. Relying on the UK Treasury (particularly post-COVID) to pay for new energy generation facilities, transport networks, home insulation and heating, reskilling and upskilling education, and the myriad other mitigation and adaptation measures, restricts Scotland's ability to pay for its own just transition.

By contrast, with the borrowing and quantitative easing powers of a central bank and fiat currency, Scotland could choose to fund its spending and reallocate existing budgets. Sitting against this clear case for financial powers, and the inadequate use of them (in climate finance terms) by Westminster, sits the Sustainable Growth Commission's report. Though contested internally, this remains the basis of the SNP's approach to a post-independence economy. It includes strict spending limits and public finance restrictions from a period of Sterlingisation. Change is clearly needed here.

The case for full powers over energy is more complex than one might immediately imagine. Scotland cannot directly influence oil and gas exploration or its taxation currently, though planning laws can be cleverly deployed if the political will exists. The performance of UK-controlled generation, transmission, distribution and supply of electricity both supports *and* argues against repatriation. Scotland outperformed the rest of the UK in terms of renewable energy generation, highlighting that we can be trusted with more powers, though this also suggests the current system can work. Supportive arguments for powers over transmission costs and contracts for difference (CFD's) will take careful development, those around energy conservation, coal exploitation and nuclear energy will be more straightforward.

It should be easy to make the case that reserved transport powers (such as vehicle standards and strategic planning for rail, marine and air) are needed to create the integrated, local, low-carbon travel options required to reduce this stubborn emissions category. Against this stands the Scottish Government's record of continued expansion of road infrastructure – for example, duelling the A9, the A96, the Aberdeen bypass and the Queensferry Crossing. The move to electric cars is, for most environmentalists understanding full lifecycle analysis, a false solution. It also ensures that infrastructure for active travel and liveable streets remains secondary to cars, irrespective of their energy source.

Powers over trade and industry, particularly around business creation, operation, regulation and dissolution, would support a rebalancing of the economy and be used to promote a wider range of business models. To this we can add consumer protection, product standards, research councils, telecommunications and internet services, and social security powers to legislate for a Universal Basic Income and a job or service guarantee. These are all required for just transition, localism and civic engagement. Repatriation of powers also brings control over the emissions associated with their administration, through for example, office real estate and direct and indirect procurement.

Building Back Better, or 'Burn, Bury and Hide'?

What does our current trajectory and plans say about our post-fossil fuel future, and what challenges do these pose the case for independence? Unfortunately, behind relative Scottish success compared with the UK and many other countries, there is much to worry about. Starkly, Scotland has missed its overall emissions reductions target for the last four years. The main path we are taking to eliminate the remaining, much tougher 48.5% is considered risky, and irrespective of success comes at a high price.

There are many different versions of how we can reach net zero by 2045. It could be the unfettered wellbeing economy path, whereby we live in 20 min suburbs or vibrant rural communities with access to skilled jobs, warm homes, local fresh food, agency in how we are governed, and time and energy for participation in life. This can bring us to net zero through reduced consumption, structural regeneration, collaboration and a heterogeneity of solutions. Of the detailed articulations, 'Our Common Home' (Common Weal, 2019) is recognised internationally as being coherent and appropriately costed. This version, and Lester Brown's Plan B series (2004, 2009) are technically and socially feasible. They are perhaps the most persuasive visions for an independent Scotland for those seeking a green, equitable and prosperous country.

Another version, which is becoming hardwired into Scotland's response, is a continued big business future in which established energy, finance and land interests sell us 'change without change'. This fossil fuel transition economy depends upon burning (or converting to electricity) hydrogen, burying emissions via carbon capture utilisation and storage (CCUS), and hiding them via offsetting. Such a 'burn, bury and hide' economic vision is large in scale, profit-driven, overhyped, over-supported and technically dubious. The emissions reduction role given to corporations in current Scottish Government plans is deeply at odds with the evidence of what they can achieve. Another view of this version is that it is a wedge tactic for ensuring that global capital profits from pretending to clean up its own mess.

Having reached the zenith of 'Build Back Better' enthusiasm in early-to mid-2020, wellbeing-based post-fossil fuel economic visions remain visible in Scottish Government documents, and visible in the Climate Challenge Fund, the Community and Renewable Energy Scheme, and the initiatives with which Scottish Green Party ministers are concerned. But underneath, and on a far greater scale, the infrastructure for the 'burn, bury, hide' version of vested interest Scotland is being enabled, funded and hardwired. This path undermines our chances of successfully addressing the climate crises at all, as well as the chances of achieving this in a fair and equitable manner.

The predominant choice of path is evident in the recent version of Scotland's pre-eminent legislation in this area, the Climate Change Plan Update (CCPU). Here, hydrogen, CCUS and offsetting are supported financially via the Energy Transition Fund. Meanwhile, the

Scottish Government's Oil and Gas and Energy Transition Strategic Leadership Group is dominated by representatives from the oil and gas industry. This gives primacy to fossil fuel companies in the just transition, rather than making the focus jobs and communities. A localised energy delivery structure via an enhanced Community and Rural Energy Scheme (CARES, funded by the Scottish Government) is a much sounder vision upon which to base just transition – instead of simply hoping oil and gas companies will become better corporate citizens.

Beyond the promise of private investment to pay for the transition, why are these solutions so seductive? Because they make (false) promises of change without actual change. Hydrogen allows the familiarity of hot water boilers and the continuation of long-haul flights. CCUS promises guilt-free consumption with the negative consequence buried out of sight and mind. Indeed, offsetting lends itself to tempting images of environmental improvement only possible through continued consumption. But offers of assurance and continuity are not matched by the required affordable engineering solutions. All three suffer under feasibility, financial and just transition-based scrutiny.

Hydrogen, offered as a replacement for fossil fuels in heating and transport, can be produced using various methods. Its energy density means it has a limited transitional role in a post-fossil fuel economy, powering certain industrial processes and acting as an interim fuel for large vehicles and long-distance air travel. But it should be facing far wider and sterner scrutiny over its environmental and financial costs.

The 'blue' or 'low carbon' version is produced by superheated steam stripping off hydrogen from fossil fuel hydrocarbons. At this point it is called grey hydrogen and has a greenhouse gas footprint 20% greater than if just the natural gas feedstock was burnt. It only becomes 'blue' through capturing waste CO_2, though the technology to do this does not yet exist. CCUS adds cost to an already costly process. So does transportation, since it cannot yet be legally added to gas networks above 0.1% concentration, because it makes pipes and joints brittle. 'Blue hydrogen' is the officially preferred version in the initial years of Scotland's Hydrogen Economy.

Meanwhile, so-called 'green' hydrogen, which is to follow, uses electricity to split water, but has a rapacious appetite for the ultimately limited supply of renewably generated electricity. This electricity, essentially to be produced by yet-to-be installed offshore wind capacity, would be more effectively utilised powering heat pumps, for example.

Talk of using hydrogen to provide a familiar form of heating distracts us from what people really want – warmth. And of course you do not need excess heating to create a warm, welcoming home, just better insulation. But achieving this across Scotland's housing stock is more complex to deliver, and (crucially) reduces the income and geopolitical power of the fossil fuel industry. This partly explains why they have lobbied so hard for hydrogen instead.

CCUS also suffers from feasibility, cost scale and control issues. Currently, according to industry figures, CCUS schemes globally can abate 0.7% of what is required by 2050. Chevron's Gorgon plant, the world's largest commercial scale project, has systematically failed to deliver the promised levels of capture – with none at all abated in its first three years, leading to threats of a \$100,000,000 fine. It can add between 2% to 68% in costs, depending on the industry (natural gas refining versus cement) and the location (\$50 per tonne in Saudi Arabia, or \$200 in Germany and Poland). These costs will lead to changes in demand, and will ultimately be passed to the customer, but for what? So we can continue to build, travel, make and consume in the very ways which are causing such harm to the planet and its inhabitants?

Finally, there is offsetting, the cornerstone of net zero (you offset the emissions you cannot reduce). For this to work it *must* demonstrate additionality, ie that money spent directly leads to additional carbon dioxide removal from the atmosphere. This is extremely difficult to prove with such a broad range of activities classed as offsetting. This includes reforestations, constructing renewable energy facilities, not cutting down forests, and providing bikes. But if these were going to be built or planted anyway – or worse, have already been built, the claimed carbon saving will exist on paper only.

Guillaume Peterson St-Laurent of the University of British Columbia sets out six limitations of offsetting: the deficiencies of carbon markets; limited economic benefits; uncertain climate effectiveness; negative public opinion; limited and uncertain property rights; and governance issues. In developing countries, offsetting schemes can reduce or remove agency from indigenous peoples, as land is used to clean up developed country lifestyles. There are also questions about size and distribution of economic benefits, as it is landowners, not tenant farmers, that benefit most. These concerns over Hydrogen, CCUS and offsetting are not new. As important as their technical and cost failings, are the companies involved.

Even the path taken to develop technologies proven to reduce emissions leads to similar concerns. The companies bidding for the Scotwind round of marine energy licenses include oil majors such as BP, Shell, TotalEnergies and ENI. Finance will be provided by banks such as Macquarie, and construction and support from large Belgian, German, French, Danish and Norwegian organisations.

So whether it is the transition path delivered by hydrogen, CCUS or Offsetting or the renewable electricity generated by our marine resources, the control of our post-fossil fuel future is being contracted to large private energy and finance interests. In the same way as Scotland's oil became theirs, so too will wind, wave and tidal, and with this it becomes harder to argue that Scotland needs new powers to reach net zero and that they will be exercised in a fair and equitable manner.

A Just Independence?

The Stop Climate Chaos (SCC) response to the Smith Commission asked directly 'whether any further devolved powers will or will not better enable Scotland to meet its climate commitments?' As a civil society organisation, they set out their view that the repatriation of powers should be a means to an end. The ends here, successfully addressing climate change through a just transition, matter.

For independence to be seen as the best way of delivering a just transition and a post-fossil fuel society, we can no longer rely on abstract ideas or well-meaning phrases such as 'we could', 'we can' or 'we would be able to'. Scotland has targets, plans and a long record of action against which visions of independence and calls for new powers will be judged.

Through work carried out by organisations such as Common Weal, the Wellbeing Economy Alliance and the Jimmy Reid Foundation, detailed versions of popular ideas concerning how a post-fossil fuel society can come about have been articulated. What unites these visions is that they call for systemic and institutional change

Solutions to the climate emergency – as with child poverty, drug deaths, underemployment and homelessness – need to address the causes of the problem at a systemic and structural level. So while Scotland does need powers it does not currently have (most notably over borrowing and money supply, energy and transport) better uses of existing powers over tax, governance, law, land and finance are needed in their own right, and to make the case for independence.

These times of crisis and liminality produced by the climate emergency, Brexit and COVID provide a rare opportunity to remake institutions and structures. However, the question of how Scotland will reach net zero threatens to become a story of the empire being invited to strike back. Backing hydrogen, CCUS and offsetting represents a kind of antidisestablishmentarianism, as active steps are taken to renew the role of established finance, land and energy companies in guiding Scotland. But if bankers, lairds and oil and gas companies still run Scotland, then ours will be a bounded independence. This is a particular challenge for a dominant SNP facing accusations of corporate capture.

In *Undoing the Revolution: Comparing Elite Subversion of Peasant Rebellions* (Temple University Press, 2019), Vasabjit Banergee explores why even successful peasant rebellions often failed to end peasant marginalisation. He asserts that rebellions only succeed if they have the support of some political and economic elites outside the incumbent government. However, the resources making these elites indispensable to the initial success of the rebellion also puts them in position to shape the post-conflict state in their own interests. So such rebellions fail to end marginalisation either because they lose without elite support, or because they succeed with it.

Will we in Scotland fail in our climate change revolution because the Scottish Government has to rely on economic elites as a result of not having the power to choose their allies? Will we fail because they did, in fact, have the power to make different choices but did not do so?

To be clear, the Scottish Government already has the power to ensure we own (enough) of the land and can create political economies organising local service-based solutions. They have the power to reshape Further and Higher education to provide the skills and knowledge needed to insulate our homes, grow our food and repurpose the transport infrastructure needed to move around.

They do not have to reach out to established power structures but as they are we can conclude that our revolution risks the same fate experienced by the rebellions studied by Banerjee.

It is not too late to change the fossil fuel path of Scotland's fossil fuel free future. We need to fight every battle regarding who delivers our just transition, who is building or retrofitting our homes, who is providing electric vehicle charging points, who controls offshore wind generation and who controls the timber we need for building and insulating.

We need a Just Independence, not just independence, and despite being told that decisions about the type of new country we want should wait until after a vote, it is increasingly apparent that if we accept this, we will end up with a Model T Ford version. Just as you could have any version of that iconic car so long as it was black, so we will be able to have any version of the future we want, as long as the establishment controls it

Section Four: The Philosophy and Practice of Independence

CHAPTER 14

Stop the World, Scotland Wants to Get On: Independence and Interdependence

Ben Jackson

THE TERMINOLOGY OF an 'independent Scotland' is, in some respects, misleading since the question posed by Scotland's constitutional status is, in fact, about which forms of political interdependence with other states and nations could best advance the democratic preferences of the Scottish electorate. The union with England, Wales and Northern Ireland is one form of such interdependence, but even outside of the union close relations would be required with other states and supranational organisations.

A new Scottish state separate from the UK would take its place within an existing global political system and accept the constraints of international power politics and economic markets. Supporters of independence have usually been conscious of this, but they have also tended to channel the conventional geopolitical wisdom of the time, even when they have presented themselves as fierce critics of it. This chapter draws on my recent book, *The Case for Scottish Independence* (2020), to reconstruct how Scottish nationalist views of Scotland's place in the world have changed over time, in response to the changing global order, and highlight the difficult dilemmas that now confront supporters of independence as they seek to adjust their prospectus to the geopolitics of the 2020s and 2030s, rather than the easier political times of the 1990s and early 2000s.

Scottish nationalism was born as a movement in the twilight of the British Empire and its early iterations in the 1930s and 1940s reflected the assumptions of British imperial world-making. An uneasy division existed within the National Party of Scotland (NPS), founded in 1928. This was between a more radical sovereigntist analysis that sought a Scottish state that had complete control over domestic and foreign policy and was firmly anti-imperialist, and a rival view. That second view supported a Scottish Parliament as a part of the British Empire, with control over domestic Scottish matters but wider 'imperial' policy remaining the province of the Parliament at Westminster.

The Scottish Party, the second, and more establishment, nationalist party that merged with the NPS to form the SNP in 1934, had many members who saw Scottish self-government as primarily about enabling Scotland to play a more active role as a distinct mother nation of the British Empire. After its foundation, SNP policy reflected these tributaries and arrived at the delicate, and purposefully vague, compromise that a new Scottish Parliament should be created to tend to Scottish affairs, while foreign, defence, and imperial policy would be determined by new joint committees shared between England and Scotland. In the course of the 1930s, this compromise frayed under pressure from more radical currents in the SNP, as the party developed a more staunchly anti-imperialist profile and key figures in the SNP ended up opposing the British war effort during the Second World War. In this phase of Scottish nationalism, then, the idea of sharing Scottish sovereignty with both the rest of the UK and the British Empire was widely canvassed and endorsed by leading figures in the movement, though it also sparked severe internal divisions (Finlay, 1992).

These strands of nationalist thought were largely focused on the relationship between Scotland, the increasingly centralised British state and economy, and the British Empire. But in the late 20th century the development of European integration, and Britain's membership of the European Economic Community (EEC), posed new questions for Scottish nationalism about the nature of sovereignty and how an independent Scotland might relate to the wider world. The SNP had been supportive of initial efforts at European integration in the 1940s and 1950s but grew more sceptical over the course of the 1960s and 1970s.

Forthright criticism of Britain's accession to the EEC was mounted by nationalist luminaries such as William Wolfe, Winnie Ewing and Gordon Wilson and they led the SNP in campaigning for a No vote in the 1975 referendum on Britain's membership. In their view, the EEC constituted a further layer of undemocratic and centralised government that would merely exacerbate the problems faced by nations on its periphery, such as Scotland. It was telling, however, that the language the SNP used against European integration was a pluralist, decentralising rhetoric, rather than a more straightforwardly nationalist one.

As Winnie Ewing argued, 'decision-makers must be where the people live, or a valuable part of the enjoyment of life to the full is lost', whereas the EEC offered 'an undemocratic community' that was 'controlled by bureaucrats' (Ewing, 1970). Scottish nationalist sceptics of the EEC perceptively noted that the pro-European case in Britain was itself one that, at times, relied on a rather conventional notion of British exceptionalism. Ewing observed that the pro-European argument seemed to be 'that Britain must be great again' by leading in Europe: 'if we want to play at influencing events, we are told, it has to be within a superpower'. But in Scotland, she said, 'we are not particularly worried that we lost the Empire' (Ewing, 1974).

Nonetheless, the Scottish nationalism of the 1970s, like the earlier version of the mid-20th century, was a product of the geopolitics of the time. On the one hand, it avowed a unilateralist critique of the Cold War and the nuclear arms race; thus purposefully standing somewhat apart from the foreign policy of the UK state. But on the other, the project of Scottish independence was understood as the assertion of the rights of a sovereign state over its territory and resources, just like the other states that had emerged all over the globe after the Second World War.

Although few nationalists seriously claimed that Scotland could be analogous to a post-colonial state, they did imagine that Scotland's geographical position on the fringes of Europe, at the juncture point of English, American, European and Soviet spheres of influence, positioned it to adopt a posture somewhat like that of Norway. That is, as a resource-rich economy that remained outside of formal membership of the common market but was nonetheless firmly a part of the community of democratic Western European states (Maxwell, 1976).

The SNP's Euroscepticism eventually gave way to a more sympathetic engagement with European integration as the Cold War reached its denouement. The EEC itself evolved in a more regionalist and welfarist direction in the 1980s, to Scotland's tangible benefit, while the British state had, of course, done the opposite. In this context, senior figures in the SNP began to rethink their initial opposition to the EEC and instead to see a putative Scottish membership of the organisation as offering a context within which independence seemed a less radical and economically fraught step. Both Gordon Wilson, who became party leader after 1979, and Winnie Ewing shifted their positions on the EEC as these advantages became clear.

The SNP officially changed its position on the EEC at its 1983 conference, recommending Scottish membership, though only after a post-independence referendum on the subject. The most powerful advocate of this change of policy was Jim Sillars who, when a Labour MP, had been an advocate of a No vote in the 1975 referendum. Sillars decisively shifted his position in favour of the EEC when he formed the ill-fated breakaway Scottish Labour Party (SLP) in 1976.

'Scotland in Europe' became a cornerstone of the SLP's ideological positioning as a means of distinguishing it from the SNP's Euroscepticism, but it also reflected Sillars's conviction that, since membership of the EEC was now resolved, separate Scottish representation in European institutions was essential to securing Scottish interests. The SLP's argument – later to become a very familiar one in Scottish politics – was that European integration had now constrained the sovereignty of all member states and that 'separate' statehood no longer existed as a viable option for either Scotland or Britain. Instead, Europe could provide a framework in which some autonomy could be exercised by a Scottish state without disrupting any of the existing trading relationships between Scotland and the rest of the UK. Sillars carried these views with him into the SNP in 1980 and continued to develop them in response to the changing character of the EEC in that same decade.

Sillars argued that global economic changes, including the rise of Pacific economies (such as Japan and China), were bringing about a new era of large economic blocs in which European nations would need to work together to form a coherent counterweight. Sillars also observed that the pace of European integration in the late 1980s was bringing about 'a process of change in the nature of national sovereignty that cannot be averted or reversed'. The arrival of a single European market in 1992, he predicted, would in due course create further pressure to integrate 'currencies, monetary policies, fiscal policies, and social policies'.

Although Sillars thought it was as yet unclear precisely how this integration would proceed, the nationalist concern was that Scottish interests could not be adequately represented in the ensuing discussions via the British state. Scotland could only have a serious role in these debates if it took its place as a full member with veto power rather than being restricted to lobbying the UK government (Sillars, 1985, 9; Sillars, 1988, 7–8; Sillars, 1989, 5–8). Sillars was broadly supportive of the signing of the Single European Act in 1986, though he warned that the single market would only work fairly for Scotland if combined with a stronger European regional policy, an independent Scottish state focused on developing a more dynamic Scottish economy, and ultimately greater democratisation of European institutions. But he did stress – and this was of great political importance – that one consequence of European integration, and the single market in particular, was that Scottish independence would no longer be vulnerable to the charge of 'separatism' from unionists.

An independent Scotland in Europe could simply retain all of its existing international links: 'continued membership means continuity in traditional trading patterns, access to markets, maintenance of the economic framework within which companies have planned their investment' and also 'continuity for the free movement of people with no barriers to the family and social relationships that exist between the peoples in the British Isles' (Sillars, 1985, 4–6; Sillars, 1988, 6–7, 13–17; Sillars, 1989, 8–15, 37–8). Membership of the EEC would therefore also preserve what Sillars termed the 'social union' between Scotland and England. In 1988 the SNP formalised its policy as 'Independence in Europe', which was also very successful as a pithy slogan that captured the essence of this strand of nationalism.

The legal philosopher and sometime SNP MEP Neil MacCormick later conceptualised the pooling and sharing of sovereignty evident in European integration in the 1980s and 1990s as the advent of the 'post-sovereign' state, in which state powers were transferred upward both to a supranational level and downwards to a regional level. MacCormick favoured an independent Scotland as a member of the EU, complemented by an intergovernmental Council of the Isles to deal with issues specific to the British archipelago. With these arrangements in place, Scotland would secure a relationship of equality with the rest of the UK, and other European states, as fellow members of the European Union. The 'process of division and combination' of national sovereignty offered by European integration thus opened the way to a model of Scottish independence in which a Scottish state would take over important powers held at Westminster, while in other domains sharing powers at a European and even British level (MacCormick, 1999, 61–2, 133, 193–9).

MacCormick's theoretical vision of a pluralist pooling of sovereignty at the national and supranational level percolated quite deeply into the practical case that nationalists articulated for Scottish independence in the early 21st century. Their enthusiastic embrace of post-sovereignty was also encouraged by a growing interest among nationalists in Ireland's successful transformation into a vibrant European economy. Ireland was thought to show that participation in Europe could enhance the power of small states and, most importantly, enable England's neighbours to stand in a relationship of equality with it for the first time in their history. George Reid, a leading figure in the SNP of the 1970s, returned from a long exile from active politics to deliver an influential Donaldson lecture to the 1995 SNP conference that made a compelling case for the importance of 'post-sovereignty' to the cause of independence.

Drawing on MacCormick's work, as well as like-minded writers such as Neal Ascherson and Tom Nairn, Reid argued that a historical 'pincer movement' was undermining the British state – on the one hand, the need for supranational structures for economic cooperation and on the other, a desire for greater local control:

> the state today is too big to address the needs of minorities like the Catalans and the Scots. It is too small, in an age of global macroeconomics, to operate the old economic particularism (Reid, 1995)

As a result, argued Reid, Scottish nationalists should abandon 'the language of the nineteenth-century state' (and the absolutist British notion of parliamentary sovereignty) and instead enthusiastically embrace the sharing of power with other European nations (Reid, 1995).

This was not just a matter of pooling resources and sharing sovereignty with the EU. Scottish nationalists were, for example, content with a new Scottish state retaining the 1603 union of the crowns and thus with Elizabeth I (of Scotland) remaining as its head of state. Membership of NATO, although a difficult issue, was accepted by the SNP at its 2012 party conference and would embed the new Scottish state in the transatlantic military alliance. Some nationalists even suggested that a number of state institutions and services might be shared by a Scottish state and the rest of the UK, such as the Ordinance Survey, DVLA, Civil Aviation Authority, or even some aspects of national defence (MacAskill, 2004, 29-30; MacLeod and Russell, 2006, 12–13, 150). These examples could also be extended to embrace the realm of macroeconomic policy, as in the run-up to the 2014 referendum the Scottish Government proposed that an independent Scotland would continue to use sterling as its currency and the Bank of England as its central bank.

Yet, as MacCormick himself noted, there was no definitive logical relationship between the advent of 'post-sovereignty' and an independent Scotland. Rather, this analysis established independence as 'one among a range of reasonable choices, not that it is a required or obligatory outcome' (MacCormick, 1999, 204). In this sense, it was certainly possible – at least before 2014 – to envisage an advanced devolutionary settlement that pooled sovereignty between Edinburgh, London and Brussels in a sufficiently flexible and pluralistic fashion to satisfy MacCormick's theoretical desiderata. Before the referendum of 2014, this was the major ideological victory of the 'gradualist' position within the SNP: Scottish autonomy had become conceptualised as an open-ended process, whereby ever greater powers could accrue to the Scottish Parliament – when Scottish public opinion demanded it – with the ultimate goal of independence representing a distant objective that would only be reached (if desired by the voters) across a long time horizon.

The opportunity to hold a referendum on Scottish independence, when it unexpectedly arose because the SNP won a majority in the 2011 Scottish Parliament elections, placed pressure on this strategic outlook, since the referendum had the effect of popularising independence as a rupture from the status quo – something that stood in tension with the SNP's previous efforts to make the enhancement of Scottish autonomy appear to be a slower and less risky proposition. The 2016 referendum on Britain's membership of the EU added a further dilemma for the advocates of 'post-sovereignty', since it confronted supporters of independence with the very forced choice that they sought to escape from by embracing European integration back in the 1980s: between an independent Scotland with unhindered economic relations with the rest of the UK out of the EU, or a Scotland separated from the UK's single market as a full member of the EU.

Advocates of independence are therefore now faced by a new and unfamiliar geopolitical context – one that presents powerful challenges to the verities of Scottish nationalism established in the late 20th century. So far, the signs are that the leaders of the SNP want to bite the bullet and present independence as a means of returning Scotland to the EU, an understandable move given the high support for EU membership in Scotland. But this is a position that carries significant political and economic costs, notably the need for a harder border between a new Scottish state and England. It was precisely because they judged such a border to be a difficult political sell that an earlier generation of nationalists embraced the promise of European integration. This is a dilemma to which independence supporters need to formulate a response, since it is a point that will be central to the case of their opponents in any second independence referendum. The British, European, and even global context that would confront an independent Scotland is rapidly shifting from the more benign circumstances of the 1990s and early 2000s, but as yet the ideology of Scottish nationalism has not managed to catch up with it.

References

Ewing, W. (1970), *Hansard*, HC Debates, fifth series, vol. 796, cols. 1086, 1088, 24 February.

Ewing, W. (1974), *Hansard*, HC Debates, fifth series, vol. 883, cols. 1956, 19 December.

Finlay, R. (1992), '"For or Against?" Scottish Nationalists and the British Empire, 1919-39', *Scottish Historical Review*, 71: 184-206.

Jackson, B. (2020), *The Case for Scottish Independence: A History of Nationalist Political Thought in Modern Scotland*, Cambridge: Cambridge University Press.

MacAskill, K. (2004), *Building a Nation: Post-Devolution Nationalism in Scotland*, Edinburgh: Luath Press.

MacCormick, N. (1999), *Questioning Sovereignty*, Oxford: Oxford University Press.

Maxwell, S. (1976), 'Scotland's Foreign Policy', *Question*, No. 12, September 1976: 5-7.

Reid, G. (1995), 'Oh, to Be in Britain?', Donaldson Lecture, Edinburgh: SNP.

MacLeod, D. and Russell, R. (2006), *Grasping the Thistle*, Glendaruel: Argyll.

Sillars, J. (1985), *Scotland: Moving on and up in Europe*, n.p.

Sillars, J. (1988), *No Turning Back: The Case for Scottish Independence within the European Community and How We Face the Challenge of 1992*, n.p.

Sillars, J. (1989), *Independence in Europe*, Glasgow: SNP.

CHAPTER 15

Independence of the Scottish Mind and the Evolution of the Public Sphere
Gerry Hassan

SCOTLAND HAS A long, rich tradition of celebrating its difference and distinctiveness, seeing in its autonomy a kind of semi-independence that is exhibited in civil society, the public sphere and public life.

Scotland's public sphere is one of the main ways we communicate, define ourselves, relate to others in public, and hold (or don't hold) power and institutions to account – hence contributing to the democratic and political process in all its richness and imperfections. It can be understood as a spatial metaphor and also described in William Mackenzie's phrase: 'community of the communicators' which emphasises the human dimension (Habermas, 1989; Mackenzie, 1978). All of this contributes to an 'independence of the Scottish mind' – an outlook that has evolved and articulated its distinctive nature in comparison to the rest of the UK, while displaying fragility and doubt (Hassan, 2014).

Some of this is due to the size of Scotland, its public life and public sphere. Some is also due to our history and traditions which, along with many positives, have at times seen a tendency to institutional groupthink and unquestioningly swallow the prevailing orthodoxies of the day – whether it be elite liberalism in the 19th century, what passed for social democracy in the late 20th century, or the politics of devolution and self-government in the early 21st century.

Another reason for fragility is the semi-autonomous nature of the public sphere here and how it has a 'dual nature', being influenced and intersected by the London-centric public sphere of the UK. Academic Philip Schlesinger observes:

> Although the Scottish and UK public spheres often overlap, key differences in political institutions, voting patterns, and agendas mean that there is built-in scope for dispute about media content, legal and regulatory competencies (2020a: 156).

This relationship is critically not one of equals, but defined by imbalances and inequalities: it is mostly one-sided, in that the London-centric public sphere communicates into and is represented in Scotland, but the Scottish public sphere has a slender footprint in London and when it does it is episodic and transient, linked to big stories or crises. London continually broadcasts stories into Scotland, such as the rise of Euroscepticism and UKIP, immigrant scare stories, and items about the London and South East economy. Scotland's one big story in a generation with UK impact has been the 2014 independence referendum.

After the 'Big Bang' of 2014

The 2011–14 independence referendum witnessed an explosion of debate and discussion that changed the parameters and contours of public life. But, in the past seven years we have seen retrenchment, retreat and a return to a restricted menu of options with similarities to pre-2014: where politics and challenging power is once again regarded as a minority interest and something to be discouraged; however, there are exceptions to this assessment such as the work of the investigative journalism site *The Ferret*, launched in May 2015.

There are numerous reasons for this return. One is the political backdrop of an SNP administration who have now been in office for over fourteen years, and the wear and tear which comes with this, as well as morphing into a political establishment. As important, this illustrates the limits of insurgency politics when the main champion of it is in office – a contrast from the twin-track the SNP ran in the 2014 campaign when they were able to portray themselves as insiders and insurgents.

Post-2014 has seen a retreat of people and participants in debate, platforms, public spaces, and in the public sphere – whether in the media or wider public conversations. This should not be seen as presenting 2014 as some kind of golden age, but merely to note that the

'Big Bang' explosion of public engagement and participation was not built upon in public life.

The long road to 2014 was one of a weakening hold by institutional Scotland – which until the 1960s and 1970s was a liberal unionist perspective – that, as it declined, provided the opening for the SNP to win office, the independence question to be brought mainstream, and issues of power and legitimacy to come centre stage. Yet, even taking this longer picture of 2014 and since, there has been retrenchment and disengagement.

Black and White Scotland

All across public life, one can witness the emergence of more abrasive debates as intolerant voices rise to the fore in discussions. This is a world of black and white Scotland, seen by its protagonists as good versus evil, the saved versus the damned, and which by its heat, lack of light and certainty has the capacity to crowd out and scare away others. Thus, we have exchanges in parts of the constitutional debate that have an Armageddon-like nature: of Scotland needing to break free as soon as possible from a rotten, corrupt, anti-democratic union and being held against its will by perfidious politicians in Westminster and Scotland (in some accounts now including the SNP).

On the other hand, the most fanatical aspects of the unionist sentiment have disappeared into their own parallel universe, equating the SNP with fascists and Nazis, hating Nicola Sturgeon to a degree beyond reason, and sometimes even embracing anti-Scottishness. One recent example has been openly refusing to support the Scottish men's football team in the Euros, instead supporting the teams Scotland were playing; the logic in this latter sentiment is that any support for Scotland plays into the independence project and has to be opposed.

Black and white thinking can be identified when people doubt the integrity of those they disagree with, or search for conspiracy theories to explain how the world, or Scotland, is not the way they want it. Thus, many who are anti-independence supporters bemoan the so-called influence of the 'cybernats', while some of the most passionate pro-independence people believe that any questioning of the project is tantamount to being a 'yoon' and hence can be dismissed.

There is a contest for legitimacy and for delegitimising the opposing side which needs to be understood beyond decrying the influence of social media and thinking all society's ills can be traced back to it. This is often the clarion call of too many mainstream media perspectives. One well-known Labour figure once told me, when researching *The Strange Death of Labour Scotland,* that he had proof that 'the most prominent cybernats were given briefings and orders from SNP headquarters' and gave an example that proved nothing of the kind (Hassan and Shaw, 2012). The point is that he saw it as proof that this tendency was organised and the official SNP was culpable for their existence and had a direct relationship with them. That is an extreme example of misunderstanding the changing media and political landscape, but there are many more.

On a more mundane level, uber-partisan perspectives on Scotland in the mainstream and social media, along with wider public discourse, have the potential to crowd out others and restrict the room for more nuanced debate. Take the example of the fall-out from the trial of Alex Salmond – where he was cleared of all charges of sexual assault in March 2020. Subsequent to this, and against a backdrop of COVID-19, for an entire year various outlandish theories were bandied about on the extent of conspiracy theories to 'destroy' and 'take down' Salmond, of female witnesses colluding and lying, and worse. All of this was based on conjecture and supposition, resulting in the blogger Craig Murray being charged with contempt of court and jailed for eight months in July 2021.

A watershed for some has been the controversy around the Gender Recognition Bill and issue of self-identification for trans people; this has become, in parts of public life, an incendiary debate defined by a lack of common ground and understanding between those who are trans supporters and those who are gender critical.

Instead of a fair debate, we see fundamentalists verbally assault each other and reduce discussion to the most simplistic banalities that are presented as non-negotiable. This does not happen in a vacuum, but has been weaponised and magnified by the forces of the reactionary right and the likes of George Galloway and Alex Salmond, blogs such as *Wings over Scotland* – which became fixated on the trans issue – as well as the *Daily Mail* and, to a lesser extent, *The Times.*

The Retreat of Public Service Broadcasting

The changing media landscape, retreat of the *BBC*, challenge to public service broadcasting, and the regulatory model overseen by Ofcom, do not assist in the vibrancy of the public sphere in Scotland or across the UK. The *BBC* is now consistently under fire from across the political spectrum – from right-wingers and the UK Tory government, from Corbynistas and the left, and in Scotland, from the SNP and independence supporters. This underlines that the *BBC's* cautious centrism and search for balance is a dangerous tightrope that it regularly falls off – aided by the ineptitude and defensiveness of senior *BBC* managers.

The spectre of *GB News* is worth noting because inept, nasty, ill-informed and unprofessional as it is, it may offer a glimpse into the future. This would be a media without much breaking news but with lots of prejudice and opinion, catering to a niche market and then looking to make waves from a small constituency and the reaction its output provokes.

This would be a media terrain where the all-encompassing national broadcasters – *BBC, ITV, SKY* – play an increasingly smaller role and instead there would be a host of partisan, specialist broadcasters and providers. Rather than just let this happen by stealth, politicians and policy makers need to recognise the changing world of the media (both internationally and in the UK) and act to aid quality, pluralism and diversity. The chances of the UK Tory government leading such a debate – given its ideological and commercial interests, as well as propensity to bash the *BBC* – is non-existent.

Scotland's public sphere is often assumed as being virtuous, without addressing realities and constraints (an exception in this is Silver, 2015). Many of the specific institutions, practices and platforms which make up the public sphere are often cited and lambasted without any reference or understanding to this wider context and landscape. For example, it is really impossible to understand *BBC Scotland* and its outlook and choices without referencing how it sits and relates to the *BBC* in London – which is ultimately about who the heads of the corporation in Scotland are accountable to, how that distorts perspectives, and how it sits in the wider media landscape here.

This is a situation of which an increasingly self-governing Scotland has to become more acutely aware because it impacts on how we hold power of any kind to account – whether political, economic, civic, or other. Today's Scotland already contains too many concentrations of power, vested interests and closed doors which debar or disincline anyone from asking too many questions or scrutinising decisions too carefully.

The public sphere in Scotland needs urgent attention, as powerful forces and interests globally are going to bring turbulence, upheaval and disruption. That means that we will need to think how to protect and preserve the diversity and pluralism that we have, but also recognise that this will not be enough. Rather, we also need to open up a debate about how we enrich and democratise our public life and public sphere, and use it for the benefit of the majority rather than the select few.

The Long Scottish Revolution

If we return to the long view of change cited earlier in this text, a suitably thoughtful perspective came from the academic Christopher Harvie, writing in the *New Statesman* in November 1975 in a piece: 'The Devolution of the Intellectuals'. Harvie characterised the decline of traditional authority and institutions, and the emergence of new ideas and voices challenging the old:

> The complacent conservatism which characterised middle class Scottish culture seems almost completely to have disappeared. The old Scottish institutions are admitted to be in dissolution; the hold of the churches has been broken; law is seen more as a restrictive practice than a national ornament; education is badly in need of reform. Political nationalism is no more prepossessing as an ideology than it was, but there is no longer a British or imperial alternative. The intelligentsia can now only create a tolerable, convivial community in its own country (Harvie, 1975: 666).

Scotland has come far in the years since those words were written. We created a parliament and a more distinctive political culture, we established distance between ourselves and the British state, and we had an independence referendum: part of an ongoing, live political debate about who we are and what we want to be. But we have also not come far enough and not been alert enough to the changing land-scape around us. For all the focus on constitutional self-government, politics and political structures, we also have to be equally aware of the importance of cultural self-determination, and issues which go well beyond traditional politics.

Moreover, there can be seen in Scotland post-1945 both great change and an element of a circular journey. The ordered, hierarchical, permission based Scotland of the 1940s and 1950s was one in which, in the words of the Norwegian sociologist Thomas Mathieson, people and issues were 'silently silenced' as the boundaries of public debate were heavily fortified by gatekeepers and normative values – with a whole variety of subjects not talked about in public and institutional settings (Mathieson, 2005). As well as this, the main traditions of political and public life exhibited a lack of interest in what could be called 'relational space' – meaning who is in and who is not in any public conversation, platform or occasion, whether it be class, gender, ethnicity, disability or another characteristic (see Barr, 2008).

Suffice to point out in the far-reaching changes that Scotland has witnessed in the decades since, one of the most prominent takes has been to regard these traditional facets as having been vanquished and that present day Scotland amounts to a free for all like some sort of Western shoot-out. This misunderstands both the legacy of the moral order and authority of the above which, having been built over centuries, carries residual respect and power and also the capacity, in a small polity, for consensus and groupthink. Hence, in today's Scotland, there are still people and issues being 'silently silenced' as well as the omissions of not recognising the importance of 'relational space' – all of which have roots in the past and draw from the socio-political realities of the present, alongside the contours of the public sphere.

Therefore, 'the new Scotland' might be remarkably different from 'the old Scotland' in numerous ways, but there are also many continuities. Over twenty years ago, the Clause 28 episode showcased what was the first ever public debate on homosexuality in the history of Scotland – one that brought forward all sorts of homophobic prejudice as well as general nervousness on the part of the political classes. Fast forward to the present, and on a host of issues – trans rights, sectarianism and anti-Irish prejudice, or the reasons for the rise in drug deaths –there is an inability to confront and get into detail in a constructive way without hyper-partisans distorting the debate.

Understanding the historical parameters of where we have come from and how they impact on the present is pivotal to addressing the voices included and excluded from public life and the public sphere. Beginning to change this has to entail, at its centre, thinking of a public sphere built on pluralism, diversity and respect for differing views, but one which also aids people listening, debating, and even changing their minds – learning how to turn down the noise and stand up to the forces of hate.

Doing this demands that not only do we have to look hard and honestly at ourselves, but also address the wider context. First, is the nature of the public sphere and its relationship to a media landscape embarking on dramatic consumption, distributional and technological changes in a platform economy? Second, how we respond to the challenge of 'the post-public sphere' – a description now increasingly used 'which designates the present, unsettled state of play' (Schlesinger, 2020b: 1557).

Third, there is the nature of Scotland's limited autonomy – both under devolution and also under independence as a small sized country. Fourth, is the nature of the Scottish Parliament and its incorporation of many of the public institutions and agencies, limiting the room for being independent and occasionally difficult. Fifth, is the regulatory and institutional reframing going on at a UK level, instigated by the age of fluidity and magnified by Brexit.

Finally, there is the broader context of the UK – namely that we are still living on a set of islands with the relics of a feudal political order intended to intimidate us into submission and make us content with being subjects, not citizens. This is not something the British establishment target Scotland with specifically but is their general attitude and arrogant worldview in relation to all the people of the UK. The difference is, we can do something about all of this if we collectively want.

References

Barr, J. (2008), *The Stranger Within: On the Idea of an Educated Public*, Rotterdam: Sense Publishers.

Habermas, J. (1989), *The Structural Transformation of the Public Sphere: An Inquiry into a Category of Bourgeois Society*, Cambridge: Polity Press.

Harvie, C. (1975), 'The Devolution of the Intellectuals', *New Statesman*, 28 November, 665-6.

Hassan, G. (2014), *Independence of the Scottish Mind: Elite Narratives, Public Spaces and the Making of a Modern Nation*, London: Palgrave Macmillan.

Hassan, G. and Shaw, E. (2012), *The Strange Death of Labour Scotland*, Edinburgh: Edinburgh University Press.

Mackenzie, W.J.M. (1978), *Political Identity*, Harmondsworth: Penguin.

Mathieson, T. (2005), *Silently Silenced: Essays on the Creation of Acquiescence in Modern Society*, Hook: Waterside Press.

Schlesinger, P. (2020a), 'Scotland's Dual Public Sphere and the Media', in Keating, M. (ed.), *The Oxford Handbook of Scottish Politics*, Oxford University Press, 156-77.

Schlesinger, P. (2020b), 'After the post-public sphere', *Media, Culture and Society*, Vol. 42 (7-8), 1545-63.

Silver, C. (2015), *Demanding Democracy: The Case for a Scottish Media*, Word Power Press.

CHAPTER 16

Reframing the Language of Independence
Joyce McMillan and Lisa Clark

This chapter revolves around material from two conversations arranged by co-editor Simon Barrow. The first is with a prominent Scottish journalist, commentator and civil society actor Joyce McMillan, who moved from No to Yes on the constitutional question, but who has retained a desire to understand the fears as well as the hopes that impact the way Scots see their future and make decisions about it.

Thinking Afresh About Scotland's Choice
Joyce McMillan

Internationalism and Pragmatism

I THINK ONE of the challenges the movement for Scottish independence is facing now is that an awful lot of the heavy lifting in terms of modernising the idea of Scottish identity, and therefore of what Scottish independence might mean, was done as a reaction to the Thatcher era. The repositioning the SNP's stance as a politics of modernity in Scotland in the 1990s, and particularly the articulation of the idea of independence in changing Scottish nationalism from a separatist movement to an internationalist and federalist one, was absolutely critical. It stopped being an essentialist nationalist movement and started saying, 'look, if you want social democracy in Scotland, the UK is about to cease to be a viable way of getting it.' Now, the problem with the pragmatic argument for Scottish independence is you have to face the fact that it means if circumstances change, your support for independence might change – say if we suddenly got a brilliantly reforming and social democratic government in Westminster, for example. I know it doesn't seem very likely at the moment, but the fact is people like me, whose top priority is social democracy, would have to think about that seriously.

So, there is a fundamentally pragmatic argument for Scottish independence that is outward looking and internationalist. I think it runs through Nicola Sturgeon like a stick of rock, although I think she is a bit more hesitant nowadays about using that language of pragmatic nationalism, because she sees the implication that she might have to change her mind about it and doesn't want to be accused of that by the more fundamentalist elements in the independence movement. However, any move away from pragmatism will damage SNP support, because most people are not that interested in nationalism of any kind. They want to know what will improve their lives – get Scotland a better future. The Yes movement has to focus quite ruthlessly on engaging the unpersuaded, the large number of people who say, 'Oh, I'm quite tempted towards Scottish independence, but I hate that flag waving.'

Brexit, Borders and Identity

Now, running a really winning campaign should, theoretically, be easier in the aftermath of Brexit, but the fact is, Brexit has not produced the surge in support for independence in the way many thought it might. People I have spoken to say, 'Well, it makes me much more depressed about being stuck in the UK. But it also makes me much more fearful of what it would be like if we had to have an EU border between Carlisle and Berwick.' People are very anxious about that. So because Brexit in itself is horribly reactionary, it forces people to make much more stark choices about identity which, in the late twentieth century, many were so relieved not to have to make any more – particularly in places like Northern Ireland. Being able to carry off both the British and Irish identity together is essential to the future of that province.

But now the fools and charlatans associated with the present Conservative government have put people in a place of having to choose, and the choice in Scotland now is much starker: create a border of some sort with England, even though we would hope it would be a very light touch border, or remain stuck outside the EU with an isolationist Westminster. So it feels like we're left with this kind of firefighting, emergency mode of devolved government, which can only deal with the situation from week to week, really. Meanwhile, people's economic confidence, which is always the crucial thing in persuading Scots to vote for change, has been absolutely hammered. So it's a really difficult situation for the independence movement just now for those who are trying to face those realities.

Security is What Enables Boldness

The kind of populist, shock wave, right-wing politics we've been witnessing in the United States, and in Britain in recent years, has led some of the progressive wing to hugely underestimate the importance of security for ordinary people. If people are living on their wages, and don't have wealth behind them, they absolutely need a reassurance that some systems – like the NHS, benefits and pensions – will stay in place, or hopefully improve. They might be pessimistic about the UK, but independence can still feel like a big risk and a leap into the unknown.

So while people can recognise, at a theoretical level, that they might be better off if Scotland could go in the direction of Norway or Denmark, they can't see the path to that without causing huge disruption. And a lot of people I've spoken to are frightened that if Scotland were to break away, politicians in England would take a really punitive attitude, refusing to buy Scottish stuff just to spite us. Money talks louder than anything when it comes to business decisions, so that may not be likely. But because of the bravado that goes with Scotland's public image, many outside the country don't realise how lacking in confidence many people are – we have been told for 300 years that this country would be a basket case without England, that we need their subsidies to survive. That, and we exist in a kind of little brother relationship to our neighbours.

It seems that many people still don't have the confidence to believe that Scotland could be a successful independent country. And there's no mainstream media source that is really even halfway to providing the little bits of that confidence that would amount to practical reporting of the issues involved. For the independence case to progress, those fears have to be addressed emotionally as well as politically and economically.

To create the environment in which progressive politics can flourish and people can feel braver, we have to see some bolder moves from the Scottish Government – I think the most obvious one would be some kind of Universal Basic Income (UBI). If people had a cast iron guarantee of a certain income, which was small but survivable, then their room for manoeuvre becomes vastly greater. People become less afraid of change; they become more willing to talk about the transition to a different kind of economy and society. And interest in UBI is surging because we've seen, during the pandemic, how some kind of floor like that makes it possible to tolerate a huge change.

Government and a Roadmap for Change

One of the variations between England and Scotland is that there is a greater sense of trust in government here, despite political differences. It's really quite remarkable, given that the Scottish Parliament has only existed for 20 years, the extent to which people see it as their primary port of call – it's become a cornerstone of life in Scotland in a relatively short amount of time. But people are less aware of how vulnerable it could be as attitudes in Westminster change and powers are curbed, as we've seen with some of the ones returning from the EU after Brexit – powers which have not come back to Scotland, but to the UK government. So the democratic case for independence, about decisions being taken here, does cut through. But the economic security case remains crucial. Environment, too. Until a majority of Scots fully understand the potential of Scotland, in terms of its natural and other resources, they won't come over to the side of independence. We need some kind of clarity on a plan about how we get there – even if it's a roadmap that has to be adjusted and changed.

We really need to understand that a vote for independence is, in the first place, a mandate for the Scottish Government to open negotiations. Then we should be absolutely clear that, given the complexity and length of the relationship with the UK, which is in part being disentangled, it will take at least a decade to do it. We can't pretend it's all going to be plain sailing, with nuclear weapons being moved off the Clyde in a matter of weeks after independence has been secured. People trust a process when it is honest and realistic, as well as positive and hopeful. There's also quite considerable opinion poll evidence that a majority of Scots, even those who support independence, don't want anything done that can't stand up in international law. That matters too.

Now, there's a huge case for saying that in 20 years' time, Scotland will be better off independent. But you need to reassure people that on Scotland's watch, the aim will be absolutely the opposite of Brexit in both outcome and process – to be clear and responsible in handling it, careful not to rush everything, and protecting vulnerable groups at every stage. And the end result should not be any fantasy of a clean break or separation between Scotland and England, which will never happen. Instead it should be the aim of a confederal British and Irish islands that enable a newly negotiated relationship between independent but interrelated nations on the basis of equality.

Scotland, England, Confederalism and Westminster

Even if we wanted to (and most people don't) we can't get away from England. They will always be our big neighbours, they will always be hugely influential on what happens in Scotland, and we will always have these very strong social links. But right in front of our eyes is an example of a country that has made the independence shift that is as closely bound to England as us, and has an even more fraught history than we have – Ireland. Yet in the last century it has made itself into a successful, independent nation within the European Union. And in the end, once the decision was made, the British government was actually quite supportive of the setting up of the Irish Free State. In spite of the differences and arguments, they realised that it was in their interest to have a successful country on their doorstep.

In other words, although independence is a big change, we can build security and gradualism into it. Scots are always minded to give the union a second chance, because they don't want the disruption of breaking it. That's why it is important to offer reassurance to the person who is much more interested in independence than he or she was 30 years ago, but is still not quite convinced, and who doesn't have the ideology that Westminster is structurally incapable of reform as many independence supporters have the from the start. People have seen Westminster deliver a significant reform in the last 25 years, in the of shaping devolution. So the case for an independent Scotland has to be positive and attractive, not just based on the idea that Westminster *can't* change. The really important point here is that Scotland *can* change. So as soon as COVID is under control, there needs to be a campaign saying, 'Look, there is a crisis, particularly an environmental crisis. Scotland needs to move on. And we've really changed. We can take out future into our own hands.'

Presenting the Yes Case Differently
Lisa Clark

We then asked a pro-independence advocate to reflect on their experience of doorstep politics, how it had changed in recent years, and how and whether their own approach would alter in approaching a future campaign on the constitutional question.

I feel as though I have been having conversations about independence all my adult life. When I was younger, this belief was sometimes treated as one of my self-conscious quirks, like my predilection for Earl Grey tea as a working-class Scot. Occasionally, though, you could be met with hostility in the most affluent parts of Edinburgh or in parts of Fife or the West Coast, but it was more usual to be confronted with a bewildered disdain. I personally feel that I have not quite adjusted to the new reality (notable from 2011 onwards) that saw votes for the SNP, if not quite independence or nationalism itself, become the default answer from those who said that they had not thought about how they were going to vote – the previous answer in those circumstances had always been Labour, across vast swathes of Scotland.

Looking forward, it is interesting and important for me to engage with those who do not see Scottish politics in this way. During the Holyrood campaign in 2019, I was involved in campaigning for an SNP candidate in a constituency with a long tradition of voting for unionist MSPs and MPs. (It also voted No in 2014.) The response on the doors, when speaking to constituents, was enlightening. Generally, in the last electoral campaign (2019), there was a strongly positive response to the Scottish Government. As always, when you chat to people in any campaign, the grumbles tend to be about the very local issues – bins, roads and the like – whatever the focus of the election. However, in this campaign, when the topic moved to the broader Scottish Government policies, especially about the response to the pandemic, there was a surprisingly up-beat response; a feeling generally of a calm satisfaction with how matters were proceeding. Not to say that they agreed with all decisions taken, but there was certainly no sense of panic or deep concern.

That is what made it particularly striking when the subject shifted to which way they intended to vote. Sometimes, almost sorrowfully, constituents would say they intended to vote for the unionist incumbent, as they 'didn't want to vote for independence'. This left me with the dilemma of saying truthfully, but it felt slightly disingenuously, that on election day they were only being asked to vote for their representative to the Scottish Parliament, not to indicate their views on the constitutional question. That response, though factually accurate, would have convinced very few people. They well knew that a strong SNP vote in the election, especially if an increased number of MSPs were elected, would be taken as a reflection of an increased support for independence – indeed, the SNP proclaimed that very proudly during the campaign.

Politics, Constitution and Identity

Gone are the days when constituents were prepared to support an SNP candidate because they liked the individual or supported the policies of the SNP in the Scottish Parliament, but could hold those views entirely separately from their beliefs around the future of the United Kingdom. In many ways, this has been one of the party's successes – to put the constitutional question front and centre in everyone's minds. However, it is clear that the strategy of hoping to win people over to the cause of independence by presenting good governance has largely gone as far as it can go. When talking about the constitution to ordinary voters, there is a feeling that they do not need to be further convinced that certain aspects of Scotland's governance can be done more effectively from Holyrood, rather than from Westminster. The present UK government can be a strong, unwitting advocate for this viewpoint.

However, this is notably different from convincing an individual that the division of the United Kingdom is the better long-term future for this nation. There are still many who 'feel' British – culturally, historically and emotionally – and who associate this with the particular polity that is the UK. To argue with people who feel this way, by advancing logical points about the advantages to Scotland of a different political settlement, feels like we are speaking a different language. A great many people who have come to believe in independence since 2014 have come to it as a pragmatic option, believing that it will ensure increased prosperity for Scotland and, even more importantly to them, ensure that left-of-centre, social democratic policies can be put in place to govern the country. As that is the way they have come to their belief, they find it hard to construct an argument on different terms.

Oddly, the 'older style Scottish nationalists', who held a more ideologically driven belief on the importance of independence, would actually understand them better, if not sharing any of the beliefs of those who regard the concept of Britishness with affection and see it as a strong norm from which it would be madness to depart. So how would one find a way in which to get people talking the same language, in order to start the process of a meaningful communication?

Gaining and Losing

Ben Jackson's book, *The Case For Scottish Independence* (University of Edinburgh, 2020), lays out very clearly the progression of the arguments around Scottish sovereignty that advanced during the 20th century until the present day. It speaks about the strand that has been present in Scottish nationalism, at least since the 1980's, that located Scotland's independence firmly within global economic interdependence. This argument, stated clearly in 2014, was summarised that Scotland was only relinquishing one of the six unions, of which it was a part.

This enthusiastic embracing of the European Union, particularly during the debates around Brexit, both allowed Scotland to stand distinct from other parts of the union, whilst also giving a clear rebuttal to some of those who had feared that a Yes vote in 2014 would isolate Scotland. This style of thinking presented a progressive nationalism, which could feel acceptable to those who had feared that an independent Scotland would be a parochial and limiting vision.

In the conversations on the doorsteps after the Brexit vote, notably during the 2019 General Election, you could sense an unprecedented willingness to accept independence from some of those who had previously voted No, but now felt that remaining within the union was emerging as the more isolating option. Further, this way of styling independence to those who were doubters, allowed a way of talking about nationalism that didn't require simply speaking positively about continuing its connection with the British state, which felt more acceptable to those who struggled with that historical picture.

However, by the time we got to 2021, this felt like it wasn't a strong enough argument to assure those who struggled with losing their Britishness. Ironically, the more strident the British state became in terms of its own creation as a post EU state, the less the talk of this style of Scottish nationalism reassured those who wanted to retain their connection to their past. A friend of mine said that he was less likely to vote for independence in a future referendum – having done so, grudgingly, in 2014 – as he felt bereft by losing the EU and the loss then of the rest of the United Kingdom would feel a loss too far.

Language, Culture and Identity

So what language should people like me use that will reach those who still see nationalism as an ideology of disconnection? One of the common doorstop tropes of 2014 was that independence would mean that people would not be able to watch *Doctor Who*. It was easy to ridicule this without respecting that underneath it lay the very real concern that people would be losing part of their cultural identity of which they were fond. More deeply, a tension emerged within the nationalist movement between those who postulated independence as the start of a 'new heaven and a new earth' for Scotland and those who were keen to present it as not meaning significant change. Neither of these extremes were of course true.

The success of the English football team in the 2020 Euros, allowed a voice to those who wanted to fight for a different style of English nationalism – more inclusive, more progressive and more caring. Figures such as Gavin Southgate, Marcus Rashford and other prominent English players spoke powerfully and proudly of this understanding of what it was to be English in the 21st century. Polling confirmed that this envisaging was widespread – 77 per cent of white people in England agreed that 'being English is open to people of different ethnic backgrounds who identify as English'. In these conversations there has often been a confusion between English and British nationalism. Moreover, this lack of divergence between Scottish and English nationalism has led to its own issues – previously Scotland has somewhat smugly understood itself to be the more caring and open nation. This is a Scottish nationalism which seemed limited to existing as a contrary to England – and Britain's – perception of themselves. Therefore, it is challenging for Scottish nationalism to engage with other more positive and similar nationalisms from other parts of the UK. However, it can also be seen as encouraging and the key to a less adversarial, and more collegiate, approach. This perspective, has acted to a challenge to ensure that Scottish nationalism is not a mere reaction to another more negative vision.

Sport has often acted as a catalyst for these conversations, and empathy is a new word that has been introduced into conversations in the previously traditionally heteronormative world of sport. If we can work with this maturity of understanding, we can apply it to the cultural, social and political backgrounds of our history. This could lead to an openness for this to play a part in the dialogue between Scottish nationalism and those who believe that their British nationalism is a core part of who they are. For the case for Scottish independence to carry with it those who do not want to abandon or repudiate a great deal of their, or the country's, past we have to find a way to truly communicate a message that the openness of Scottish nationalism extends to our border to the south, as well as into Europe. That when we see positive ideas of Britishness, whether it be from culture or in ideology, we can embrace and incorporate them into the new Scotland. Obviously, this becomes more problematic while another, more negative, view of Britishness is on the rise politically. But just as Scottish nationalism is far broader and deeper than the current SNP and its policies, Britishness is not contained by whatever government is in power at Westminster. This attitude to both of these nationalism needs to be part of the discourse of the movement towards independence, and the political and constitutional debate of which it is part.

CHAPTER 17

Leadership, the SNP and the
Politics of Incumbency
Dani Garavelli

IN OCTOBER 2020 – WITH COVID-19 raging and Nicola Sturgeon's approval ratings soaring – I went to Dreghorn in North Ayrshire and Linlithgow in West Lothian to talk to people on the street about the spike in support for independence.

I had chosen those towns for obvious reasons: Dreghorn is where Sturgeon grew up; Linlithgow, the birthplace of her predecessor, Alex Salmond. The parliamentary inquiry into the way the Scottish Government handled sexual harassment allegations against Salmond had begun. Talk of schisms and feuds dominated the political bubble. I thought it would be interesting to see what people made of their contrasting leadership styles, and also how they rated Sturgeon against her UK counterpart, Boris Johnson.

It was, indeed, interesting. At that moment, Sturgeon appeared to be unassailable. Yes voters, No voters, Remainers and Leavers were united in praise for her handling of the pandemic, remarking – in particular – on her communication skills, her empathy and her willingness to apologise when she got things wrong. They had little time for Salmond, whom they saw as toxic and 'yesterday's man', and even less for Johnson – admittedly, the bar was low. The Tory leader's performance during lockdown had been woeful – a confection of lies and misjudgements, which allowed Sturgeon to shine. But even so, such a universal endorsement of any politician seemed remarkable.

It was not just on the streets of Scotland that Sturgeon's leadership was attracting attention either. A few months earlier, she had been named as the fifth most eloquent leader in the world. The accolade had been bestowed upon her by professional development coaches from Acuity Training, who described her as 'clear, calm and compassionate,' adding that she was 'not afraid to be tough or emotional' and that she had 'a great sense of humour'. These are qualities that have marked her out from the moment she became SNP leader and First Minister. In those heady days of the 2014 rockstar stadium tour, when she posed for selfies with anyone who asked, commentators were already talking about her 'relatability'.

With her appointment, came a sense the party was modernising. The narrative was that while Salmond had been the man to bring Scotland to the brink of independence, Sturgeon was the woman to deliver it (with an emphasis on the word 'woman'). Part of Sturgeon's appeal lay in her lack of male ego or entitlement; for all his political abilities, polls had suggested Salmond was off-putting to female voters. Sturgeon's ascendancy marked a move away from an old macho politics towards something more outward-looking and inclusive.

It is worth noting that three of Acuity Training's top five eloquent leaders were women, the others being New Zealand's Prime Minister Jacinda Ardern and German Chancellor Angela Merkel, who were ranked first and second respectively. Claims about a 'female' style of leadership can seem a bit facile – Merkel is nothing like Ardern. And yet, it did make me wonder if there was something about these women's approach that was particularly suited to steering a country through a health emergency. A heightened sensitivity to people's distress, perhaps?

There are those who dismiss Sturgeon's pandemic performance as spin. They point out, with some justification, that she made many of the same policy mistakes as Johnson. But the importance of empathy should not be underestimated in a crisis where people crave clarity and a sympathetic ear, and where persuading people to follow the restrictions you introduce is of paramount importance.

Nicola Sturgeon's Leadership

Even so, the skills required to lead a country during a pandemic are not necessarily the same as those required to tackle a drugs epidemic or to lay the ground for a second independence referendum. And the skills required to be a good first minister are not necessarily the same as those required to lead a party. In fact, the day-to-day demands of governing may well conflict with the demands of grassroots members who would like more say over the policy agenda.

Outside of the pandemic, Sturgeon's leadership abilities are more contested, with some such as journalist and Yes campaigner Ruth Wishart criticising a lack of ambition and attributing her pre-eminence to a lack of any real competition:

> If you look around Holyrood post-election, there is no obvious contender – no one with her skill set and qualities to challenge her inside or outside her own party. That's unhealthy for Scotland, the SNP and politics generally.

Professor James Mitchell, at Edinburgh University, claims Sturgeon is arguably one of the best debaters in modern politics:

> 'Give her an idea or policy, or even a difficult position to defend, and she will do it superbly. But this is also her weakness as it allows her to deflect criticism, which can lead to a failure to address the underlying issue. She works very hard, is one of the best in terms of mastering detail. But it is rare for a politician to master detail and see the broader position and think strategically. She can't, and does not have anyone around her capable of filling that gap.

While Salmond surrounded himself with people, inviting favoured journalists to drinks parties at Bute House, and liked to have his ideas challenged, Sturgeon operates within a small coterie of close confidantes, including her old Glasgow University friend Shona Robison – brought back into the Cabinet after the last election as social justice secretary – and her chief of staff, Liz Lloyd.

There are those who welcomed the end of Salmond's 'Big Beast' leadership, but who are still wary of this more controlling, centralised approach which, Mitchell says, began under Salmond post-2004, and intensified under Sturgeon. Much of the disquiet has focused on Sturgeon's marriage to Peter Murrell, chief executive of the party. Even those who like and respect them as individuals see the potential dangers of having the two most important positions in the party held by a husband and wife.

If they did not before, then the parliamentary inquiry – to which Murrell and Sturgeon gave sometimes diverging evidence – and the police inquiry into the whereabouts of £600,000 donated to an independence fund, have brought it into sharp relief. With this centralisation has come a perceived lack of transparency – again highlighted during the inquiry – and a failure to harness the energy and ideas of those working-class members who propelled the party into power.

The need for a reorganisation to engage the membership post-2014 was recognised early on by MP Tommy Sheppard. 'Members are our biggest asset and we need structures that allow them to get more involved,' Sheppard said when he stood for deputy leader in 2016. 'They are central to our continuing success as a party and a movement.'

'We need to prepare as many people as possible to play an active role in campaigns. I believe we need to refocus our basic unit – the party branch – to include much more political discussion and action. We need to spend money on professional organisers – at HQ and in a regional network – to support branch activities and members' training. We need to bring together all our elected representatives – MPs, MSPs and councillors – in coherent teams providing political leadership to our communities. We need to rethink how we make policy, involving as many members as possible in a continuous process.'

In the end, Sheppard lost to Angus Robertson and those structural changes were not made. Some of the working-class members who joined the SNP because 'Labour left them' now feel similarly taken for granted by their new party. They believe the SNP has abandoned the left-wing policies they were seduced by to chase soft No votes and insist party conferences have become little more than rallies, with important issues, such as fracking and a Plan B, rejected for debate. The question is: what can and should be done to reassure them? Would a change of leader help? Or are the pressures of government pre-destined to stifle any move towards democratisation?

Strategy

Sturgeon's leadership style is a fusion of personality and political calculation. Unlike Salmond, who liked to gamble, she is cautious by nature. But she also knows global uncertainty over climate change and automation is creating a hunger for stability. So, while her predecessor was always thinking up some new political wheeze, Sturgeon's game plan has been to demonstrate her party's capacity for efficient devolved government.

Musician and writer Pat Kane says of Sturgeon:

> She knows how to project her personality and she
> knows how it fits with a politics that is about display-
> ing reassurance and competence. What is often referred
> to as 'the golden thread of competence' is a big and
> deep idea in this current SNP leadership. That's how
> they believe they will get the cringe-beset population
> over the line.

There is a clear logic to Sturgeon's strategy, and for a time it worked.
She walked a tightrope, distancing herself from the 'marching tendency' she felt was off-putting to swithering No voters, while holding
out enough hope of a referendum to keep them on board. Holding
such a disparate group together was an impressive feat; however it is
also a strategy with pitfalls. What if, for example, despite your cau-
tion, or perhaps because of it, you fail to demonstrate your competence? What if you 'take your eye off the ball' and allow a drug crisis
to spiral, until you have the highest drug death rate in Europe? What
if you stake your reputation on narrowing the education attainment
gap but that gap remains?

On the one hand, the more cautious voters you hoped to win
over may be unimpressed. On the other, those voters who looked to
you for something more radical may start to resent what has been
lost in a desire not to rock the boat. They might ask themselves:
'What could have been achieved if the leadership had been willing to
take more risks?' Activist John Shafi states:

> The SNP has held near hegemonic political power in
> Scotland for some years, and yet when you actually
> look at the reforms that have been made, they have
> been minimal. Council tax still exists, there's been a
> lack of movement on land reform, and instead of our
> energy resources being taken into public hands, they
> are in the process of being sold off to international
> investors. While there is a veneer of social and eco-
> nomic progress, the fundamentals of the economy and
> how it's run have remained intact.
> The irony is that the SNP gained this hegemonic position
> from a huge switch in working-class support towards

the party, but the return in terms of an industrial strategy, in terms of real reform, isn't there.

The fragile unity that Sturgeon brokered has been further damaged by the way the Gender Recognition Reform Bill has been handled. No one who pushed the policy, which makes it easier for trans people to gain legal recognition of their lived gender, seemed to foresee the backlash it would cause or do anything to mediate between pro-trans and gender critical activists.

This mismanagement has led to polarisation, with both 'sides' feeling let down and ignored. The pro-trans lobby believes transphobia has been tolerated, while those who oppose the new bill (or have reservations over some aspects of it) believe Sturgeon is in thrall to the 'wokerati' and allowing women's hard-earned rights to be eroded. The debate has become so toxic, it will need a combination of strong leadership and UN-scale conciliation skills to find a way forward.

But the greatest source of frustration is being caused by a perceived stasis over a second independence referendum. The promises of a fresh vote have worn thin for some such as Mitchell in the absence of any sense of urgency or contingency plan in the face of Westminster's continued blocking:

> There will always be a fringe demanding a referendum tomorrow. Smart leadership manages this and can even make use of it politically. The problem is a lack of strategy. [Sturgeon] misread public opinion in the aftermath of Brexit and marched the troops to the top of the hill then down again (more than once).

The momentum the 2014 referendum provided has been dissipated. And, though the Holyrood elections returned a clear pro-independence majority, polls suggest public support for independence – which stood at 58 per cent in October 2020 – was back down to 48 per cent by June 2021, although varying a little towards 50 per cent since then. 'The sense, now, is of a leader who is going through the paces, but hoping that opinion will shift towards independence based on opposition to Boris Johnson,' Mitchell states.

Though Sturgeon insists there will be a second referendum in this parliamentary term, there is no obvious evidence of work being done on issues like currency, borders, and finance, which would need to be agreed and sold to voters before the referendum. Wishart's assessment is this:

> The problem is most of the people beavering away on these issues are not members of the Government and, furthermore, I don't think the Government pays much attention to them.

The resignation in late May of Marco Biagi as head of the recently-founded independence task force, designed to kickstart a grassroots campaign, did not augur well. The new SNP President Mike Russell has taken charge; he is understood to be reaching out to grassroots organisations, but it is early days and he has his work cut out for him. Though the SNP mainstream does not seem too worried about the frustrations of members whose votes they have already mentally banked, their disaffection is having a destabilising effect.

In December 2020, more than 20 activists, councillors and MPs critical of Sturgeon's leadership were elected to the National Executive Committee (NEC) – the party's ruling body. These dissenters sought to exert more influence over policy. But then – shortly before the May election – some of them moved over to Alba. On one level, their defection did the SNP a favour: Alba's failure to make any electoral impact neutralised them as a threat and left them in the political wilderness. They were replaced on the NEC by Sturgeon allies, including Fiona Robertson and Rhiannon Spear.

But the internal tensions continue to fester. The same week Biagi quit his post, SNP National Treasurer Douglas Chapman and MP Joanna Cherry resigned from the NEC. They had both supported the Common Weal Group inside the SNP which called for more transparency, a greater role for members and more pressing work to be carried out building the case for independence.

The Changing SNP

Since the inception of Holyrood in 1999, the SNP has moved from the fringes to the mainstream to the core of the Scottish establishment. Inevitably, leadership styles have changed in tandem with its new position and aspirations. Salmond, who was in his element as the leader of a rebel force, began to curb his insurgent tendencies as the party came into power in 2007 and won a majority in 2011.

Having delivered a referendum and increased support for independence, Salmond's leadership could not be considered anything but a success; yet, it was clear his risk-taking was not suited to take the party to the next stage. In contrast, Sturgeon possessed a broad appeal to the thousands of new members who joined in the wake of the defeat and a statesman-like quality that meant she was taken seriously by the international community. If you believe – as many do – that the best way to gain independence is to behave as if you are already independent, then she was the woman for the job. But the last few years have not been easy – success has brought a new weight of expectation against the difficult backdrop of Brexit, the pandemic and the fall-out from the Alex Salmond trial.

Some feel a managerialism has crept into the SNP –they believe Sturgeon and those around her have grown so attached to governing that they are no longer invested in independence. Shafi states:

> I think Sturgeon's priority will be retaining political power rather than taking a risk on a referendum. I can imagine her advisers saying: 'You won [the election] by focusing on the pandemic. Those who were more fundamentalist in their approach [those who joined Alba for example] barely registered electorally. People trust you.' That's the way they will frame it.

It is not surprising then, that some members have begun to look to the short and long-term future and ask: what next? Formal collaboration with the Scottish Greens – with Green MSPs appointed as ministers in the Scottish Government – has now been established. Such a pact can help push the Gender Recognition Reform Bill through, consolidate the pro-independence majority and increase the SNP's environmental credentials in the run-up to COP26. But could it also mark a shift towards a more pluralist, 'grown-up' style of government? Views will vary.

Then, there is the question of the succession. In 2014, there was no doubt who would take over the leadership; Sturgeon had been groomed for the role. This time round, there is no clear successor. Those most frequently mentioned – Humza Yousaf and Kate Forbes – seem unlikely, at least in the short term, Yousaf because he is considered gaffe-prone and Forbes because, while well-respected, she still lacks experience.

The reader can see this as a failure. Surely every leader should have an eye on the future. Then again, perhaps a competition rather than a coronation would be good for the party. Imagine, for example, if Sheppard was to stand, and consider what this would do to the dynamics. Shafi considers such an outcome:

> A lot of people [who are critical of the party] have zoomed in on Nicola as if to say: 'If we didn't have Nicola as leader, if we had person X instead, it would be radically different'. That isn't my view. I am very critical of her leadership but the idea that switching to, say, Angus Robertson is going to address the concerns of someone like me? That's not going to happen.

How do the extra-parliamentary campaigns and organisations make an impact on the party and its policies? Shafi's focus is similar to Sheppard's:

> I think there has been a view: 'We have these voters in the bag, so we can pivot looking to the business people and boardrooms', but that becomes very difficult to hold together. Though it is true to say the SNP's Holyrood electoral success was substantial, I do think there is an expectancy for there to be movement around the independence question even from people who have been, up until now, pretty loyal to the leadership.

Wishart says one of the first ways to democratise must be for the SNP to open up its conference to its members:

> The party doesn't belong to the leadership, it belongs to its members as any party should. The way the party membership was excluded from debating independence last time round was entirely counterproductive.

Speaking with those in the parliamentary party, there does seem to be a degree of complacency towards the grassroots faithful; a sense that, no matter how discontented they become, they are not going to vote No. That may be true, but they may also become less zealous advocates for the cause – when the time comes, as Wishart believes, they may be less willing to give their all to the campaign:

> This softly, softly catchee monkey approach is all very well but if, in the meantime, your core membership is disappearing like snow off a dyke then you have got something wrong. My worry is not so much that people who get cheesed off will set up another party, it is that they will just sit on their hands and not bother going out and doing any of the work that needs to be done to win.

The SNP may increasingly be the political establishment, but they are going to have think carefully about how they change and do politics if they are to maintain popularity and be successful in government, while acting as the leading advocates for independence.

Section Five: After the United Kingdom

CHAPTER 18

England and Scottish Independence
Gavin Esler

IRANIAN REVOLUTIONARY MOBS know they hate us, but they seem unclear about who exactly 'we' are. The front page of *The Times* reported the following incident in January 2020:

> Iranian protesters burnt the union Jack outside the British embassy in Tehran last night as the diplomatic crisis over the arrest of the UK ambassador grew. A crowd of hard-line religion students and regime supporters chanted 'Death to England.'

One can feel sympathy, not for the protesters' cause, but for their confusion. In just two sentences a British newspaper describes 'us' – citizens of these islands – as having a 'British' embassy but a 'UK' ambassador and suffering offensive chants of death to 'England.' And it's not just Iranians who are confused about the differences between England, the United Kingdom of Great Britain and Northern Ireland, and the idea of being British. Earlier in 2021, I was invited on radio and TV programmes to discuss my new book about the UK drifting apart, entitled *How Britain Ends*. Nations are sometimes described as 'imagined communities,' and I wrote the book because the UK is suffering an acute failure of imagination. Historically, the idea of Britishness was based on three pillars – Protestantism, Empire and War – and has successfully reinvented itself as a result of conflicts or crises every century since its foundation (in 1707, 1801 and 1922). Another reinvention is overdue, but without significant changes, the UK as currently constituted may come to an end. Yet on a London-based radio show, the presenter introduced me as the author of a book supposedly called *How England Ends*. 'England?' I laughed. 'The book is called *How Britain Ends* .... as the old song says, "There will *Always* be an England."'

The presenter did not understand either my feeble joke or the correction. Instead, she thanked me for writing, once more, *How England Ends*, eliding England with Britain in a way no person from Scotland, Northern Ireland, the Irish Republic or Wales is likely to do. And yet it is understandable – England's population is 84 per cent of the entire UK. The Scottish broadcaster and author Ludovic Kennedy described England as 'the elephant in the bed' of the union. The elephant is becoming increasingly restless, and yet English politicians are astonishingly reluctant to consider or even contemplate what an independent Scotland would mean for England itself. Scottish independence will inevitably bring a series of profound practical and psychological shocks for the biggest part of the UK, yet no one prominent in English politics appears to be either interested or concerned.

Scots have thought and argued about independence for decades. People in Northern Ireland and Wales have also considered the implications of significant constitutional changes, but in England the idea (as it is often phrased) of Scotland 'breaking away' elicits three complacent responses: the first is to ignore or deny it – it will not or cannot happen; the second is to say it will not or cannot work; the third is to conclude that whether it works or not, it would be better for England to get rid of those troublesome Scots, the ungrateful hordes who take 'our money' and then complain. All these responses lack any sense of realism about the shocks Scottish independence will deliver to a largely unprepared England.

The Scottish Questions

The 'deniers' include the former Chancellor George Osborne. In London's *Evening Standard*, Osborne wrote that the way to prevent independence is for Westminster to stop Scots voting on it. Well, possibly. But that is not a positive English case for the union – it is defeatism. Nevertheless, Osborne does begin to contemplate some impact on England:

> ... the rest of the world would instantly see that we were no longer a front-rank power, or even in the second row. We would instead be one of the great majority of countries who are on the receiving end of the decisions made by a few, subject to the values of others.

We would become another historically interesting case study in how successful nations can perform unexpected acts of national suicide (2021).

The second English political response – that independence cannot work – is based on the idea that a small northern European country of five million people is unlikely to prosper. Ireland, Norway and Denmark, in per capita GDP are all now richer than the UK, so they disprove that argument. Although William Hague, the former Conservative leader, does offer some genuinely important caveats. Hague asks what he calls four 'fundamental' questions. First – currency. Will an independent Scotland keep the pound and therefore be subject to decisions from the Bank of England? Or will Scotland invent its own currency and prepare to join the euro? Second, as Hague puts it, 'since tax revenues per head are about £300 lower in Scotland than UK-wide and government expenditure about £1600 higher' is the answer higher taxes in Scotland or more borrowing? Third, what kind of border will there be between an independent Scotland and England, especially if Scotland joins the EU? Fourth, security: NATO sets a target of 2 per cent of GDP spent on defence. How can Scotland find the money? These important questions are tricky and contentious and they do require answers, but at least Scots have considered such issues for as long as I can remember.

The third response to Scottish independence – 'good riddance' – comes from English nationalists. English nationalists sometimes dress up their England-only world view as if it were 'British' nationalism, but an articulate expression of genuine England-alone considerations comes from the author of *Captain Corelli's Mandolin*. Writing in *The Times*, Louis De Bernieres argued:

> The logic of Brexit should take us further. It has been increasingly obvious to me and fellow Leavers for years that the English would be better off on their own. It seems ever more obvious that Ireland can be reunified because all the very good reasons for the North resisting this have gone; the Republic is no longer a corrupt, backward country, it is an energetic vibrant place where anyone would love to live, including me. We are an important trading partner; if Ireland were being strictly rational it would also leave the EU and

> opt for an Anglo-Irish economic zone. England has no good reason to want to cling on to Northern Ireland or to Scotland either. The English attachment to Scotland is a sentimental one, but the Scots have fallen out of love with us, and inevitably the English will sooner or later have had enough of the grandstanding of the nationalists. The English have noticed that their own nationalism is the only one that is routinely denigrated and despised, and that also grates. The English have developed their own 'cultural cringe.' (Times Letters, 29 January 2021).

The self-pity of a broken love affair aside, all these arguments from an English perspective simply point to a debilitating lack of realism about the post-independence future of England or England and Wales. What follows, then, are obvious questions that Scottish independence poses for 84 per cent of the UK's population – the English.

The English Questions

First: the land. Scottish independence means the UK would lose a third – 32 per cent – of its existing land mass. This would be a profound psychological shock. When Germany was defeated in the First World War, under the crippling terms of the Treaty of Versailles in 1919, it was stripped of 13 per cent of its total land mass. This led to years of bitterness, revanchism, the rise of Hitler and ultimately the Second World War. Scottish independence would rewrite the map of the UK much more fundamentally than the Treaty of Versailles did Germany.

Second: the seas. Scotland has 900 islands, of which 118 are inhabited, stretching from Shetland to the Western Isles and the Bass Rock. Marine Scotland puts Scotland's coastline at 18,743 km at the high water line and the area of Scotland's seas at roughly 460,000 km sq or two-thirds (63 per cent) of the UK total. The seas around Scotland are nearly six times the size of Scotland itself, and twice as vast as the seas around England (230,000 km sq or 32 per cent of the UK total). Who would fish where? In 2021, Boris Johnson sent two geriatric gunboats to 'protect' Jersey fishermen from French fishing boats. Would he divert them to Rockall? What was Westminster's plan? Either way, Scottish independence means a geographical transition from 'Great Britain' to 'Little England'.

Third: defence. SNP policy is to get rid of all nuclear weapons based at Faslane, on the Clyde. Where would England put Trident submarines, or their successors? Who would accept these Cold War relics? Boris Johnson's government announced, in March 2021, cuts reducing the British Army to just 72,500 soldiers by 2025; the National Army Museum says these cuts take the British Army to the lowest level since the war of the Spanish Succession in 1714. The Johnson plan is to 'pivot' defence away from Europe, towards the Indian ocean and Pacific. Is this a serious or credible strategy? How far does 'pivoting' to the other side of the world fit with the biggest recognisable threat to British security, which national security experts have agreed is Russia – a sense which has now come to disturbing fruition?

Fourth: while Scottish independence supporters do have big questions to answer about a border between Carlisle and Glasgow, so does England. Would an EU border on the island we share be as chaotic, cumbersome and irritating as the badly organised customs border affecting Northern Ireland? Would we need passports? The Queen might be exempt when she visits Balmoral, but what about everyone else?

Fifth: when the Soviet Union disintegrated, Russia applied to the UN to retain Permanent Five status on the Security Council. There were no objections. After Scottish independence, would England (or England and Wales) realistically inherit the UK seat, and its veto, on the P5? Would those coveting a seat – Brazil, India and Nigeria – object? Would Russia? China? France? I have discussed this at the UN with an English diplomat who responded to the threat of losing the veto by saying 'we would veto it.' He was joking; I'm not. There is absolutely no certainty that England (or England and Wales) will automatically inherit a permanent UN Security Council seat.

Sixth: the biggest upset of all will be the blow to England's self-confidence and the pleasant delusions of English exceptionalism. The British imperialist Cecil Rhodes once said:

> Ask any man what nationality he would prefer to be, and 99 out of 100 will tell you that they would prefer to be Englishmen.

Rhodes never tested that theory in a Glasgow, Cardiff or Belfast pub. He also advised, 'remember that you are an Englishman, and have consequently won first prize in the lottery of life.'

Post-empire, post-Brexit post-Scottish independence, the Government in Westminster risks achieving – by complacency and inattention –precisely the kind of isolation and relative weakness that every English leader since Henry VIII fought and plotted against. English foreign policy since Tudor times was designed around one big idea, or rather, big fear: historically England's leaders always tried to prevent any power or alliance uniting Europe and leaving England isolated. The union of 1707 – which created Great Britain – worked with others against the Catholic powers of Europe – most notably France – until Waterloo in 1815, then against Germany in 1914 and in 1939. The UK helped create the alliance of NATO against Soviet domination in Europe for the same reason. As the old diplomatic joke has it, NATO is 'to keep the Americans in, the Russians out, and the Germans down.' Scottish independence, with Scotland joining the European Union, would leave England surrounded by a trading bloc of European powers from Ireland to Poland, from Shetland to Cyprus, overturning the strategic aims of every Westminster government in British history.

And seventh: the European football championship, Euro 2020, showed clearly the difference between English patriotism and toxic forms of English nationalism. The England team (diverse, talented, committed) gave us reasons to be proud of many of the great things about England. Patriotism is positive – it's about 'us,' and gives reasons why 'we' should celebrate our country, whatever way it is defined. But toxic nationalism is always negative and about 'them' – booing the German and Danish national anthems, attacking Italian fans leaving Wembley stadium, racist social media attacks on talented England players of colour. If Scottish independence becomes a reality, will England find a positive new patriotism, or sink back into the toxic swamp of boorish 'little England' nationalism?

For now, such concerns have no resonance in English politics. Instead, we hear the repeated yet empty slogan of 'Global Britain' while the Johnson Government has irritated friends and allies in Scotland, Wales, both parts of Ireland, the Biden administration, most of the EU, and also Russia, China, and developing countries which have lost British aid. An articulate *English* voice for the union is hard to find. In one striking 2019 poll organised by the Conservative donor Lord Ashcroft, three-quarters (76 per cent) of English Brexit voters prioritised leaving the European Union over the unity of the UK. As Ashcroft put it:

> When asked what they would do if they had to choose between going ahead with Brexit and keeping Scotland and Northern Ireland in the union, most Leave voters chose Brexit.

Informed English commentators – none of them active in party politics – do understand the problem. The historian David Edgerton, writing in *The New York Times* puts it somewhat wryly:

> Freed from the grip of the decayed British nation and British state, England could finally be done with its delusions of grandeur. Fanciful beliefs about British importance in the world would crumble. England would be only around the eighth-largest economy in the world. And it would probably have to give up its nuclear weapons – the United Kingdom's nuclear submarine base is in Scotland. England need not be, as many fear, a rump United Kingdom, parochial, perhaps even irredentist. Less cocksure and more understanding of its real place in the world, it may soon rethink its hostility to the European Union (2020)

This is a thoughtful description, but it is couched in uncertainty. This future England 'could be ... probably ... need not be ... perhaps ... it may'. Nobody knows; perhaps few even care.

Drifting Apart

The tectonic plates of the union of the UK have been shifting for years. In the 2015 election the largest party representing voters in England was the Conservatives; in Northern Ireland, the Democratic Unionist Party (DUP); in Wales, Labour; in Scotland, the SNP. Four nations, four very different parties. A year later, in the Brexit referendum of 2016, there was an even clearer divergence, with Scotland and Northern Ireland voting to remain and England and Wales voting to Leave. Even coronavirus, a common threat to all the UK and beyond, has not stitched the union back together. Devolved governments in Belfast, Cardiff, and Edinburgh adopted different coronavirus measures at different times and at a different pace.

Wales' First Minister Mark Drakeford, – a Labour politician and pro-union – told the parliamentary Welsh Affairs Committee:

> What we have to do.... is we have to recognise that the union as it is, is over. We have to create a new union. We have to demonstrate to people how we can re-craft the UK in a way that recognises it as a voluntary association of four nations, in which we choose to pool our sovereignty for common purposes and for common benefits (2021).

Drakeford added that the relatively 'random basis' on which the UK government engages with the devolved Welsh, Scottish and Northern Ireland administrations 'is not a satisfactory basis to sustain the future of the United Kingdom'.

While it is obviously impossible to predict the future, one possible parallel with the recent past was noted by the British historian Norman Davies. In 1999, Davies published his monumental study of the UK and Ireland, *The Isles: A History*. He ends his historic overview by suggesting that the people of the UK should consider a peculiar similarity with the collapse of the Soviet Union. In most respects, Davies thinks there are no parallels, except this: The USSR and the UK were both 'composite states of imperial origin.' In those states, when the biggest player – Russia or England – has much to offer, 'the popular nations will sink back into the status of regional curiosities.' But where the big player, 'the imperial nation, loses the citizens' trust, the popular nations will revive, turn militant, and restore their sovereign status.' Other 'composite states' – the Austro-Hungarian Empire, the Ottoman Empire and Yugoslavia – have experienced similar stresses and have also broken apart. Davies concludes that 'the most ominous sign for the health of the United Kingdom' can be summed up as 'the fading of belief in the British nation' (Davies, 1999).

Davies was a historian, not a fortune teller. The UK may yet reform and reinvent itself for another century, but that would demand that the elephant in the bed – England itself – wakes from its slumber. Westminster politicians have failed even to begin to engage with the problems ahead, adopting instead the Osborne Ostrich strategy – don't let the Scots vote and it will go away. But it will not.

English politicians have often congratulated themselves that they just 'muddle through' to manage change gradually. They did not 'muddle through' when Ireland left the UK in 1922 after a war. And, as with Brexit, in recent years 'muddling through' has seemed less a strategy and more like a destination. Complacency and muddling may therefore be how Britain ends. As I reminded the radio presenter, there will always be an England. Whether there will always be a UK is a very different question, with potentially a very different answer.

References

Davies, N. (1999), *The Isles: A History*, Oxford: Oxford University Press.

Drakeford, M. (2021), 'United Kingdom 'as it is, is over', says Wales First Minister', *Wales Online*, 3 March, https://www.walesonline.co.uk/news/uk-news/united-kingdom-as-is-over-19966832

Edgerton, D. (2020), 'Boris Johnson Might Break Up the UK. That's a Good Thing', *New York Times*, 10 January, https://www.nytimes.com/2020/01/10/opinion/brexit-scotland-northern-ireland.html

Osborne, G. (2021), 'Unleashing nationalism has made the future of the UK the central issue', *Evening Standard*, 19 January, https://www.standard.co.uk/comment/nationalism-union-brexit-b900299.html

CHAPTER 19

The British Left, Neoliberalism and the Potential of Scottish Independence
Paul Mason

THE FIRST TIME I realised the UK would cease to exist was about a week before the first independence referendum. I was interviewing Glasgow school students for *Channel 4 News*, some just turned 16 and newly eligible to vote. 'I'm all for independence', said one, 'even though I support the wrong football team'. He didn't have to say the word Rangers, or mention religion – the whole class knew what he meant and so did I. In the car park at Glasgow Airport the next day, I passed the union Jack and the Saltire drooping amid the drizzle, and understood that within my lifetime one of them would be taken down.

The 16-year-olds of the first referendum will have their own children by the time the second happens. By the time those children are 16, I expect the Sark, the Esk and the Tweed to mark an international border, and not a particularly soft one.

But the UK's disintegration will be just one strand of a multi-layered crisis. Class-based voting behaviours, having been eroded slowly for years by education and demographic change, have been rapidly replaced by polarisation over cultural values. That, in turn, is fragmenting labourism, which for more than a century has been just as strong a pillar of the British state in Scotland.

Meanwhile as the Afghan debacle shows, the rules-based global order is also disintegrating, with the increasingly strong rival 'poles' of the multipolar world now exerting a strong influence into Britain's political reality. And climate chaos is approaching. Amid the uncertainty, there is a clear and achievable task: to replace the neo-liberal economic model that is driving this fragmentation process with something more sustainable for the planet, and more socially just. And to do so in all the states that succeed the UK.

Neo-liberalism is best defined by the Goldsmiths University economist Will Davies as the 'disenchantment of politics by economics' (2017). It created an economic model whereby finance dominates and dictates all social priorities, where credit displaces wages and the wage share of GDP falls, where wealth inequalities soar and productivity stagnates. What's more, Davies points out, it was created coercively, through the imposition of market norms and behaviours across large parts of society where they have never existed.

This 30-year economic reality, in turn, created an ethos: a sense of self revolving around money, consumption, narcissism, and back-stabbing competition. Then, after the 2008 crisis, when the model ceased to function, and could only be kept alive through borrowing and money creation on a massive scale, millions of people experienced what I've called 'the crisis of the neo-liberal self'.

Everything that Generation X and the Boomers were told was permanent is vanishing: the unipolar world, 'the End of History', 'Cool Britannia', social mobility and the contents of their pension funds. If the UK itself were to vanish from Google Maps, sometime in the late 2020s, it would not exactly seem like a 'Black Swan' event.

After the Neo-liberal Wreckage and the Agenda for an Emergent Scottish State

What can be rescued and what can be achieved? Neo-liberalism, as a global system, cannot be dismantled one country at a time. But just as it was coerced into existence, by Thatcher, Pinochet and Reagan, it can be coerced out of existence by countries that choose radical action plans aligned to decarbonisation, the promotion of the commons, and state-led industrial strategy.

In the short term, everything depends on the precise economic vision settled on by the pro-independence Scottish *polis*. By this I mean everything from the SNP-Green political alliance at Holyrood, to the city councils, to the legal and academic world, to trade unions, and the wider demos that sit in permanent session via Twitter and Facebook.

The 2013 white paper 'Scotland's Future' was a fiction whose believability, like the best works of literature, rested on what it did not say (Scottish Government, 2013). A new white paper for the 2020s has to be concrete: it has to spell out the pathways and the costs of fiscal and monetary independence. It has to contain not just numbers but a project plan, with clear phases and risk assessments. Its centrepiece has to be an explanation of how an independent Scotland would achieve the goals it is committed to by COP26, and how it ensures both sovereignty and national security in a world order characterised by volatility and power-grabs.

Without this, it is still possible that the Scottish people would vote for a kind of 'hit-and-hope independence' offered in 2014 – but the process following a narrow referendum victory would be ripe for exploitation by a Conservative government in Westminster. Just as Johnson exploited a non-specific Brexit commitment, and drove it to the maximum point of disruption, it would allow a UK Tory government to dictate economic, diplomatic and political forms to the emergent Scottish state, if there were no specific economic or geopolitical commitments embodied in the result.

The options are stark. A Scotland whose currency is backed by the Bank of England will not just be a monetary colony but a fiscal colony as well. Its real economy – from farms to universities, betting shops to artificial intelligence labs – would be just as subject to the dictates of global finance as before. It would be obliged to maintain just as hard an economic border with Europe as it has today.

A Scotland whose destination is EU membership, however, would be a satellite of the eurozone from the very start, subject to the same fiscal imperialism that was applied to Greece in 2015, and – unless something dramatic changes in England – it would require a hard economic border with the rest of the UK.

There are those on the Scottish left who believe a third outcome is possible: Scotland as a Hibernian Cuba, declaring radical independence from both the major states and economies bordering it. A softer version of this is the 'warm south of Scandinavia' model – joining Norway as a semi-detached, resource-rich and fiscally balanced economy at the edge of the EU.

The fragmentation of the global order, COVID-19, and the need for Europe to emerge as a strong regional superstate puts paid to that. The fact that 'strategic autonomy' and 'technological sovereignty' have emerged as buzzwords in Paris, Madrid and Brussels tells us all we need to know. A Scottish national independence project has to be either aligned with European strategic autonomy, or in friction with it.

That is why I am convinced the medium-term destination for Scotland, should its people choose independence, has to be the EU and the eurozone. In that context, the key that unlocks the route beyond neo-liberalism is a green industrial revolution. An independent Scotland could, and should, move faster and in a bespoke way towards net zero carbon than the pathway on offer from Johnson and Sunak in Westminster.

Since Scotland's fiscal dynamics would be heavily dependent on fossil fuel revenues, and they need to decline towards zero, that means embracing a deficit-funded Green New Deal. It would involve rapid decarbonisation, alongside radical changes in transport, infrastructure, housing and urban design. It would need to be supported by expansionary, money creation policies by a central bank.

There is no other realistic path. The Growth Commission's proposal – to embark on a programme of austerity in order to shrink the inherited deficit – was wrong in 2018, and is doubly impossible today, when the UK Treasury has borrowed in excess of £300 billion in a single year to combat COVID-19 (Sustainable Growth Commission, 2018).

So the art of statecraft, for those who want to run the emergent Scottish state, is to create the conditions in which a deficit-led green expansion programme can happen: a non-hostile government in London; a remainder UK (rUK) state in which Wales and the English regions gain significant power, restraining the financial elite in London; and a willing fiscal partner in Brussels and a willing monetary partner in Frankfurt, prepared to extend support to Scotland's transition process.

Today, most of the major democracies are running on the 'gas and air' of borrowing and quantitative easing. That's created a form of zombie neo-liberalism, in which the finance sector gets money for free and expands its capital through a mixture of speculative property, asset price inflation and technological monopoly. The central banks of the USA, Switzerland, the eurozone, Britain, and Japan are all playing the same game, and the financial elites of these countries have adapted to it.

But it is a dead end. The answer is not to stop borrowing, or to stop creating money, but to start vectoring resources towards the planned decarbonisation of the real economy, growing the wage share of GDP and suppressing wealth inequality through asset taxation.

It should go without saying that this is unachievable with a Scottish currency created by fiat on day one of independence.

The Need for a UK-wide Progressive Alliance to Aid Independence

Instead of turning their backs on Westminster politics, in a mixture of disdain and disgust, those advocating independence need to engage with the task of building a progressive alliance government in London, and movement throughout Britain. To save the planet, to reverse out of Johnson's hard Brexit and to ensure the security of the UK's constituent nations, even as they choose to separate, we need to lock English conservatism out of power for decades.

Labour alone has become incapable of doing this. Parts of its social base in the ex-industrial towns, with older voters in the vanguard, are morally and culturally alienated from the party's social liberalism. Hostility to Scottish nationalism played well among this group in 2015, and will do so again, for the simple fact that they have become culturally attached to English nationalism. And as Labour adapts its rhetoric to the task of winning those voters back, prioritising crime, defence, and fixing the potholes in the road over radical language on climate change and social justice, it is bleeding voters to the Lib Dems, Greens and Plaid Cymru.

To break the logjam, the whole of UK progressive politics has to engage with the constitutional challenge. I have no doubt, as a second independence referendum approaches, Labour will throw out yet another last minute offer involving fiscal autonomy, or even federalism, all designed to desperately head off independence.

Instead, Labour – and indeed the Lib Dems, Greens, Plaid, Sinn Fein and the SDLP – needs to focus on what a post-independence constitutional settlement with Scotland might look like. For most of the British left this has been a 'deal with it if it happens' issue. By proactively engaging with a post-independence reality we can bring all parts of it – fiscal, monetary, trade, defence and energy policies – to the same table.

We are dealing, in essence, with three legislatures: a post-independence Holyrood; a Westminster government led by Labour but involving Green, Lib Dem and Plaid Cymru MPs in the Cabinet; and a Welsh legislature where a de facto coalition of Labour and Plaid can lock out the reactionaries.

These parties should, in advance of the second referendum, design a treaty: its centrepiece should be a clean, no-penalty independence process for Scotland permitting, for example, equal membership of the board of a central bank of sterling for all four legislatures, replacing the Bank of England. It should commit its signatories to shared decarbonisation targets, and equitable sharing of the energy generated throughout the whole former UK. It should commit to re-entering the European single market, allowing Scotland to pursue the path to eurozone membership and full EU membership.

Its centrepiece should be a cross-border economic plan to decarbonise the economy and reduce inequality. Its capstone should be a mutual defence treaty, with all signatories remaining part of NATO, or aligned to it, and strong collaboration against terrorism, organised crime and hybrid warfare activities by Russia, China and others.

In retrospect, the problem for both the English and Scottish left since 2010 has been their refusal to think beyond independence, fuelled by the suspicion and hope that it will not happen. A Yes vote in a second referendum need not be the trigger for constitutional chaos: it can be the signal for all four units of the UK to begin moving in the same direction – beyond neo-liberal economics, beyond delusions of post-imperial grandeur and beyond parliamentary systems rigged for centuries in favour of a Conservative elite and its mass base.

A treaty process, and a political convention of progressive parties to design and debate it, could bring realism to all sides. It would force politicians in Cardiff and London to confront the reality of independence and what being left without Scotland might entail for them, their politics and how they reshape their democracy.

It would force the majority parties at Holyrood to ditch the fantasy blueprints of 2013 and 2018 and recognise the cold fact: either you attack the power of global finance and big energy, placing deficit-funded expansion at the heart of the post-independence project, or become a puppet state of something else. The choice is a Scotland where independence and self-government are about real power and substance, or merely empty symbols and platitudes while power continues to lie in the entrenched elites of the present. This is a debate whose success matters not just to Scotland but every single person on the British left.

References

Davies, W. (2017), 'Populism and the Limits of Neo-liberalism', *LSE Blog*, 30 April, accessed at: https://
blogs.lse.ac.uk/europpblog/2017/04/30/
essay-populism-and-the-limits-of-neoliberalism-by-william-davies/

Scottish Government (2013), *Scotland's Future: Your Guide to an
Independent Scotland*, Edinburgh; Scottish Government.

Sustainable Growth Commission (2018), *Scotland: The New Case for
Optimism*, Edinburgh: Sustainable Growth Commission.

CHAPTER 20

The Labour Party and Class, Nation and State
Seán Patrick Griffin

The Crisis of the British State

THE UK, ONCE a political union that was the foremost global power and creator of the largest empire in world history, is now fighting a struggle for its own survival and relevance. But to understand its present trajectory, we must understand its past. The British state was founded upon, and built for, defending the three pillars of the union: Crown, Church, and Empire (Smyth, 2001; Levack, 1987). The UK had a powerful narrative and story to tell; an imagined community was constructed at home to advance the monarchy, Protestantism, and imperialism abroad. However, as the stonemasonry of each of these pillars began to evince hairline cracks in the twilight of the 20th century, the union started to appear precarious.

The onward march of decolonisation and secularisation, coupled with the waning importance of British royalty, rendered the original raison d'être of the union obsolete. The noble lie peddled by the ruling class of the British duty to spread Christianity, commerce, and civilisation to the wider world seemed to belong to another age. The popular mythology that was built up around the idea of the union faded in the public consciousness of its citizens and thus its foundations and institutions were seriously undermined. The UK lost its narrative.

Despite these seismic epochal shifts, changes in British society and in the UK's sense of self, the British state has constitutionally remained largely static, devolution notwithstanding. The UK is stuck with the relic of an imperial state in a post-imperial world. While socially, culturally, and economically the UK is well down the road of a journey (for some a painful one), transitioning from imperial power to middle-sized European nation, the state itself is wedded to the power-hoarding constitution of its vainglorious past.

In his 1976 Richard Dimbleby lecture at the BBC, the late Lord Hailsham warned against the dangers of the British state being captured by an elective dictatorship in Westminster. He noted that the only limitations on the sovereign will of Parliament are political and moral, not legally binding. Alluding to the UK's political constitution, he pointed out that the only limitations on this power 'are found in the consciences of members, in the necessity for periodical elections, and in the so-called checks and balances inherent in the composition, structure and practice of Parliament itself' (Hailsham, 1976).

This power to which Hailsham was referring is of course the sovereignty of Parliament – the foundational principle of British constitutional law which remains, in theory at least, absolute. Hailsham was more concerned with what he perceived to be the anti-democratic nature of governments with slim majorities being able to control Parliament (not least the Wilson government at the time of his lecture). However, his borrowed term, 'elective dictatorship', is an apt description of the British constitution from top to bottom immutably for all time, not a fleeting epithet applying to one government at a particular point in history.

The British state is one of the most centralised in the Western world. In the absence of the safeguards offered by codified and entrenched constitutional arrangements, all ultimate sovereign power is concentrated in and exclusive to the singularity of the sovereignty of Parliament. Like a democratic black hole, all power, control, and checks and balances in the body politic are swallowed up by the Crown-in-Parliament. Nothing can escape its authority, no one can challenge it, and devolution is at its mercy (Dicey, 1885).

One may argue that in a parliamentary democracy, this is the way it ought to be. A democratically elected legislature with supreme and unassailable law-making power should be sacrosanct (leaving aside the unelected House of Lords). The trouble with this theory is that in practice the chokehold the government has on Parliament means that Parliament's will is effectively the Government's will and a British prime minister with an overall majority in the House of Commons has, in effect, untrammelled constitutional power. This arrangement may be suited to administering the far-flung colonies of a sprawling empire on which the sun never sets, but it is nothing short of disastrous in a modern multinational state in a post-devolution and post-Brexit world.

It is not only power that is concentrated in the hands of the few – the UK's monocephalic model is not restricted to its constitution. All the principal organs of government are geographically centralised too, situated in London in the SW1 postcode, including Parliament itself, the Supreme Court, the headquarters of the prime minister as well as most UK government departments. The City is the financial services and banking centre of the UK; London is the location of the central Bank of England, the media centre of the UK, and the UK's centre for music and the arts.

The broader UK economy is massively imbalanced. The UK is one of the most centralised states and regionally imbalanced economies in the world. London and the South East of England are by far the wealthiest parts of the UK, boasting over 300,000 millionaires, while in the North East of England that figure is 14,000, and less than 40,000 for the whole of Scotland. On virtually every economic measure, London and the South East of England vastly outstrips the rest of the UK in terms of GDP, GVA (Gross Value Added) per head, employment, enterprise figures, household expenditure, and number of millionaires (Barclays Prosperity Index, 2016). Both power and wealth are concentrated and centralised in the UK in a way that is difficult to imagine in most Western democracies, including the states of the UK's closest allies such as the US, Canada, or Australia.

In recent years, the state of the union has deteriorated further, from a state of precarity towards existential crisis. As well as renewed demand for independence in Scotland post-Brexit, there is also growing appetite in Wales for independence or, at the very least, radical devolution and reform of the centre of power. In the English regions, too, there is growing discontent and resentment towards Westminster's cavalier disregard for local interests, as has been evident during the COVID-19 pandemic. In Northern Ireland, demographic changes and the fallout from Brexit have precipitated growing demand for Irish unity and a border poll on the island of Ireland. Although the case of Northern Ireland is unique in many ways, the underlying aetiology of this decay is shared across the entire UK. It is the result of decades of centralised power and wealth, a sense of lack of control in the lives of ordinary people, and a fundamental alienation from our democratic institutions of government.

This all against the backdrop of a failure by our political leaders to reimagine and redefine the UK's purpose and narrative in the post-imperial world. As if backfilling that void, the old constitution is now creaking under the weight of competing nationalisms, identity politics, and a disconnect between citizens and the British political and economic elite centred on Westminster and the City of London. Where does the UK go from here?

Labour

It is not only the British state grappling with questions over its purpose and narrative. For different but related reasons, the Labour Party is facing similar soul-searching questions about what it is for, who it represents, and how it regalvanises its electoral base to avoid mortal decline (Audickas et al, 2020). Labour is not alone – social democracy across Europe has been in retreat since the turn of the century. The origins of this decline are multifarious and, in some cases, idiosyncratic to local circumstances. However, the rise of neo-liberalism in the second half of the 20th century and with it the evisceration of industrial working-class communities, trade unions, and class solidarity, are shared experiences across the continent. Not only did the rise of this ideology result in damaging partisan dealignment for centre-left parties, but those parties themselves also got caught up in the whirlwind, renouncing democratic socialism in favour of unfettered markets, privatisation, and a blistering rate of globalisation. In the process, they managed to alienate many voters in their traditional working-class heartlands.

In the UK this has been keenly felt by Labour, particularly in Scotland where the party's embrace of neo-liberalism, despite the Corbyn interregnum, has become intrinsically linked to the problems of the British state and the constitutional question. Labour has gone from hegemonic control of Scottish politics for much of the latter 20th and early 21st centuries to having one solitary MP in the Commons and sitting in third place in Holyrood.

The view of many progressive voters in Scotland in the run-up to the independence referendum and subsequently was that austerity and the twin forces of neo-liberalism and globalisation, which were perceived to be at least partly responsible for the financial crisis and resulting great recession, were ideas synonymous with the British state, and one way to reverse the tide of right-wing economic policy was to break up this state. The politics of right and left were subsumed into constitutional politics, the nature of the British state itself, and Scotland's place in it (Foley and Ramand, 2014).

This was not merely a view shared by radical socialists but also by many centre and centre-left voters in Scotland, who viewed the austerity programme imposed by the Conservative Government at Westminster as extreme, thus making an alternative to Westminster increasingly attractive. In addition to many Labour voters, a large number of Liberal Democrat voters also decided to vote for independence, while three-quarters of all Yes voters stated that disaffection with Westminster politics was one of the two or three most important reasons for voting Yes (Ashcroft, 2014). It is not an overstatement to say that a large part of the Yes vote can be viewed as an implicit rejection of the British state rather than an explicit endorsement of Scottish nationalism.

It is impossible to resist the conclusion that the absence of a serious democratic socialist challenge from Labour at Westminster has been a significant contributory factor in allowing this worldview to hold water. The sense of abandonment felt by many working-class communities in Scotland towards Labour meant that there was no electoral alternative to Tory Britain. Within Scotland, this lack of alternative turbo-charged the pre-existing grievances levelled against the British state of centralised power and wealth mentioned earlier and has ultimately translated into the working class using their vote en masse in an attempt to replace the state with a new one. The result is now that, in Scotland, almost all politics is viewed through the prism of the constitutional question.

Incredibly given the circumstances, rather than offering a serious alternative vision to the British state, Labour – particularly Scottish Labour – have been among the loudest cheerleaders for the union status quo. This manifested itself in the disastrous decision to share a platform with the Tories in the infamous Better Together campaign in the run-up to the independence referendum. More recently, the party has taken an ultra-hard line against the prospect of a second independence referendum, while simultaneously failing to put forward a radical constitutional reform agenda.

While this may seem incredible, it is hardly surprising. It has been said that of the political parties claiming socialism to be their aim, the Labour Party has been one of the most dogmatic – not about socialism, but about the parliamentary system as the means of achieving it (Miliband, 1964). The British state has not only been viewed as the favoured but also, in fact, the exclusive route to advance the interests of the working class. One may have assumed, therefore, that a democratic socialist party so committed to parliamentary democracy as the sole vehicle for change would have a thoroughgoing constitutional transformation agenda at its heart. In truth, Labour has historically taken a very conservative view of the state and curiously has found no contradiction in its vehement defence of the British constitution and its ambitions to transform society (Plant, 2012).

This position is no longer sustainable for two main reasons. Firstly, the British state's institutional structures and power-hoarding constitutional arrangements are simply not capable of coping with the complexity of governing a multinational state in a post-devolution and post-Brexit context. Failure to bring about radical change will result in never-ending constitutional collisions and wrangling, and sooner or later an implosion into constitutional calamity. It goes without saying that the Labour Party is the only political force in the UK capable of implementing a transformational, constitutional reform agenda; therefore the mantle falls to the party to pursue it.

Secondly, the Labour Party must find ways to reconnect with its traditional working-class heartlands, particularly in Scotland, lest it face its own existential crisis. The notion that this can be achieved by moving Labour to the centre ground is baffling. Lessons from the continent show that the social democratic parties that have been able to stave off Pasokification most effectively are those that have embraced radical policies (Lapavistas and Trickett, 2021). A transformative agenda that seeks to redistribute power and wealth across the UK and empower people and local communities in a project of democratic renewal is an important starting point for Labour in that endeavour.

Constitutional Radicalism

Labour must seize the opportunity to pursue constitutional radicalism before it is too late. While the New Labour reforms tinkered with siloed constitutional plumbing to stop leakages in the system, what is now required is new constitutional architecture. There is a recognition in some quarters of the acute need to move in this direction. For example, while leader of the Labour party, Jeremy Corbyn – jointly with Richard Leonard as leader of Scottish Labour – commissioned a report on exploring ideas around replacing the union state with a progressive federal settlement for the UK, combined with a democratic socialist perspective on the constitution (Griffin, 2020). In Scotland, the Red Paper Collective (Bryan and Kane, 2014) and in Wales, the Radical Federalism group (Antoniw et al, 2021) make/made a similar case arguing for a sweeping new round of devolution but also, crucially, reform of the centre of power at Westminster.

Specifically in relation to Scotland, the report commissioned by Corbyn recognises the need to radically devolve further powers to the Scottish Parliament. For example, it suggests devolving borrowing powers to allow the Scottish Government to invest in the economy to alleviate poverty and tackle inequality. It also suggests devolving the following powers: tax powers over alcohol and tobacco products to improve public health outcomes; powers over employment law to improve workers' rights; powers over drugs policies to enable the Scottish Parliament to address Scotland's drug deaths epidemic, unique in its scale in Europe; and powers over social security administration to end the punitive sanctions regime of the Department for Work and Pensions. The report also suggests innovative powers for the Scottish Parliament such as the power to set a Scottish Wealth Tax, issue graduate work visas to international students at Scottish universities, and a power for the Scottish Parliament to enter international treaties with other nations in devolved areas of competence such as the environment and employment rights.

The report also addresses the subject of England and its place in a federal settlement for the UK. It suggests radical devolution to the English regions by allowing local authorities across England to voluntarily combine into Combined Regional Authorities. These could then draw down on funding and suites of powers over spatial and planning issues, transport, housing, health and social care integration, education, local taxation, and social security. The report also suggests ways England as a nation could be adequately accommodated in a federal constitutional arrangement. It suggests that the now-defunct parliamentary procedure of English Votes for English Laws should be replaced with a more formal territorial division on voting in the UK Parliament. This would finally provide an answer to the West Lothian Question, and also suggests ways in which the English regions could be represented effectively at Westminster.

The report directly ties in the devolution settlements in Scotland, Wales, and Northern Ireland, as well as devolution to the English regions, with reform of the Second Chamber at Westminster. There is a proposal to abolish the House of Lords and replace it with an elected Senate of the Nations and Regions which would be the primary federal organ of the new federal state. Its composition could either be directly elected by proportional representation from the nations and regions, or indirectly elected with the devolved institutions themselves returning senators to represent the devolution settlements at Westminster. The Senate could be given significant new powers including a veto over certain types of bills, such as those that alter the relationship between the UK government and Parliament and the nations and regions. Or, bills that fall into areas of devolved legislative competence with a cross-territorial element, including in policy areas of the repatriated powers returning from the EU. The Senate could also be given powers to ratify international treaties including new trade deals and the power to confirm judicial appointments to the Supreme Court.

The report also recommends the adoption of a codified and legally entrenched constitution, with the courts being given the power to strike down primary legislation from Westminster that is deemed unconstitutional. The idea of the sovereignty of Parliament discussed earlier would therefore be supplanted by a supreme constitutional law founded on the popular sovereignty of the people of all the nations and regions of the UK. The elective dictatorship at Westminster would thereby be brought to an abrupt end.

In order to secure a progressive constitutional settlement, the report also suggests a number of measures: international human rights standards, including economic and social rights, should be incorporated into the constitution; a national investment bank should be established as part of the constitution to ensure that investment in the UK economy is directed across the country according to need and spread across the nations and regions equitably; the constitution should also seek to protect and reinvigorate local government to bring power closer to the people based on a principle of subsidiarity.

While these developments are encouraging, at present there is limited movement in this direction officially at a UK level. At a time when social democracy is failing across Europe and as we venture into the middle of the 21st century, the political left lacks a narrative, a story to tell, a vision. In the UK, that vision should be, to paraphrase the late Tony Benn, to reshape and repurpose the state itself to secure a fundamental and irreversible shift in the balance of wealth and power in favour of working people. For Labour, it is the unfinished business of devolution. By reclaiming its own narrative, Labour could not only save itself but also help save the UK.

References

Antoniw, Mick et al (2021), *We, the People, the case for Radical Federalism*, Radical Federalism Collective.

Ashcroft, Lord (2014), 'How Scotland Voted, and Why', 19 September, https://lordashcroftpolls.com/2014/09/scotland-voted/

Audickas, Lukas; Cracknell, Richard; and Loft, Philip (2020), *UK Elections Statistics: 1918-2019: A Century of Elections*, House of Commons Library Briefing Paper, Number CBP7529.

Barclays (2016), *Prosperity Index*, https://home.barclays/news/2016/08/all-regions-of-uk-more-prosperous-than-last-year/

Bryan, Pauline and Kane, Tommy (2014), *Class, Nation and Socialism: The Red Paper on Scotland*, Glasgow: Glasgow Caledonian University.

Dicey, A.V. (1885), *The Law of the Constitution*, Reprint, Oxford: Oxford University Press, 2013.

Foley, James and Ramand, Pete (2014), *Yes: The Radical Case for Scottish Independence*, London: Pluto Press.

Griffin, Seán Patrick (2020), *Remaking the British State: For the Many, Not the Few*, Glasgow: Red Paper Collective.

Hailsham, Lord (1976), BBC Richard Dimbleby Lecture, 14 October, https://genome.ch.bbc.co.uk/9474f2a73e814142ae93290b9e55bf72

Lapavistas, Costas and Trickett, Jon (2021), 'Britain's Labour Party Can't Become Another PASOK', *Jacobin*, 23 April, https://www.jacobinmag.com/2021/04/uk-labour-party-greece-pasok-brexit-syriza

Levack, Brian (1987), *The Formation of the British State: England, Scotland and the Union, 1603-1707*, Oxford: Clarendon Press.

Miliband, Ralph (1964), *Parliamentary Socialism*, Reprint, Pontypool: Merlin, 2009.

Plant, Raymond (2012), *The Neo-liberal State*, Oxford: Oxford University Press.

Smyth, Jim (2001), *The Making of the United Kingdom 1660-1800*, London: Longman.

Section Six: Frontiers, People and Power

CHAPTER 21

Trade and Scotland's Place In The World
Craig Dalzell

AT ITS MOST fundamental level, all of the sound and fury of the debates around Scottish independence (and around statehood for any state anywhere) is a debate around drawing a fairly arbitrary blob on a map of the world; declaring that one set of laws and regulations applies within that blob, as distinct from the laws and regulations that apply to various parts of the world outwith that blob; determining who should make those laws and regulations; and how that blob interacts with the other blobs around it. Whether trying to create a social democratic nation state, a mercantile city state or an autocratic, multi-ethnic empire, those absolute core tenants remain.

In Scotland's case, the last item on that list contains the most unknowns and will involve the greatest degree of change. Scotland's relatively stable position compared to other countries means that our physical place in the world is pretty well defined (especially compared to many other European nations that have experienced significant border changes or have come into existence entirely within living memory). Even within the union that formed the United Kingdom, Scotland (distinct from the other members of that union) has a distinct legal system that will be largely preserved by independence. Although, there will undoubtedly be debate around some kind of 'withdrawal act' that determines how currently reserved legislation is translated into Scots law upon independence, and the odds of Scotland breaking down into city states (sorry Edinburgh) or embarking on a despotic, expansionistic, imperial crusade are slim at best.

Scotland's Trade Data

Scotland therefore needs to have a discussion – well ahead of independence – about the place it wants to fill in the world and how it wants to interact with its neighbours. This means looking at the geopolitics of Scottish independence and looking at our trade with the rest of the world – right now, how it will change as a result of independence, and how it will have change forced upon it as a result of a changing world.

Unfortunately, the data on Scotland's current trade patterns are not good enough. The best data we have on trade comes from the annual Export Statistics Scotland (ESS) report which, as the name implies, only covers exports from Scotland.

Even within this export data, the data can be limited. This was the case even before the 2020 COVID pandemic that caused, amongst a great deal of other problems in trade, a suspension of the ESS programme. ESS is based on self-reported surveys which are more effective in certain sectors (especially manufactured goods where receipts are easy to trade) than in others. The overall survey return rate is low at the best of times – the most recent survey had a total response rate of just 17 per cent of companies asked to respond. The highest returns came from companies exporting agriculture, forestry and fishing goods with 33.7 per cent of companies returning their export data, but the lowest came from financial services where just 9.3 per cent of companies returned their data. It has been noted that in some sectors it can be difficult to obtain data at all, with particular difficulties noted in retail (a shopper from Newcastle buying groceries across the border represents a retail goods export but the supermarket is unlikely to track where they came from, or where they took the goods when they left the store) and in tourism (it may be surprising to some even in the sector that a non-Scottish person staying in a Scottish hotel represents a tourist services export with respect to the country of origin of the guest).

If the data on exports could be improved, the data on imports is almost non-existent and what little there is is based on fairly loose proxy measurements. This is not a problem unique to the UK – many countries find it easier to measure their exports than their imports, to the point that there is a known problem in trade accounting circles where Country X's measured exports to Country Y are often very different to the amount measured by Country Y of their imports from Country X (the two numbers should, of course, be identical).

What this all means for Scotland is that perennial news stories are generated on the amount of Scotland's trade that leaves for destinations in the rest of the UK, to the EU or to the rest of the world but few ever ask what Scotland's trade balance is with those countries. This is just as important as trade volume because trade policy can be influenced a great deal by whether you are a net importer or a net exporter of goods to another country.

Scotland's Customers

To the best of our current knowledge around 60 per cent of Scotland's total exports go to the rest of the UK, around 19 per cent to the EU and around 20 per cent to the rest of the world. For goods, these ratios are almost reversed. Around 60 per cent of exported Scottish goods go to the rest of the world whereas only 40 per cent goes to the UK outwith Scotland. In services – which make up the majority of Scottish exports – the UK is a much more prominent customer with around 70 per cent of Scottish service exports going to the UK.

It makes sense that so many exported Scottish services go to the rest of a UK – it is a result of that sector's high degree of 'trade gravity' (the tendency for volume of trade to reduce in proportion to distance travelled from the exporting country). In today's fairly globalised and increasingly trade-liberal world, the biggest hurdle involved in moving goods to an external market is getting them to the port. Once a container is loaded onto a ship or lorry, it is comparatively easy to move it anywhere. The trade gravity for goods has been reducing steadily, but the same is not true for services. Services such as utilities (electricity, gas and water) require a direct pipe or cable connection to the customer, which limits exports. Information and communication services may face language barriers which could be limiting in many cases (except perhaps where translation is part of the service being sold). Financial services in particular have significant gravity given that they face language, currency, and regulatory barriers. If someone in Scotland is considering buying a house in Germany, it's highly unlikely that they would use a Scotland-based real estate agent to do so, nor are they likely to go to anywhere other than a German bank for the mortgage. If a Scottish financial services company found itself in a position to be doing a lot of this kind of financial trading in Germany or another country, it may be simple good business sense to move part or all of the company to that country – or create a subsidiary such that the services could be based within the language, regulatory, time zone and other barriers rather than trading across them. Such a service would then no longer be an export but simply part of the internal trade of that country.

When it comes to considering the importance of these present trading patterns and discussing them in the context of Scottish independence it must be emphasised again that Scotland lacks a lot of basic data on these service trades, particularly in the case of trades within the UK. A Scot buying a house in Scotland might not approach a German bank to arrange their mortgage but it is entirely reasonable to assume they could consider taking their mortgage out with a bank whose headquarters are somewhere in the UK other than Scotland. Not only do we not know the relative trade balance between Scotland and the rest of the UK, but we also do not know how much of that trade is not easily transferable if a trade barrier renders it unviable. For instance, if a Scottish bank provides loans or mortgages to an English customer and an English bank provides the same for a Scottish customer, could those two customers simply swap banks and receive their required services without any substantial interruption or net reduction in the volume of trade in the respective countries?

However, just because for some tradeable items independence may be more a matter of realigning the accounts, this does not mean it will be the same for all. The choices that Scotland makes here will fundamentally define the challenge of how Scotland rises to those choices.

Building Borders

While the world has slowly been moving towards freer and more globalised trade the process is far from complete, may never be complete, and is happening on a much more regionalised basis than is often assumed. Rather than a unified global movement towards free trade, the world as of 2021 appears to be moving towards a multipolar world of trade blocs. Blocs like the European Union, the Southern Common Market (Mercosur), the South African Customs Union, the Greater Arab Free Trade Area and others explore a spectrum of economic and monetary unions which aim to reduce tariff and regulatory barriers as far as possible within their bloc – sometimes to the point of complete unity – and can act as a united front in negotiating on trading conditions between blocs. Members of these blocs generally consider the benefits of membership – greatly reduced trade barriers with their closest and often largest volume trading partners as well as somewhat reduced barriers elsewhere – to outweigh the costs, which include loss of national sovereignty to set their own regulations, possible inability to counter policies that undercut national standards or 'trade away' a competitive advantage for the greater good of the trade bloc. Scottish fisheries are perhaps a particularly sensitive subject in this regard.

This multipolar trading bloc model leads to a conundrum for countries that wish to focus on their own national sovereignty, or attempt to withdraw from trading blocs entirely and negotiate trading deals unilaterally with other nations or, indeed, with the larger trading blocs. This is a topic that the United Kingdom as a whole is having to rapidly learn as a result of its withdrawal from the European Union. In its re-engagement with the world on its own it may find that its halcyon days of mercantile imperialism have long departed the stage, that its largely service-based economy has little to offer other countries for the reasons outlined above, and its own substantial trade deficit means that it has fewer goods to offer than the goods it needs to buy from other nations.

Unless global trading patterns change substantially, an independent Scotland may find itself essentially choosing between three futures. The first involves closely aligning itself to its current largest customer – the remaining United Kingdom – and essentially trying to preserve as much of the present trading integration as possible. This could involve maintaining free movement of goods, capital, services and people between the two countries – essentially forming a British single market and customs union – and would necessarily involve the remaining UK taking a leading role in defining the monetary, financial and other regulations that create this Union. Given little motivation to change what they are currently used to, and less to modify it to suit Scotland's ongoing trading needs, may lead to an 'independent' Scotland that is little changed from the status quo with most of the changes being the loss of what little accountability and democratic power it currently has within the union. This may well be a price worth paying if the gains in other areas are substantial enough and if the mandate to preserve much of Scotland's current economic structure are powerful enough. But it may also be that this future offers little to those for whom the chance to change an economy that does not work for them is a substantial opportunity for independence.

Also that the withdrawal of Scotland's current levers of power in this sphere through legislation like the Internal Market Act 2020 represents a deterrent to the current constitutional arrangement.

The second future involves Scotland closely aligning with its second closest and largest customer, the European Union. This may mean full EU membership or it may mean a looser relationship defined by EFTA and/or EEA membership but the overall idea is similar in all instances. This would involve Scotland remaining aligned or realigning with EU standards, regulations and other strictures while the remaining UK diverges. This could preserve and restore the economic markets lost as a result of Brexit but could also act to corrode the links between Scotland and the remaining UK. This choice may, again, be worth the costs especially if the markets between Scotland and the remaining UK are different enough that one, they are not directly competing, and two, the lowering of barriers in one field does not result in the raising of barriers in others.

As we have seen above in what we know of Scotland's exports, the 'shape' of goods traded to the EU is substantially different from the goods shipped to the UK, so it may be that it is possible to preserve a kind of best of both worlds. This is, of course, an incredibly complex area and determining this definitively is well beyond the scope of what can be done in this chapter or even in this book as a whole. Services present a different problem entirely and getting to grips with these will likely remain a substantial challenge for independence and for the teams negotiating it once the democratic mandate for it is granted.

Shifting Trade Winds

One major challenge for an independent Scotland when it comes to trade is the reliance on England, not necessarily as a customer but as a route to the rest of the world. Once a major direct trading nation in its own right, Scotland no longer has many significant trading ports. The vast majority of Scotland's exports and imports are transhipped through England. International trading rules do allow for transhipment of goods through countries without having to pay tariffs or duties but the paperwork and additional checks to ensure that these routes are not used as a mechanism for smuggling into the country they are passing through can be onerous. This is before one considers the vulnerability a country may face if critical goods like food or energy could potentially be cut off if diplomatic relations break down – however unlikely such an event may seem.

These factors are what have induced Ireland to develop direct trading routes to the rest of the EU as a result of Brexit. Scotland would do well to learn those lessons and study how its own routes can be rapidly developed upon, or even before, independence. This is especially important if Scotland wants to factor its Green New Deal into trade policy as doing so will – at the very least – involve factoring transport emissions into goods exports and imports. If Scotland wants to accelerate a global shift in cutting said emissions then it could, for example, invest in developing electric and green hydrogen refuelling stations at the ports. But this is something that may not be effective if it is still reliant on moving goods by lorry from England if England has not made similar investments and therefore cannot support Scotland's electric and hydrogen transport fleet.

However, the Green New Deal must mean more than just doing old things in a slightly 'greener' way. Whilst Scotland has made some progress towards reducing its domestic greenhouse gas emissions, a large fraction of that has come by offshoring those emissions, by reducing domestic production and increasing imports. In 2021, the Scottish Climate Assembly – a panel made of a representative sample of Scotland's population – called for the deliberate reduction of imports to Scotland so that transport emissions could be reduced and so that domestic laws and regulations can be employed to ensure that the goods are produced to the highest possible standards and that the full environmental costs of producing them can be accounted for. They also called for the reduction in the demand for various goods and services by moving from a consumer society to a sharing society. Resources libraries would allow people to access goods like DIY equipment without everyone having to buy a cheap power tool that almost no one ever uses. Creating a Circular Economy is mostly framed around reducing resource extraction and waste production, but it will also have to address the need to move goods around the world especially when it involves resources being extracted and moved to one country, sent to another to be manufactured, sent to a third to be used and then disposed of in a fourth.

And finally, Scotland must not only reckon with its imports but also with its exports too. The three highest profile exports from Scotland are oil, whisky and salmon. The first is contributing to the global catastrophe that is the climate emergency, the second contributes to a health crisis both globally and domestically, and the third contributes to at least a regional environmental crisis whether it involves the over-exploitation of wild habitats or via intensive farming done in a way that causes significant environmental damage. Scotland is not an innocent victim of the harms caused by our current economy but a direct contributor to them. The answer of what Scotland should produce for export instead of these will perhaps be the greatest challenge of the question of independence and trade because it strikes to the very heart of what these prestige exports are often about – how Scotland finds its place in the world, and what it stands ready to contribute to the global community.

CHAPTER 22

Moving to Smart Borders and Customs
Bill Austin

THE 2014 REFERENDUM showed that the issue of borders is a stick those arguing for Scotland to continue to be part of the UK will attempt to use to beat down the case for independence. However, the next referendum will likely be a very different experience. When faced with a damaging Brexit and with Scotland having no financial or border controls of its own during times of pandemic, the border argument is reshaped. The specific question of arrangements for trade and transit between Scotland and England needs to be re-examined in that wider context.

The key point about modern borders is that, beyond demarking and establishing the legal jurisdiction and geographic extent of a country, they have a number of revenue, immigration and safety functions. Crucially, each of these functions can occur at the place where validity needs to be checked and this does not have to occur at a particular point where the goods or people cross a line on a map. This allows a country to create 'smart borders' to check this validity in the most appropriate, cost-effective and convenient real or virtual space.

The very notion of a 'hard border' where everything and everyone is stopped and searched is a ridiculous and almost cartoonish fiction, not resembling reality in any other European nation. Indeed, it is not a concept recognised by the World Customs Organisation. A departure from the UK's approach to borders, allowing us to reimagine them for ourselves, is actually one of the key advantages independence could bring. The UK Border Force focuses disproportionately on illegal immigration at the expense of controlling customs and revenues. This political choice by the UK Government means that an estimated £120 billion per year has been lost due to a failure to collect customs revenues. Ineffective smuggling prevention also results in approximately £40 million of fake Scotch whisky entering our country each year. Think of what NHS Scotland or even the Scottish National Investment Bank could do if they were allocated additional spending because of this new revenue.

Borders, Customs and the Deficiencies of the UK System

Borders have always been synonymous with collecting import and export revenues. Such revenues, however, are only one important cog within the national revenues wheel, and cannot exist in isolation within a Scottish revenue strategy. The question arises as to what the role of a customs officer is. In short, they are empowered by statute, as a law enforcement officer, to collect and protect national revenues and enforce customs and other related laws. The World Customs Organisation (WCO) and World Trade Organisation (WTO) recognise this role within trade facilitation and revenue collection.

So, how much import and export revenues does Scotland generate annually? In short, we do not know at present, and that provides another benefit of controlling our own system. No statistical data is collated for Scotland as a discrete geographical area. All three UK government agencies, responsible for the collection of excise duty, HMRC, UK Border Force (UKBF) or Office for National Statistics (ONS), only produce data for the UK as a whole.

This highlights the dysfunctionality of the UK system for excise duty collection. HMRC, reporting to HM Treasury, is not located at UK borders but situated at various inland locations. Relevant Treasury departments are responsible for international customs services and are located at ports and airports. As is the UKBF; the principal department at ports, airports etc, and responsible to The Home Office. With 90 per cent of their work focused on anti-immigration initiatives, revenue protection and collection has tended to be of secondary consideration, again evidencing UK dysfunctionality in this area. Borders controlled by an independent Scotland could do more than this and ensure that due tax is paid and product and services standards are marinated.

Incredibly, very few UKBF officers are empowered, by law, to carry out customs tasks. The customs service, consistently referred to in Westminster documents pertaining to Brexit before 2021 no longer exists despite customs import revenue controls being carried out. There have been no customs officers in Glasgow or Edinburgh since 2005. It is the UKBF immigration service that staffs ports and airports, not customs and Excise. HMRC and UKBF have been shedding staff and closing offices since 2005. At independence, a new Scottish government would expect to be allocated Scotland's customs service officials and staff as well as the existing infrastructure within the UK system at the time of independence. HMRC and the UKBF however, have been shedding staff and closing offices since 2005. The Scottish Government white paper, *Scotland's Future 2014*, suggested replication of this broken, ineffective system, mirroring the current UK taxation regime – this should be avoided.

The UK approach has long been characterised by nebulous Brexit borders/customs controls with zero evidence of resources to cope with the tsunami of import/export transactions and attendant delays which came into force on 1st January 2021. In 2005, Labour Chancellor Gordon Brown, amalgamated HM Customs and Excise (HMCE) with HM Inland Revenue to form HMRC. He did this shortly after the USA had carried out a similar exercise with the US Customs Service, changing its name into the Bureau of Customs and Border Protection. This was a reaction to 9/11 attacks and the revelation that US agencies were not sharing information on intelligence that may have prevented the attack. An unintentional effect, however, was to significantly reduce revenue protection and help facilitate multinational corruption. Indeed, corruption is alleged at the heart of HMG/HMRC decision-making. The proof is in UK endemic, institutionalised tax avoidance and evasion.

'Smart' Not 'Hard' Borders

It is commonly accepted that an independent Scotland will seek to rejoin pan-European institutions, either as part of EFTA or the EU. The opportunity here is to work towards the EU definition of integrated borders management – 'national and international coordination among all relevant authorities and agencies involved in border security and trade facilitation to establish effective, efficient and coordinated border management at the external EU borders, in order to reach the objective of open, but well-controlled and secure borders.' This will facilitate international trade and make Scotland a highly attractive location for organisations seeking to sell their goods and services into Europe.

Moving to 'smart borders' means that 90 per cent of import customs revenue and legislative controls can be collected and legally enforced within our authority – giving Scotland clear evidence of fulfilling EU membership requirements. This dispels the notion that when independent, Scotland would be forced into accepting a border arrangement that England decides. Scotland can create and manage a border of its own making and it will be up to England to do likewise.

Static border controls are easily evaded; they are the result of historical events and as such, in modern societies and in the light digital technologies, are outdated in protecting economies and raising revenues. Professor Hiroshi Motomura (UCLA) argues that there is a long-established legal precedent for 'functional borders'. A border can be conceptualised, according to his analysis 'not as a fixed location but rather wherever a government chooses to perform border functions'. In that context the 'hard border' is a misconception and a distraction. It focuses on a 150 km stretch of land between the Solway and the Tweed and misrepresents reality; the coastline of metropolitan France is 3,500 km while Scotland's coastline, at high tide, is 18,672 km.

Excessive attention to imports crossing into Scotland that must combat barbed-wire, guard posts and bureaucratic, aggressive delays also miss the point. Scottish exports are more of an important priority to our economy. The concept of functional or 'smart borders' means that up to 90 per cent of national revenues and legislative controls can be carried out inland, within Scottish jurisdiction.

To assist revenue collection, anti-smuggling controls could focus on Intelligence Preparation of the Border (IPB) within a modern integrated border management, intelligence-led analysis and risk system. The emphasis must be on mobile controls, in-depth, covering the whole customs jurisdiction of an independent Scotland. The crucial aspect being the whole of Scotland is 'borderland', subject to customs controls. Scottish customs officers could secure tax payments wherever they are due in Scotland, or abroad, within their legal powers and statute of limitations.

A Scottish customs service should prioritise the training and hiring of custom staff, in contrast to the job losses experienced under the governance of the UK. Scotland can benefit by doing things differently. Currently HMRC costs around one penny for every pound collected, but this impressive efficiency is undermined by the small number of dedicated staff. For example, whereas the Department

of Work and Pensions (DWP) has approximately 3,000 investigators, the HMRC has only 300 spread across the whole of the UK to
deal with massive revenue frauds. An independent Scotland should
aim to maintain this collection ratio while increasing the number
of staff.

It cannot be overemphasised that the creation of a revenue
department, including a customs service, would be a golden opportunity for Scotland. The economic stresses and hardships caused by
the pandemic and a hard Brexit could be mitigated by an independent Scotland creating a tax revenues system built to meet the needs
of the Scottish economy and raising the revenues required to support
and protect our communities.

Tax, Legal Compliance, Logistics, Transport and Trade

A constitution for an independent Scotland could and should
enshrine the concept of Right Tax at the Right Time to ensure tax
compliance of every individual and trader within our jurisdiction
liable to pay taxes. Fundamentally, fair and equitable collection of
due revenues and taxes must be the guiding principle throughout.
Revenues due by individuals, traders and multinational companies
anywhere in Scotland must be paid correctly and on time to support
government expenditure. Relevant income that is liable for tax must
be calculated applying only Scottish taxation laws and regardless of
any foreign directives for the calculation of taxable income.

Logically and for practical reasons, customs should have legal
primacy in jurisdictional matters pertaining to Scotland's border and
be responsible for collection of all revenues payable within the jurisdiction of Scots law. Customs must also be included in the Resilience
Division leading on emergency planning, response and recovery on
behalf of the Scottish Government.

The Scottish Government should establish a specialist team to
assist in a review of such laws as soon as transition is implemented
in order that they are written in clear, modern and simple language
to better facilitate their understanding by traders and the general
public, as well as their consistent application by customs personnel.

The Scottish Government should prioritise investing in and
developing a modern logistics strategy and transport infrastructure,
making Scotland an effective and attractive trading location. Necessarily, this would have to focus on a holistic approach encompassing

sea, air, road and rail transport, paying particular attention to Nordic and European links via the East Coast routes with particular attention paid to the development of roll-on/roll-off facilities and the supporting infrastructures.

In 2017, for example, Ireland introduced a Dublin–Zeebrugge Ro-Ro-Ro vessel MV *Celine* capable of ferrying 600 trailers. This can be done by developing multimodal transport hubs, including setting up a certification programme for approving qualifying goods that meet standard specification, set down by appropriate government departments. Such systems, although well established in other countries, require a wide range of support services, including banking, logistics, and customs, all working together with their respective regulatory agencies in order to maximise revenues at the points of import and export activity.

Scotland is strategically placed to benefit from any expansion of trade along the North Sea Route emanating along the Arctic coast of Russia. This is the maritime route that is likely to be free of ice first and thus represents the highest commercial potential. It would reduce the maritime journey between East Asia and Western Europe from 21,000 km using the Suez Canal to 12,800 km, cutting transit time by 1015 days. The Scottish Government must anticipate attracting sea-trade from this route in order to maximise revenues.

A Maritime Nation

Scotland is pre-eminently a maritime nation whose territorial waters are more than five times larger than its landmass. It has over 11,000 km of highly indented coastline, accounting for approximately 61 per cent of the total UK coastline, and over 800 islands. Scotland's territorial waters, together with her exclusive economic zone as set by the 1982 Convention on the Law of the Sea, extend 200 nautical miles outwards from the coast. The waters within this boundary constitute Scotland's recognised fishing limits: a total sea area of 468,994 square km. By contrast, relatively narrow bodies of water – the English Channel and the North Channel in the Irish Sea – are all that separate Scotland from continental Europe and Ireland respectively. Scotland's physical characteristics and location confer many benefits but they also confer risk, and a newly independent Scotland should look to develop its defence model around those risks.

By managing Scotland's maritime borders properly, Scotland can require ships to protect our coastline – providing much-needed work for our shipyards. As mentioned above, Scotland's coastline is in fact five times longer than that of France and yet Scotland has no revenue vessels patrolling our coast or stationed in our ports. This is an opportunity for an independent Scotland to defend our coastline and increase prospective revenues.

No single customs Service or jurisdiction can operate effectively in isolation; therefore, regional cooperation is essential. This must be achieved from government strategic levels to operational and tactical level through regular training exercises and establishment of liaison officers. Ensuring harmonisation of taxation across both Scottish and rUK jurisdictions will remove the incentive to smuggle as funding for criminality, irrespective of south to north or vice versa, and also reduce requirement for border controls. Then there is the question of the EU and EFTA hard border: EU accession requires compliance with customs requirements within EU Acquis35. There is zero mention, nor requirement, for a 'hard border' within Acquis. Finally, EU Acquis is specific about what is required of an aspiring EU member, but is not proscriptive about the 'how'. This is left to the individual EU member to ensure compliance, with or without border controls.

Conclusion: Fresh Opportunities for Scotland

We must think of self-governing Scotland as an independent legal jurisdiction that has internationally recognised legal boundaries. A customs officer at an immobile customs station, in an open-borders 21st century Europe, has very little impact and misses the point, which is that 'hard borders' as we conventionally think of them are very largely irrelevant.

A 'smart borders' approach means that the majority of customs controls for an independent Scotland would occur inland, often near transit depots for efficiency; an arbitrary line on a map is not the principal or smart place to carry out border controls. France collects 90 per cent of its customs and taxation through post-clearance inland controls; on our coast, customs officers would deploy maritime assets to patrol and protect our borders using flexible, mobile customs teams.

This work is not just important for revenue – it is also vital for keeping us all safe. The smuggling of drugs, weapons, illicit tobacco and alcohol using Scotland's coast line is a long lasting and serious problem, affecting communities across the country, but the UK has ignored its damaging impact. Customs officers, working alongside defence and police services, are crucial for the protection of society.

Manufacturing and exports will continue to be crucial to Scotland's economic success after independence. Scotland continues to have a trade surplus in contrast to England's consistent trade deficit, and Scotland's exports are intrinsically linked to EU trade, with 41 per cent of our overall food and drinks exports going to the EU. That would continue whether we are members of EFTA or the EU. Scottish waters produce 20 per cent of the EU's seafood catch, which amounts to 62 per cent of all seafood landed in the UK, two-thirds of which are exported to the EU. Allocation of customs resources can be prioritised towards simplification and enactment of customs export legislation in order to support our economy.

In summary, independence would bring Scotland the opportunity to build the institutions required by a new country. We have the opportunity to build our customs and borders infrastructure and approach based on modern best practice, fit for our priorities and requirements. We can and should avoid replicating the overly complex, inefficient, and inhumane UK system. By letting go of the hostile environment policy, and by implementing an integrated, internationally aligned 'smart border' approach, an independent Scotland has the opportunity to secure our country, claim significant sums in lost revenue and create thousands of high-paying, self-funding jobs. This is a challenge, for sure, but one that can create huge opportunities.

Addendum

In February 2022 UK in a Changing Europe published an important paper entitled 'An EU border across Britain: Scotland's borders after independence'. This focuses on complementary and supplementary questions to the kind raised by Bill Austin and others, starting from the assumption that if an independent Scotland joined the European Union, the trading relationship between Scotland and England/Wales would become that between the Britain and the EU, governed by the terms of the UK-EU Trade and Cooperation Agreement (TCA).

However, it points out, the UK-EU trading relationship at a point at which Scotland transitions to independence within the EU could be very different from the one we see today. The rules governing that relationship would shape the nature of the border between Scotland and the rest of the UK, and the scale of the task required to manage it.

The challenges of a harder border are not just felt 'at' a borderline itself, the executive summary stresses. The terms of the TCA may also mean that there would be no automatic retention of free movement of services, capital or (increasingly) digital data between Scotland and the rest of Britain, because these policy arenas are becoming ever more subject to the competence of the EU.

However, EU border controls would not be necessary between Scotland and Northern Ireland if the Protocol on Ireland/Northern Ireland was fully operational at the same time as Scotland became a full EU member state, and whereas an independent Scotland's membership of the EU would pose new challenges for Scotland's trading relationship with its closest neighbour, it would have a 'de-bordering' effect in its relations with Europe, opening up the markets of the 31 countries in the European single market. This could revive opportunities for the free movement of Scottish goods, services, people and finance across Europe, and *vice versa*.

The report also anticipates that an independent Scotland negotiating entry to the European Union would be likely to secure an opt-out from the EU Schengen Agreement on a similar basis to Ireland. This would enable continued participation in the Common Travel Area, which permits British and Irish citizens to move freely and live, work, study and access services across the two isles.

Note: This paper is an edited version of the late Bill Austin's lengthier paper on 'Independent Scotland's Smart Borders', referenced below, and the article he wrote jointly with Professor Iain Black in November 2020.

Further reading

Austin, W J, December 2020, 'Independent Scotland's Smart Borders', Scottish Independence Convention. https://independenceconvention.scot/wp-content/uploads/2020/12/Smart-Borders.pdf

Austin, B, and Black, I, 24 November 2020, 'Borders can help an independent Scotland to prosper', The National, https://www.thenational.scot/news/18892915.borders-can-help-independent-scotland-prosper/

Austin, B, 'Scotland's Borders', 26 November 2020, podcast on *Voices for Scotland*. https://play.acast.com/s/the-voices-for-scotland-podcast/scotlands-borders-with-bill-austin

Austin, W J, *Front Line Duty: iScotland's Revenues, Borders and Defence* (2nd edition), Cambridge, Searching Finance Ltd.

Austin, B, and Henderson, P, 12 January 2017, 'A "smart" border, not a "hard" one, will help an independent Scotland prosper', *The National*. https://www.thenational.scot/news/15017065.bill-austin-and-peter-henderson-a-smart-border-not-a-hard-one-will-help-an-independent-scotland-prosper/

Hayward, K, and McEwen, N, 3 February 2022, 'An EU border across Britain: Scotland's borders after independence', London, UK in a Changing Europe.

CHAPTER 23

A Fresh Approach to Migration
Tanja Bueltmann

MIGRATION HAS SHAPED Scotland, its society, culture and communities all around the country, for many centuries – from the emigration of Highlanders cleared from the lands they had worked, to the immigration of EU citizens exercising freedom of movement rights pre-Brexit.

Viewed through the prism of these outward and inward movements, Scotland has long since been a global diasporic nation (Bueltmann et al., 2013). But migration is more than the patterns of departure and arrival: it is also about the needs of a country, from addressing demographic issues to labour market needs, and about the contributions of immigrants in the communities where they live. There is also, however, a much more fundamental issue to consider, namely: what kind of society one wants to build in terms of values, specifically values of openness, tolerance and inclusion; the last mentioned point also relates to the question of who can, and is enabled, to actively participate in a nation.

This chapter explores these questions in the context of the Scottish independence debate, highlighting what opportunities an independent Scotland has in developing a more progressive, holistic and inclusive approach to immigration that can both meet the needs Scotland has while also being value-based in a way that enables the building of what is defined here as a participatory nation.

The chapter begins by examining the impact of Brexit, situating the migration challenge it triggered for Scotland in a brief overview of migration patterns since the 1950s. While there are some similarities in attitudes, research showed that – even prior to the EU referendum – people in Scotland held distinct views on immigration and 'are less likely to want immigration reduced, more likely to see it as good for the country' (The Migration Observatory,

2014). This is followed by an assessment of Scotland's population needs – in terms of economic and demographic questions, but also in relation to the needs of particular regions – to argue how independence now offers the only route to developing an immigration policy that actually serves those needs. The final section concludes with an exploration of how such a fresh approach to immigration could look.

Understanding Scotland's Migration Challenge Post-Brexit

While migration to Scotland has long since been a question of interest (Allen, 2013; Devine and McCarthy, 2018), the EU referendum and the UK's subsequent departure from the EU has triggered an unprecedented migration challenge for Scotland that directly impacts many spheres of life, the economy and Scottish communities.

Brexit ended the right to freedom of movement and this, as freedom of movement is a reciprocal right, has already had significant consequences for both Scots, who have now lost this right, and for EU citizens. Those EU citizens who lived in Scotland prior to 31st December 2020 had to apply to the EU Settlement Scheme to secure their status post-Brexit; given the nature of the scheme – a retrospective application process rather than an automatic protection of rights – many EU citizens will continue to be negatively impacted by this for decades. There will be some who are without status, for example, but do not even know this yet (likely among some children in care), but also there will be practical issues to do with the new, digital-only status.

Accounts of discrimination and problems have already been accumulating for some time (Bueltmann, 2020). It is worth highlighting these issues because they are a good illustration of the problem Scotland is continually faced with when it comes to immigration policy: the fact that it is a reserved matter. So while the Scottish Government has always been opposed to a retrospective application process for EU citizens, there was no option for implementing a different policy as immigration is not devolved. The only choice available was around implementing mitigation strategies, for instance by providing additional financial support for Scottish charities and organisations that helped EU citizens with their applications. While beneficial for EU citizens in Scotland, these mitigation strategies, like others, do not affect policy change.

This is not a new problem – immigration has always been a reserved matter. However, post-Brexit the impact of this will be felt much more strongly and immediately. The first reason for this lies in the direct impact that Brexit will have on immigration numbers. While it is difficult to predict precise patterns – not least because the pandemic continues to contribute new challenges – it is likely that there will be a noticeable decline given that a plurality of new arrivals who migrated to Scotland in the last decade, 45 per cent of them, came from EU countries, utilising freedom of movement rights. This is no longer possible. Instead, Scotland is tied to the UK Government's immigration approach designed to reduce numbers. It is critical that we recognise this context: estimates by the Scottish Government's Expert Advisory Group on Migration and Population indicate that we may see 'a reduction of net migration of between 30-50 per cent' (Boswell et al., 2020) as a result.

Such a reduction has the potential to undo significant advances. Between the late 1950s and the late 1980s, Scotland saw 'a period of negative net migration' (Boswell et al., 2019) as 'the dominant Scottish demographic narrative...remained one of large-scale emigration rather than immigration' (Devine and McCarthy, 2018). This changed only from the late 1990s and most fundamentally so since the early 2000s, when net migration figures firmly went into the positive. This was primarily a result of EU enlargement and the accession of Poland, Estonia, Latvia, Lithuania, Czech Republic, Hungary, Slovakia and Slovenia, opening up free movement opportunities for these countries. In the decade 2001–2011, Scotland's foreign-born population nearly doubled, increasing from 3.8 per cent to seven per cent, with Polish EU citizens becoming Scotland's largest immigrant community from outside of the British and Irish Isles, rising in number from 2,505 in 2001 to 55,231 in 2011 (Devine and McCarthy, 2018). Polish EU citizens also account for the highest proportion, among different immigrant groups, in the Scottish workforce (Scottish Government, 2017). Regardless of nationality group, a majority of immigrant arrivals came for work; figures for 2013–17 indicate that 67 per cent either already had a job offer or came to look for work (Boswell et al., 2019), while a recent survey of EU citizens specifically also reveals this pattern (Bueltmann and Bulat, 2021). This is important because it highlights labour market needs, but also reflects how immigrants are, on average, younger in their age profile, and hence, bring significant longer-term potential in economic activity.

Brexit threatens Scotland benefitting from this in future as the end of freedom of movement, coupled with the UK's new immigration system based on restrictive criteria designed to reduce immigration numbers, will have negative impacts. These impacts will become increasingly visible in Scottish communities and demonstrate how reserved policy matters often translate into impacts in devolved policy areas. The extent of this problem becomes clearer when looking at more specific examples relating to Scotland's population and economic needs.

Scotland's Population and Economic Needs and Why Immigration Policy Matters

The new UK's immigration system is a points-based system that includes a range of restrictive criteria – certainly when compared to freedom of movement – most notably, a salary threshold. While provisions are made for addressing shortages, providing some level of flexibility, it remains, overall, a rigid system given the barriers that are built-in by default. The impact of this will not be uniform across Scotland but show sector-specific patterns as well as different impacts in different regions of Scotland. A cancer scientist who wants to take up a position at one of Scotland's universities, for example, is very likely to have a high number of points in the skilled workers points-based system; there might also be a route via the so-called Global Talent scheme. A hospitality worker who wants to work in a hotel on the Outer Hebrides, on the other hand, is much less likely to have the required points, unless their role is listed on the shortage occupation list.

This will have immediate impacts on the labour market but is likely to also change the composition of Scotland's immigrant population in the long term. For some sectors, for example the health and care sector, the likely changes are particularly problematic if immigration numbers reduce in line with estimates. Scotland is already faced with a shortage of nurses, for example, and a significant proportion of those who work as nurses are from abroad – nearly 10 per cent; of these, nearly 40 per cent used to come from the EU (Boswell et al., 2019). While there is a specific Health and Care Worker visa route and while some roles, for instance that of senior care worker, are currently included on the shortage occupation list, these specific schemes and lists can change and decisions will be made by the UK government. Therein lies a continuous risk for Scotland, as decisions may not reflect Scotland's needs.

A rigid salary threshold is also likely to have wider impacts relating to where in Scotland immigrants move to. Some of Scotland's rural and remoter areas, for example, are characterised by lower salary levels compared to Scotland's cities, so there is likely to be an even stronger impact of changes on these areas. These are the types of challenges remote rural and island areas are already familiar with given past depopulation patterns. But, post-Brexit, there is likely to be even less opportunity to compensate the negative natural demographic change that has been happening in these communities with inward movements by immigrants, given that these areas are much less likely to offer jobs that meet relevant thresholds and criteria. As Boswell et al noted, 'these areas of Scotland seem to be facing a demographic 'double whammy' in leaving the EU and ending free movement which is likely to have far-reaching implications for economic activity, the provision of services, and levels of general well-being' (Bosewell et al., 2019).

This highlights that this is not just a question about labour market needs and fiscal contributions immigrants make. In many of Scotland's remoter areas, the demographic profile is such that immigration is the only means through which local populations can be sustained. Even when Scotland was a member of the EU and benefitted from freedom of movement this was a challenge as remote rural and island areas do not usually offer many of the traditional pull factors that attract immigrants, but at least mobility rights were open and flexible for Scotland's main source of inward migration. Brexit restricts these to the tune of the hostile environment, making it harder to address region-specific needs in Scotland.

An independent Scotland with the ability to shape its own immigration policy would have the opportunity to develop solutions that combine immigration and economic policies to address these issues. This is impossible within the UK constitutional set-up, certainly under present conditions. For Scotland, this means a lost opportunity for building sustainable communities in rural areas in particular, but also of pursuing a much more holistic approach to economic regeneration and community-building that is intrinsically coupled with social wellbeing. Immigration can facilitate this because of the age structure of immigrants, but also because of the resilience immigrants can bring to communities. This is enhanced further if immigration routes include clear pathways to permanent settlement.

Building a Participatory Nation

The concept of a participatory nation used in this chapter draws from the idea of a *'Bürgerhaushalt'*: *Bürger* is the German word for the legally recognised inhabitant of a country or even a city, but it does not necessarily mean citizenship per se as it can also refer to residents more broadly. For the *'Bürgerhaushalt'*, the idea was the *'Bürger'* of specific cities would, in their role as such, participate in deciding what some of the city's money was being spent on. The underlying principle, therefore, is direct and active participation. As we debate the feasibility and possible future of an independent Scotland, this focus on the principle of direct and active participation deserves consideration in the context of immigration policy. On one critical level – that of participation in the political process – recent policy changes have already pushed Scotland forward on this route, extending the franchise for Scottish elections. So in that sense, the place where someone was born already plays a much smaller role in determining participation than it does, for instance, in England.

But this is a point about the status quo and the political process, while the idea of building a participatory nation relates to the ambitions an independent Scotland could pursue more broadly. At this point it is worth remembering the implications of immigration policy being reserved, and hence, grounded in the hostile environment approach – a system that is, in fact, hostile from the get-go and about compliance, checks and limiting rights, as the EU Settlement Scheme has demonstrated, for instance. Under new UK immigration rules this will get worse – new rules erect new barriers. In particular, tier 5 short-term work visas, for example, do not even enable immigrants to consider permanent settlement, effectively establishing an insurmountable hurdle for a participatory nation for a large proportion of immigrants. By enabling temporary routes expressly designed to prevent permanent settlement, there will be new challenges moving forward, including a greater turnover in Scotland's immigrant populations. This is likely to have a negative impact on communities as this effectively makes transience a default feature. As the Expert Advisory Group on Migration and population pointed out, support services will need to adapt to this and 'local authorities and employers are likely to struggle to meet these challenges' (Boswell et al., 2019).

An independent Scotland could reject this approach entirely, building an immigration system that enables a participatory nation for at least a majority of immigrants. This would be possible by devising a policy that does two things at the same time: select immigrants based on characteristics – this could, but does not have to be – via a points system, and/or specific needs. But alongside this there could also be an approach to attract immigrants via different pathways to settlement that are designed to facilitate permanent residence. For remote rural areas in particular, such an approach – especially if coupled with economic investment, for instance in renewable energy – would also bring new jobs to these areas. Canada's Atlantic Immigration Pilot Programme offers an example of this type of scheme.

Encouraging and enabling at least a long-term settlement in Scotland is already a principle that has driven Scottish Government discussions. This has focused on enabling immigrants to raise families here, become part of communities and contribute what they have to offer. In an independent Scotland where immigration policy is controlled directly, schemes with clear settlement pathways can make a real difference, investing communities, employers and/or sectors with a buy-in that can also positively enhance participation in society at a more local level, and improve integration of immigrants. Such a system too will need some forms of control to prevent abuse and exploitation, but it would rest on the principles of being easy to navigate and barrier-free in the sense that it can focus on just on the contribution immigrants make in fiscal terms, but also the wider societal value of their immigration to Scotland.

Immigration policy that, at the core, is focused not just on attracting immigrants but also on retaining them can be a game changer in this respect. This is, in essence, what the idea of building a participatory nation is about: if immigrants are offered clear pathways to settlement and becoming a member of a community in which they can participate fully, they are more likely to stay. While such a scheme would require support systems, and hence, investment, the benefits can be significant, addressing Scotland's population, sectoral and geographic needs while building new levels of inclusion. Such an approach, especially if coupled with economic policies designed to enable a more balanced population profile and investment across rural and island areas in Scotland, offers a holistic route forward for Scotland to thrive – one that it cannot realise within the existing constitutional set-up of the UK.

References

Allen, W. (2013), 'Long-Term International Migration Flows to and from Scotland', Migration Observatory Briefing, https://migrationobservatory.ox.ac.uk/resources/briefings/long-term-international-migration-flows-to-and-from-scotland/

Boswell, C., Bell, D., Copus, A., Kay, R. and Kulu, H. (2020), 'UK Immigration Policy after Leaving the EU: Impacts on Scotland's Economy, Population and Society – July 2020 Update', Expert Advisory Group on Migration and Population, https://www.gov.scot/publications/uk-immigration-policy-leaving-eu-impacts-scot-lands-economy-population-society-july-2020-update/

Boswell, C., Bell, D., Copus, A., Kay, R. and Kulu, H. (2019), 'UK immigration policy after leaving the EU: impacts on Scotland's economy, population and society', https://www.gov.scot/publications/uk-immigra-tion-policy-leaving-eu-impacts-scotlands-economy-population-society/documents/

Bueltmann, T. (2020), 'Experiences and impact of the EU Settlement Scheme: report on the3million Settled Status Survey', https://thisi-sourhome.uk/research

Bueltmann, T. and Bulat, A. (2021), 'EU citizens' identity, belonging and representation post-Brexit – interim report', https://thisisourhome.uk/research

Bueltmann, T., Hinson, A. and Morton, G. (2013), *The Scottish Dias-pora*, Edinburgh University Press.

Devine, T.M. and McCarthy, A. (eds) (2018), *New Scots: Scotland's Immigrant Communities since 1945*, Edinburgh University Press.

The Migration Observatory (2014), Report 'Immigration and inde-pendence: Public opinion on immigration in Scotland in the context of the referendum debate', https://migrationobservatory.ox.ac.uk/wp-content/uploads/2016/04/Report-Immigration_Inde-pendence.pdf

Scottish Government (2017), 'The Contribution of EEA citizens to Scotland: The Scottish Government response to the Migration Advisory Committee call for evidence on the role of EEA workers in the UK labour market', https://www.gov.scot/publications/contribution-eea-citizens-scotland-scottish-governments-response-migration-advisory-committee-9781788514057/documents/

CHAPTER 24

An Independent Scotland in Europe
Kirsty Hughes

SCOTLAND'S EUROPEAN RELATIONS are in a much more positive place than those of the UK post-Brexit. And, despite foreign policy being reserved, the Scottish Government has a fairly clear, if light, European strategy or para-diplomacy. All this can be helpful both as arguments for independence are made and as an independent Scotland aims to rejoin the EU – the goal of the current Scottish Government.

European relations are, though, more challenging in many ways since the UK left the EU, and Brexit also creates more challenges for independence in the EU than it did in 2014, not least in terms of borders. There may also be some tensions between internal debates and arguments on independence and the EU, and the image and relationships that the Scottish Government is aiming to build with EU member states and in Brussels. This is not a Scotland-specific problem – all member states and aspiring candidates for accession have to be mindful of the fact that arguments that may go down well at home will not necessarily all be taken as positive in Brussels, and vice versa.

In this chapter, we look at how some of the key arguments around independence in the EU face new challenges post-Brexit, and at the potential interaction between the Scottish Government's current European strategy and the arguments that will need to be made in the context of a push for independence.

Current European Para-Diplomacy

The Scottish Government's range of European policy positions since the 2016 Brexit vote could not be more distinct from those of the UK government. Scotland's government and voters were opposed to Brexit – voting 62 per cent for Remain in 2016. The Scottish

Government argued for a second referendum on staying in or leaving the EU. It argued for a compromise of a 'soft' Brexit of staying in the EU's single market and customs union, or in the absence of that for Scotland to stay in the EU's single market even while part of the UK (Scottish Government, 2016).

None of these political and policy goals succeeded as the UK government under Boris Johnson went for a hard Brexit as set out in the Trade and Cooperation Agreement and the Withdrawal Agreement. Nor did more specific goals succeed, such as for the UK to stay within the EU's Erasmus programme – or at least for Scotland to do so. But the Scottish Government's approach was certainly noticed in the EU – and there has been considerable sympathy for Scotland since 2016 as a pro-European country taken out of the EU by the UK vote to Leave.

At the same time, UK relations with the EU have been increasingly fractious. Those who hoped for a more constructive relationship once the UK left and a trade agreement was in place were disappointed. The UK has positioned itself provocatively and dangerously on the Northern Ireland protocol and its arrangements for the internal border between Britain and Northern Ireland agreed by Johnson (in place of Theresa May's EU withdrawal agreement which allowed for the whole UK to stay, indefinitely, in the EU customs union).

That the UK's reputation, trustworthiness and influence has been hugely damaged by Brexit is incontestable – European observers ask where the professional and pragmatic UK has gone. But Scotland has successfully distinguished itself from this negative EU view of the UK (Hughes, 2020a). There is not only sympathy for Scotland but some observers note that they now have a better understanding of arguments for independence. And where EU commentators ask where the professional and pragmatic UK has gone, Scotland has a chance to show that it retains a constructive, professional and pragmatic European para-diplomacy.

These European views might be seen as a shift away from the 'negative neutrality' that the EU, or at least Brussels, showed towards independence in 2014, with the European Commission's then president Jose Manuel Barroso emphasising how difficult rejoining the EU would be for an independent Scotland. There is, in a sense, a more 'positive neutrality' in the EU – sympathy and understanding and a greater likelihood of finding some EU actors who might say that an independent Scotland would face a normal EU accession process.

However, there are limits to this more benign outlook. The EU wants to build a constructive relationship with the UK post-Brexit and, while it remains fractious, the EU wants to handle it as best it can with least negative fallout. The UK is still a large economy, and a not insignificant foreign policy player and European neighbour. For France, or the Netherlands or Ireland, their relations with the UK are important and a focus of state-to-state diplomacy. So EU neutrality on independence will continue and some in the EU are observing with concern the potential for the UK to fragment.

Scotland's European Strategy

The Scottish Government set out its overarching European strategy in early 2020 (see 'The European Union's Strategic Agenda 2020-2024: Scotland's Perspective', 2020). It emphasised the priorities of: the environment and net-zero, wellbeing, innovation, and rights – for both Scotland and for the EU. More broadly, the Scottish Government's European para-diplomacy is one that clearly aims to situate itself both in the existing status quo and with respect to the goal of independence in the EU. The Scottish Government aims to present Scotland as a constructive, creative, open and participative pro-European country. In broad terms, that has obvious potential benefits for Scotland–EU relations both now and in a potential future as an independent country.

The Scottish Government and SNP politicians at Holyrood and Westminster, not least the foreign and defence spokespeople at Westminster, maintain a range of contacts in Brussels and across the EU. There are also Scottish Government hubs in Brussels, Berlin, Dublin and Paris (the last three mentioned having been established over the last few years) – and located within British embassies in those countries. These are investment and innovation hubs, with some also putting an emphasis on promoting culture and educational links. It's a soft para-diplomacy but it's one that some see as a forerunner of potential future Scottish embassies in the EU. Even in this relatively soft format, the hubs are somewhat neuralgic for the UK government and a potential source of future conflict on their activities and role between the Scottish and UK governments (Hughes, 2021).

The Scottish Government is fully aware that the EU and its member state governments do not wish to be drawn into constitutional debates in the UK and Scotland. So their para-diplomacy aims to respect that EU neutrality and present Scotland as a constructive, serious player that is not asking EU member states to take sides or favour Scotland in any particular way.

One other major distinction between Scotland and England, in the Brexit context, has been the Scottish Government's insistence on how welcome EU citizens are to remain in Scotland – and its efforts (rejected by the UK government) to argue for devolution of some aspects of migration policy to allow Scotland to continue to benefit from something close to EU free movement of people.

This Scottish para-diplomacy, however soft, stands in a rather stark contradistinction to the UK's approach to EU relations and its 'Global Britain' foreign policy. Even outwith the constitutional divide, many in Scotland would compare the country to near European neighbours such as Ireland, Denmark or Finland, or support remaining as engaged as possible with EU programmes, or support the Scottish Government's policy of remaining aligned with EU law as far as possible in devolved areas.

This latter policy of aligning to EU laws, another clear demonstration of Scotland's intention of maintaining close relations with the EU, is an unusual one for a country that is not a state nor on the path to being a candidate for EU accession. How far Scotland does remain aligned, time will tell. The UK Internal Market Act, which in recreating an internal market post-Brexit undermined some devolved powers, may make alignment tricky at times. Equally, exactly how to align in specific areas may not always be straightforward for a country outside the EU without full access to its single market. Overall, the policy is meant to keep Scotland close to EU laws, show good will on European policies, and indicate a state of readiness for EU accession if and when Scotland is independent. It also means a certain amount of communication between EU and Scottish officials on particular policy areas, so building a two-way relationship, even though there is, of course, no formal overarching EU–Scotland context within which to discuss the alignment route agreed by the Scottish Parliament now being implemented by the Government.

The Scottish Government's European para-diplomacy underlines that Scotland is a European country and partner and that it will remain active in engaging positively across the EU – both in governmental and non-governmental formats. But Brexit has, inevitably, put limits on this para-diplomacy and put barriers in the way, not only of trade but also of wider relationships. It has also put new challenges in the path of accession to the EU as an independent country to which we now turn.

Challenges on the Path to Independence in the EU

Rejoining the EU is one of the big positive arguments that can be made for independence. Independence in the EU would restore Scotland to EU membership, this time as a full member state, and mean Scotland once again had all the economic, political, social and cultural benefits of membership.

Brexit was inherently an isolationist move – despite the UK government's 'Global Britain' rhetoric. It cut the UK off from its main European allies, damaged its international reputation and influence and is inflicting growing damage on its economy. In contrast to 2014, where the debate was about whether Scotland would be able effectively to stay in the EU as it transitioned to being an independent state, the independence debate now has to focus on how Scotland could rejoin (Hughes, 2020b).

There are substantial issues to consider here – from time-scale, to the implications of the rest of the UK being outside the EU including the border question, to currency, deficits and more. But the top-level arguments need to be about the broad political, economic, security, cultural and social benefits of being part of a bloc of 27 countries – 28 with Scotland – that has a population of almost half a billion people and is a major European and international player.

Some argue that smaller member states have little influence in the EU –the evidence suggests the opposite. Smaller member states are at all the EU's tables, with a voice and vote, in the European Parliament, Commission and Council (Hughes, 2020c). It is telling that while Norway stayed in the EEA, alongside Liechtenstein and Iceland, its government having lost a referendum to join the EU in 1994, other European countries chose to join the EU (and not the EEA – although Switzerland stayed outside the EEA). Since the original six formed the EU in 1957, 22 states have joined and one (the UK) left. In the last 30 years, sixteen states joined: three former EFTA countries – Austria, Finland and Sweden – and eleven Central and Eastern European countries, plus Cyprus and Malta. Most of these accession countries are smaller states, all of them saw the benefits of being fully inside the EU.

There are various challenges here for independence debates. There is, to begin with, no advance guarantee of EU membership. The latest EU treaty (Lisbon) makes it clear that any European country can apply to join and the EU is open to enlargement, as the accession of 22 states in its lifetime shows. So an independent Scotland can apply and is highly likely to be rapidly given candidate status and face a fairly speedy accession as it was part of an EU member state for 47 years and since – if independence is in the next few years – it will remain already fairly well aligned to EU laws in many areas (Hughes, 2020b). Independence debates have to have the maturity to recognise that rejoining the EU is highly likely but it is a process to go through, not an open offer ahead of time.

EU accession is a process that takes time. Work has been done by the Scottish Government on this process but it was suspended at the start of the COVID-19 pandemic and so has not yet seen the light of day. An independent Scotland will need to follow the well-trodden route of other states who have joined – it will have to apply for membership, get candidate status, and then negotiate through the wide-ranging EU laws, regulations and conditions that candidates must meet. All EU member states have a veto over this process but one that has rarely been used (though France used it against the UK in its first two membership bids in the 1960s). If Scotland has become independent through a legal and constitutionally agreed process, then it is unlikely to face any serious political challenge joining the EU as a small northern European democracy.

There are serious issues to address here in terms of how to handle the various transitions an independent Scotland will face: transition out of the UK, into full statehood, and back into the EU. More work is needed on whether, for instance, there should be a transition after independence of staying part of the EU–UK Trade and Cooperation Agreement for a year or two before concurring on an association agreement with the EU tailored to Scotland's specific path towards becoming an EU member state. Some have argued that Scotland should first aim at being part of the EEA for its transition. But this is an alternative to the EU, not a transition route. What there should be, after EU accession negotiations are complete, is a referendum to confirm that there is public support in an independent Scotland for rejoining as negotiated (something almost all acceding states have done).

Key questions for independence, including currency and the likely deficit an independent Scotland will have, will also impact on its route into the EU. If an independent Scotland was using sterling at the time of its application, this would be unprecedented for the EU. The EU might insist Scotland should have its own currency at the point of accession – alongside a commitment to join the euro in the future – or it might, if asked, agree a transition period whereby Scotland used the pound for a brief period on accession. It will also have to meet or be near to meeting the EU's fiscal rules by the time of accession (Gow, 2020).

There are contradictions in how the independence debate views a future independent Scotland in the EU. There is an image of a constructive, participative Scotland playing a role just as Ireland or Finland or Austria do. But these three member states are in the core of the EU as they all joined the euro – altogether 19 of the 27 member states currently use the euro. Scotland would be unlikely to meet the criteria for joining the euro at the time of accession but would have to commit to joining eventually. Unlike Ireland, the debate in Scotland views joining the euro tentatively at best or, for some, as something to avoid by never quite meeting the criteria (as Sweden has done without having a formal opt-out like Denmark). There needs to be more openness in this debate. There is a risk that too much discussion about never joining the euro in practice could label Scotland as too like the opted-out, semi-detached UK.

An independent Scotland would be likely to get just one opt-out: from the Schengen border-free zone. Like Ireland, it would need that to remain part of the Ireland–UK Common Travel Area so avoiding passport controls between Scotland and the rest of the UK. This would need EU agreement for the Schengen opt-out and rUK–Ireland agreement to stay in the Common Travel Area. It would be a win-win on free movement of people – both in the EU and across the UK.

Another challenge will be for an independent Scotland to show the EU that it has good relations with its neighbours – the nearest being rUK and Ireland. Whatever state EU–UK relations are in at the time when Scotland joined the EU, Brussels will want to be sure that Scotland's accession will not make these relations worse. It will, of

course, be in an independent Scotland's interests to have good relations with the rest of the UK, but after a potentially bruising referendum and divorce talks, there needs to be much more detailed
thinking around what those relations would look like and how to
make them as positive as possible. In the case of Scotland–Ireland
relations, these are already good, constructive and likely to stay so
despite the challenges Brexit poses to the UK–Ireland relationship.

Good relations with rUK are not just about the challenge of having an EU external border between Scotland and the rest of the UK,
but handling that border as well as possible will be vital. If Scotland
remains in the Common Travel Area, that will certainly facilitate the
border. And by the time an independent Scotland joined the EU, there
will have been years of experience of managing the post-Brexit border under the Trade and Cooperation Agreement (or any successor).
But there are serious questions that need more analysis here, particularly on services trade between Scotland and rUK (the majority of
Scotland–rUK trade) after Scotland joined the EU and how that can
be facilitated in the face of the barriers that would then exist and to
reduce the economic costs that a border will introduce.

In the EU, Scotland would contribute to the formation of the EU's
common foreign and security policy. It will bring its own priorities
and need to show that it will contribute in a constructive way. The
current policy of joining NATO after independence already sends a
message. Ireland, though not in NATO, shows a path for an independent Scotland of how to be an active, constructive, full EU member
state while also maintaining as healthy relations as possible with the
UK (deeply challenged by Brexit), while also having an active, global
foreign policy, not least towards the US.

Overall, the Scottish Government has a current European
para-diplomacy that is fairly light but constructive and intent on
maintaining and developing European relations even post-Brexit.
Deepening this strategic approach would be advisable in the coming
years. This para-diplomacy also contributes to Scotland's potential
path to EU accession as an independent state. Independence in the EU
throws up a range of challenges and issues that need fuller and more
open debate. But given Scotland was in the EU until 2020 and in its
single market and customs union to the end of 2020, if independence
happened in the next few years, then Scotland would be likely to
face a fairly swift accession process, perhaps one taking just four to

five years. Certainly, the EU's history of enlargement suggests that an independent Scotland would rather rapidly be able to rejoin the EU as a full member state.

References

Gow, D. (2020), 'The EU's Fiscal Criteria: Debt, Deficit and Currency Questions', in Hughes, K. (ed.), *An Independent Scotland in the EU: Issues for Accession,* Scottish Centre on European Relations.

Hughes, K. (2020a) (ed.), *An Independent Scotland in the EU: Issues for Accession,* Scottish Centre on European Relations.

Hughes, K. (2020b), 'European Union Views of the UK post-Brexit and of the Future EU-UK Relationship', Policy Paper, Scottish Centre on European Relations, November, https://www.scer.scot/database/ident-12883

Hughes, K. (2020c), 'Smaller States' Strategies and Influence in an EU of 27: Lessons for Scotland', Policy Paper, Scottish Centre on European Relations and University College London European Institute, https://www.scer.scot/wp-content/uploads/Small-States-Policy-Paper-pdf-ucl-scer.pdf

Hughes, K. (2021), 'Scotland's European Relations: Where Next?', Policy Paper, *Scottish Centre on European Relations*

Scottish Government (2016), *Scotland's Place in Europe,* December, https://www.gov.scot/publications/scotlands-place-europe/

Scottish Government (2020), *The European Union's Strategic Agenda for 2020-24: Scotland's Perspective,* 31 January, https://www.gov.scot/publications/european-unions-strategic-agenda-2020-24-scotlands-perspective/pages/2/

Section Seven: Where Scotland Sits Geopolitically

CHAPTER 25

Scottish Security in an Age of Political Warfare
David Clark

THE NEW ERA of Great Power rivalry defined by the authoritarian challenge of Russia and China is different from the Cold War in many respects. Yet, it shares at least one important feature in common. Aware of what a direct conflict between nuclear-armed adversaries would entail, and notwithstanding the risk of escalation in Russia's war against Ukraine, the antagonists have so far chosen to compete using largely indirect methods. Some of these are familiar, such as proxy wars and political subversion. Others are new, including cyber-attacks and 'troll farms'. Learning how to respond to these threats is one of the most important security tasks we face.

An independent Scotland would not be immune to these pressures. Even without courting hostility, the young Scottish state would be a target of interest for authoritarian regimes keen to explore its potential as an entry point or base of operations within the West. Its location at the centre of NATO's zone of maritime operations would make it additionally attractive whether it chose to be part of the Alliance or not. Scotland would, therefore, need to be ready from the moment of independence to recognise these threats and counter them.

Aims and Methods of Political Warfare

A variety of labels have been used to describe the strategies states deploy in targeting their opponents using non-military means, such as information warfare, disinformation, influence operations, psy-ops, active measures and hybrid warfare. None of these is entirely satisfactory for our purposes. Disinformation describes only part of the problem. Hybrid warfare, on the other hand, refers to conflicts in which military and non-military methods are combined. Although the willingness of Russia, in particular, to use violence is clear, we are concerned here primarily with the use of non-military means as an alternative, rather than as a complement, to conventional military force. The term chosen to describe this is political warfare.

Countries have long sought to compete with each other below the threshold of military conflict by attempting to influence and subvert each other's political systems using covert and deniable means. These rivalries have been particularly intense during periods of sharp ideological division within the international system. The Russian revolution in 1917 raised this form of competition to a new level. An underground revolutionary movement schooled in conspiratorial methods seized power and began applying the lessons of its political struggle to the field of international relations (McKnight, 2002). China still formally adheres to the ideology of Marxism-Leninism. In Russia, the operational legacy of Bolshevism lives on in the 'Chekist' traditions of its intelligence and security apparatus and those, like Putin and many others in the Russian elite, who served in its ranks (Weiner, 2020).

The common roots of Russian and Chinese approaches to political warfare are reflected in the similarity of techniques used. These are aimed at dominating or distorting the political and media environments in order to influence public opinion and the decision-making structures of target states. Where possible, the goal is to manipulate those states into adopting policies inimical to their own interests and favourable to the interests of the targeting state. Where this proves impossible, the goal is to paralyse decision-making structures or slow down response times to the point where the target state is no longer capable of acting as a potential source of opposition. This is achieved by sowing division, confusion and apathy. This is evident in the way that Russia has attempted to manipulate the information environment in relation to its war against Ukraine, for example by encouraging war crimes denial.

Disinformation and propaganda campaigns utilise a wide range of platforms and technologies in a pyramid structure. At the apex are state-controlled new agencies and broadcasters, such as RIAN, Russia Today (RT), Xinhua News Agency and China Global News Network (CGTN), which publish and broadcast heavily slanted content aimed at foreign audiences. A second tier of activity is made up of a larger number of proxy websites posing as independent news organisations, blogs, think tanks or NGOs (Department of State, 2020). These disseminate messages and content similar to the official propaganda channels, but usually in a cruder and more aggressive form, including conspiracy theories. These platforms operate with fewer regulatory constraints, are deniable and can be tailored to specific audiences.

The base of the disinformation pyramid is formed by armies of keyboard warriors who post comments and share content on social media using fake identities. These are the so-called 'troll farms' made famous by the St Petersburg-based Internet Research Agency. Some are private entities that may also engage in commercial social media manipulation for profit. Others are operated directly by state security agencies. China's social media operations targeting Taiwan, for example, are believed to be organised by the cyber warfare unit of the People's Liberation Army – the Strategic Support Force – which has 300,000 troops under its command (Rand, 2020).

All three tiers of the disinformation pyramid are designed to work together, reinforcing and amplifying each other's content while attempting to attract third party attention and engagement. The objectives of these campaigns vary. Sometimes the aim is to deflect, or counter criticism of the originating state, or promote its image. Offensive objectives include smearing and undermining high-profile critics, attacking specific target states, turning Western countries against each other, fostering hostility to Western influence globally, promoting politicians and movements advocating policies advantageous to the originating state, and encouraging political division and cynicism about the democratic process. Online operations are sometimes used to draw attention to compromising materials. These include the use of forged documents and hack-and-leak operations in which materials obtained by the intelligence services of the originating state are released in a way designed to cause maximum damage to the intended target.

Despite similarities in the methods used, there are important differences of emphasis in the objectives behind Chinese and Russian political warfare activities. Whereas China is mainly interested in furthering its national interests in a narrow sense, Russian activities are more disruptive because they actively seek to destabilise and weaken target states. For example, while both countries have spread disinformation during the COVID-19 pandemic to promote their own vaccines and denigrate Western alternatives, Russia has also pursued a broader set of goals, such sowing division within and between Western countries by encouraging opposition to public health measures and spreading conspiracy narratives blaming the virus on US bioweapons research (CEPA, 2021). China has encouraged confusion about the origins of the pandemic primarily to deflect attention from its own responsibility.

Both countries use front organisations, the covert funding of foreign political allies and the cultivation of agents of influence as part of their political warfare armouries, again for slightly different purposes. With the exception of Taiwan, where aggressive attempts are made to influence electoral outcomes, China is mainly concerned with building networks of support for its policies. Russia engages in election interference on a much wider front with the aim of installing friendly governments where it can and causing maximum disruption where it cannot. The radical fringes of left and right are mobilised simultaneously using linking narratives of anti-globalism and anti-liberalism. Nevertheless, the Kremlin has a clear preference for working with right-wing populists and movements promoting sovereigntism, ethnic nationalism, social conservatism and hostility to immigrants, which offer a better ideological fit with Putin's priorities and greater disruptive potential (Shekhovstov, 2018).

Russia and China both make extensive use of business relations. China is mainly concerned with cultivating foreign business lobbies prepared to advocate closer economic ties and oppose criticism of Chinese policy (Hamilton and Ohlberg, 2020). Russia does the same, but also uses business deals to supply covert funding to foreign politicians and movements considered useful to its interests. For example, a scheme to channel up to $65,000,000 to the Italian right-wing populist party, Lega Nord, exposed in 2019, included the use of a proposed oil deal between Russia and the Italian company, Eni, as cover (Buzzfeed, 2019). Academia is another area of interest to both countries, particularly China, which uses funding and academic cooperation as levers of influence to reward or punish Western educational institutions depending on their behaviour.

The Challenge for an Independent Scotland

There is no evidence that Russia or China have so far targeted Scotland in any systematic way. That would almost certainly change with independence and the acquisition an autonomous role in world affairs. The geopolitical reality of Scotland's position alongside one of the North Atlantic's main maritime communications routes and the debate about membership of NATO would attract the interest of Russia in particular. Preventing NATO enlargement and disrupting its internal cohesion has been among Putin's top foreign policy priorities for many years. Blocking Scotland's accession and creating a vacuum at the heart of NATO's theatre of operations would be a prize too tempting to ignore.

In the Western Balkans, Russia's efforts to obstruct NATO enlargement have included an attempted coup orchestrated by Russian military intelligence in Montenegro in 2016 and violent protests that led to the storming of the North Macedonian Parliament in 2017 (Warsaw Institute, 2019). Russian operations targeting an independent Scotland would be more likely to follow the template of those launched against Sweden in 2014–6 to coincide with the adoption of its cooperation agreement with NATO (Kragh and Asberg, 2017). Although stopping short of violent actions, the campaign deployed a full array of hostile tactics including the release of forged documents, the systematic use of fake social media accounts to promote disinformation, the aggressive targeting of Swedish politicians by Russian state media, the harassment of Swedish journalists and diplomats based in Russia, activity by pro-Russian organisations and cyber-attacks against mainstream media outlets (Buzzfeed, 2018).

Aggressive moves towards both Sweden and Finland have escalated as NATO membership has been considered in response to Russia's invasion of Ukraine. An independent Scotland could expect to receive similar attention in the process of joining Atlantic Alliance. The continued presence of the UK's nuclear deterrent, even for a transitional period, would be an additional factor. Russia would deploy its resources to encourage anti-NATO and anti-nuclear sentiment by promoting a neutralist vision of Scotland's future outside Western institutions. While much of this would be designed to appeal to the traditional left, Russia would also work to encourage the growth of activism on the populist and radical right. Scotland's need for higher rates of immigration, as well debates around EU membership and LGTBQ+ rights, would provide the most likely rallying points for those efforts.

Policy Responses

Although meeting this challenge will require significant effort and preparation, there is one sense of which the prospect of independence represents a major advantage. It comes from the opportunity afforded by the process of state design. The methods of political warfare deployed by Russia and China are now well understood. The thing that has hampered Western responses more than anything is the extent to which the issue has become an arena of partisan conflict. Donald Trump actively blocked the US government efforts to counter foreign interference ahead of the 2020 election. Similar considerations of self-interest make serious reform of political finance or media regulation in the UK nearly impossible. Independence provides Scotland with a one-off opportunity to write its rulebook from scratch and build greater democratic resilience into the foundations of its own statehood.

Before considering specifics, one thing needs to be acknowledged. Putin and other hostile actors haven't created any of the problems currently afflicting Western democracies. What they have done is exploit the problems Western democracies have created for themselves. In confronting the malign influence of authoritarian regimes, policies to tackle poverty and entrenched pockets alienation are more important than measures to counter 'troll farms'. That said, targeted policies to strengthen political security and prevent external interference are needed as part of a wider strategy to build a healthy democratic environment.

Media Regulation

As one study has shown, foreign disinformation campaigns flourish in media environments where the immune system has already been weakened by hyper-partisanship and the influence of vested interests (Benkler, Faris and Roberts, 2018). The first challenge, therefore, is effective regulation of the domestic media market. Legislation should be used to break-up or prevent concentrations of media ownership of the kind that have long existed in the UK. Ownership of media assets should be limited to domestic residents and taxpayers, and ownership separated from editorial control. Creative solutions should be explored to expand public interest journalism, perhaps using lottery funding.

Priority should be given to disrupting and dismantling the disinformation pyramid used by authoritarian regimes. Outlets like RT and CGTN are not legitimate media organisations. They are disinformation and propaganda fronts for regimes that suppress media freedom at home and should not be allowed to operate abroad, either directly or using proxies. A list of states denied broadcasting privileges should be updated by the Scottish Foreign Ministry as part of its regular human rights reporting.

The only real solution to tackling disinformation is for social media companies to take more responsibility for regulating the content that appears on their platforms. If they will not do this voluntarily, it should be required in law. Political advertising should be banned. Social media operators should be quicker and more diligent at removing hate speech and closing down inauthentic accounts. Stopping the circulation of forged materials should be a priority given technological advances in the generation of 'deepfake' videos. The timely blocking of hacked material targeting Joe Biden in the 2020 election should be a model for the future. Disinformation awareness should be taught in schools as part of a wider push to improve social media literacy.

Political Funding

Tough rules on transparency and campaign financing should be used to remove the influence of 'dark money' from politics. On their own, bans on the foreign funding are ineffective since hostile state actors are able to use ostensibly legitimate business deals to channel funds to permitted donors. It is also known that the Russian intelligence services make extensive use of opaque financial vehicles like cryptocurrencies to fund foreign operations. An independent Scotland should introduce the state funding of political parties on the German model and impose a low ceiling on annual personal donations. This would limit the influence of money in general and inhibit the ability of foreign governments to bankroll interference campaigns. Funding disclosure rules should also apply to NGOs, think tanks and campaign groups with a significant presence in the public debate.

Agents of Influence

Even in the internet age, political warfare campaigns rely on the participation and support of local proxies in the target states, recruited using a variety of financial or political inducements. They include lawyers, lobbyists, PR specialists, academics, journalists, social media influencers, activists and politicians, to name the most obvious. Some of these activities are regulated in the US using the Foreign Agents Registration Act. An independent Scotland should adopt similar legislation, but with an updated and expanded definition of 'foreign agent' that captures a wider range of activities. Legitimate activities, including legal representation and some lobbying, should be allowed provided they are registered. Other activities designed to further the hostile intent of foreign regimes, such as witting participation in campaigns of disinformation or political interference, should be illegal. The terms under which academic institutions accept funding from hostile states and their proxies need tighter regulation, including strict rules protecting academic freedom.

Intelligence Structures

Commentary about the intelligence structures of an independent Scotland tends to focus on what Scotland would supposedly lose from leaving the UK (Mackay, 2020). This includes access to the 'Five Eyes' intelligence sharing network of Anglophone countries highly rated among intelligence watchers, especially those who have never had access to its output. In truth, the major western intelligence agencies have responded sluggishly and with limited success to the new era of political warfare. The US intelligence community was slow to detect Russian interference in the 2016 presidential election and the Russia Report published by Parliament's Intelligence and Security Committee in 2020 showed that the UK intelligence agencies were disinterested to the point of negligence in their approach to Russian interference in the 2016 Brexit referendum (ISC, 2020).

The countries that have responded most effectively to the challenge of political warfare include small European states that established new intelligence agencies from scratch after freeing themselves from communism, notably Estonia and the Czech Republic (CSIS, 2020). History and proximity have given them particular insight into Russian methods and operations. Other small states with good intelligence capabilities include the Netherlands, Norway, Sweden and Denmark. The development of intelligence partnerships with these countries would give an independent Scotland access to experience it can draw on to create effective intelligence structures of its own.

Lessons can also be learned from the new breed of citizen investigators, like Bellingcat, who have developed creative techniques for combining open source research with leaked data to expose the hostile operations of authoritarian regimes.

Conclusion

There will be other security threats that an independent Scotland has to deal with, such as terrorism and industrial espionage. The challenge of political warfare is one that will have to be confronted at an early stage, possibly even before the date of independence itself. The ideas suggested above provide, at best, a rough sketch of the kinds of measures that will need to be considered if Scotland is able to respond effectively. Much additional thought and preparation will be required before that point.

References

Benkler, Y., Faris, R. and Roberts, H. (2018), *Network Propaganda: Manipulation, Disinformation, and Radicalisation in American Politics*, Oxford: Oxford University Press

Collier, K. and Leopold, J. (2018), 'Russian Hackers Targeted Swedish News Sites In 2016, State Department Cable Says', *Buzzfeed*, 10 August.

Center for Strategic and International Studies (CSIS) (2020), *Countering Russian Disinformation*, Washington: CSIS, 23 September.

GEC Special Report (2020), *Pillars of Russia's Disinformation and Propaganda Ecosystem,* Washington: US Department of State.

Hamilton, C. and Ohlberg, M. (2020), *Hidden Hand: Exposing How the Chinese Communist Party is Reshaping the World*, London: One World.

Harold, S.W., Beauchamp-Mustafaga, N. and Hornung, J.W. (2021), Chinese Disinformation Efforts on Social Media, Santa Monica: The RAND Corporation'.

Intelligence and Security Committee of Parliament (ISC) (2020), *Russia Report*, London: ISC, HC632, 21 July.

Kragh, M. and Asberg, S. (2017), 'Russia's strategy for influence through public diplomacy and active measures: the Swedish case', *Journal of Strategic Studies*, 5 January.

Lucas, E. Morris, J. and Rebegea, C. (2021), *Information Bedlam: Russian and Chinese Information Operations During Covid-19*, Washington: The Center for European Policy Analysis.

Mackay, N. (2020), 'Could Scotland go it alone in a world of espionage? Former spymaster gives his view', *The Herald*, 8 November.

McKnight, D. (2002), *Espionage and the Roots of the Cold War: The Conspiratorial Heritage*, London: Frank Cass Publishers.

Nardelli, A. (2019), "Revealed: The Explosive Secret Recording That Shows How Russia Tried To Funnel Millions To The "European Trump"', *Buzzfeed*, 10 July.

Shekhovstov, A. (2018), *Russia and the Western Far Right*, Oxford: Routledge.

Weiner, T. (2020), The Folly and the Glory: America, Russia and Political Warfare 1945-2020, Tim Weiner, New York: Henry Holt and Company.

The Warsaw Institute (2019), *Russia's Hybrid Warfare in the Western Balkans*, Warsaw: The Warsaw Institute, 26 March.

CHAPTER 26

Defence and Scottish Independence
Phillips P. O'Brien

DEFENCE ISSUES WERE not uppermost in the minds of most Scottish voters during the 2014 referendum, but with the crisis brought about by the invasion of Russia's invasion of Ukraine, it is likely that they would be profiled rather differently if there is another vote in the future.

Even with the well-known issue of basing Trident nuclear submarines on the Clyde, defence played second fiddle to issues such as identity, sovereignty and economic interest in the Scottish referendum, to say nothing of the relationship of an independent Scotland to the European Union. In fact, the Yes campaign worked to de-emphasise discussions of defence in most cases by reducing the areas of friction between itself and the Scottish electorate as a whole.

Before 2012 the SNP position was that an independent Scotland should not be a full member of NATO but instead should join its subsidiary organisation, Partners for Peace, which includes such nations as Ukraine. However that year the party made a very public turn away from this long-standing position. In a move that was internally contentious for many members the party, under strong pressure exerted by its leadership, voted by 426–332 during its 2012 Autumn conference to call for an independent Scotland to remain a full military member of the NATO Alliance (*BBC*, 2012). It was a move done to appeal to two different constituents. In the first case there were NATO member states that would be important partners of an independent Scotland, such as those in Western and Northern Europe, and the centre of the Scottish electorate which seems to be relatively happy with NATO membership.

The 'Scotland's Future' white paper, produced to describe how an independent Scotland would function, was deliberately vague on certain issues concerning defence (Scottish Government, 2013).

On the one hand it highlighted a relatively robust stance, pledging that Scotland would remain a full member of NATO while starting with a relatively large defence budget of £2.5 billion (placing it near the top of European defence spending on a per capita basis). On the other hand, it said Scotland would be a 'non-nuclear' member of NATO, which ambiguously addressed the difficult question if other nuclear-armed members of the alliance, crucially the USA, would be allowed to send ships into Scottish waters. The USA, for example, refuses to confirm or deny whether any of its vessels are indeed nuclear-armed.

This kind of political tightrope walking highlighted that issues of defence, even if they do not always receive the coverage that is regularly given to issues of identity or economics, remain a potential headache for both a new Yes campaign and an independent Scotland if the vote went that way. To understand why that would be, it is important to understand that any independent Scotland would result in things that would present serious issues for its fellow European partners: one would be that it would mark a serious diminution for the UK as a power, in terms of territory, resources, capabilities and most likely internal and external perception.

Though the UK is no longer a first-rank global power and has not been so for decades, it has been Western Europe's most reliable, capable contributor to NATO since the alliance's founding in 1949. UK forces have been a mainstay of NATO operations in Europe and around the globe, and have established a close relationship with US and other European forces. The UK – even with the most recent round of defence cuts and the Brexit decision which has brought awareness from some European allies that the country's reliability is not what it was – maintains amongst the most high-quality frontline forces in Europe, ones that have shown themselves to be adaptable in such new areas as cyber. In that sense, it would be hard to find a NATO state (and this includes major players in the EU who have cooled on the UK since Brexit) who would favour the diminution or separation of the UK.

If Scotland were to leave the UK, it would add an issue of strategic instability into their worlds that has little attraction and some serious possible drawbacks. From Norway and Denmark, through Germany and the Netherlands and even to France, the end of the UK as a united strategic partner is not seen as a positive – those campaigning for an independent Scotland need to understand that.

Map of Scottish Exclusive Economic Zone that would be claimed after independence (BBC, 2013).

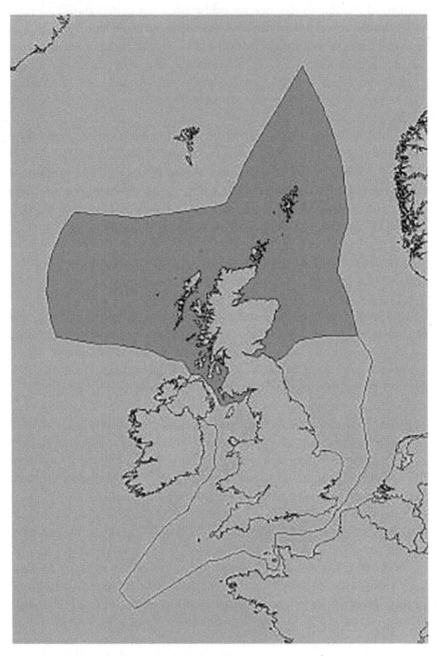

The other issue is that an independent Scotland would not only have led to the break-up of the UK, it would also find itself sitting in an extremely important strategic location that its neighbours would want protected. Scotland sits astride the North Atlantic shipping and air routes into and out of Europe. It provides key basing facilities for both air and sea forces, ones which allow for the protection of trade in vital waterways during peace and potentially during times of conflict. An independent Scotland, because of the reach of Scottish Islands such as the Shetlands and Outer Hebrides, would be in possession of an extremely large area Exclusive Economic Zone – significantly larger than that of the rUK, as it turns out. Scotland would have rich fisheries, wind farms and oil fields in its territorial waters that would need patrolling.

The need to reassure NATO partners and provide credible strategic control over these valuable and strategic water and airways were one of the key reasons that the SNP leadership felt the need to change policy and embrace full NATO membership in 2012, even over the reluctance of many of its more committed members. It was an important lesson (one that Brexit Britain is now learning) that political independence does not somehow magically bestow freedom of choice to whatever we want – in many ways it means a nation has to work even harder to please more powerful states and have far less freedom of action than expected.

In the case of Scottish independence this need to please would probably be most keenly felt in the relationship Scotland would have to carve out with the rUK, and defence would be a crucial element of that new relationship. An independent Scotland would have to establish a productive and co-operative defence relationship with the UK, not least to ease its transition into NATO, which would be such a high priority to NATO-members Norway, Denmark, Germany, France etc, with whom an independent Scotland would have to have a good relationship.

The defence negotiations between an independent Scotland and rUK need not be contentious – in most respects they present solvable issues that could be worked out with good will on both sides. However in one respect they could lead to acrimony, distrust and a crisis capable of derailing many of the international hopes and expectations of the backers of Scottish independence – this will be the politically charged question of the UK's Trident nuclear submarines now based not far from Glasgow at HM Naval Base Faslane on the Clyde.

The problems that Trident presents to an independent Scotland are not difficult to see. One of the most committed groups supporting independence are those who want nuclear weapons removed from Scotland quickly after independence. To this day, the SNP is left having to balance between its anti-nuclear wing and the more pro-NATO wing of the Scottish electorate. Removing nuclear weapons is not *a* reason that many of the anti-nuclear supporters have flocked to Scottish independence, it is *the* reason. For instance, the Campaign for Nuclear Disarmament (CND) in Scotland is resolutely opposed to considering a form of devo-max (self-government for Scotland in all areas short of foreign and defence policy) precisely because Trident would therefore remain untouched. The Chair of Scottish CND Lynn Jamieson said in June 2021 that 'such a route (devo-max) can effect none of the transformation that we need for a wholesome and peace-loving nation' (*Ban the Bomb*, 2021).

The SNP, partly inspired by the commitment of this group, makes sure to argue for a strongly non-nuclear position whenever possible. In the UK Parliament it regularly votes against Trident renewal on the ground of ethics and cost (SNP, 2021). However it also is careful not to give any sort of precise timetable for removal, saying, as its Westminster defence spokesperson Stewart McDonald did in 2019, that any removal would have to be done 'quickly, sensibly and securely as possible' (SNP 2021). This proviso, the importance of which cannot be underestimated, affords the party enough wiggle room in the case of independence to try and come up with a solution to the Trident dilemma that would please both its core anti-nuclear support and the British government.

The reality is that the Government of the rUK will want and need time to consider its future – and its nuclear status will be one of the most important things for it to ponder. The shock of Scotland voting to leave the UK is still something that will be difficult to anticipate. Losing its second largest constituent nation, with more than half its coastline, much of its valuable resource base, and an area which provided a great deal of the UK's historic military culture, cannot but help to result in a period of self-assessment – the end result of which is difficult to judge. One thing that the rUK will not want to be immediately forced to do is decide what it will do with Trident. If an independent Scotland somehow demanded that the rUK remove the weapons before this process of assessment could occur, the potential for strained independence negotiations is very real – and Scotland would pay the price.

Using the recently and only partially concluded Brexit negotiations as a guide, it is pretty obvious that in discussions of this type, the smaller, weaker power (such as the UK in comparison to the EU) ends up making most of the sacrifices to achieve a deal. The Brexiteer boast of 'holding all the cards' and being able to dictate terms to the EU was shown to be hollow, and the reverse was far more the truth. In negotiations over Trident, the rUK would have the dominant hand to play, and it would certainly be rash of an independent Scotland to try and force Trident out before the UK was ready and could poison the negotiations. Though those who most passionately believe forcing Trident out quickly is the best way to make the rUK abandon nuclear weapons, it's just if not more likely to lead to the preservation of the Trident system. An rUK forced to choose quickly to hold onto Trident or not could very well initially opt to try and keep it to maintain its present status as a UN Security Council permanent member. In other words, trying to impose a non-nuclear result on the rUK is as likely to save Trident as it is to end it.

Scotland After Independence

If a mutually acceptable compromise could be reached over Trident, one that might see the system stay longer on the Clyde than many would prefer before being removed (or even decommissioned), it would allow an independent Scotland time to adjust to its new status and set up its defence forces accordingly. Some of the present UK defence assets based in Scotland could help form the nucleus of an independent Scotland's armed forces; however, to make the transfer smooth, there would have to be some significant repurposing and negotiations would have to be conducted amicably. Scotland certainly would very much want some of what is in the nation now, but would also prefer that other responsibilities be taken away by the rUK.

Take Faslane for instance. An excellent submarine base with access to the North Atlantic and the world's oceans, it is actually about as poorly placed a facility as one could imagine to patrol Scotland's innate natural resource priorities which lie to the north and east.

Having to sail around the Mull of Kintyre and the Inner Hebrides means that naval bases in England and Norway would actually be closer in sailing time than Faslane when it comes to patrolling North Sea oil fields and shipping transport lanes. Any rationally planned Scottish defence force would therefore have to maintain a naval facility on the East Coast – where indeed there exists many superb harbour areas from the Firths of Forth and Tay, through Aberdeen and up to Inverness.

However the Clyde facilities, which actually include two bases – Faslane where the nuclear submarines are based and maintained and Coulport where the nuclear warheads are stored and protected – are the largest employer in an area that is not well off, supporting up to 6000 personnel (HMNB Clyde, 2021). In 2014, the Yes campaign was left trying to appeal to this region by stating that Faslane would be maintained as an independent Scotland's major naval facility – perhaps politically astute but impractical in reality. You could base certain elements of an independent Scotland's

UK military bases in Scotland at the time of the 2014 independence referendum (Stratfor, 2014).

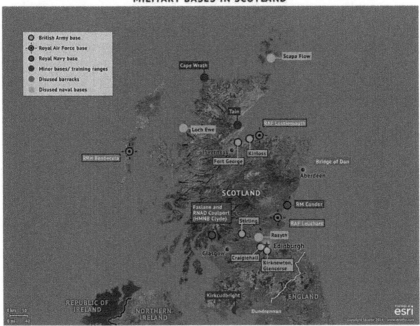

MILITARY BASES IN SCOTLAND

military capabilities in Faslane, but Scotland would need something on the East Coast as well.

Indeed in constructing a new defence force for an independent Scotland, the new state would have to balance defence requirements with domestic and international politics. It would have to construct affordable forces to fulfil limited, defined roles while making a useful contribution to NATO and providing security in home areas. What it would not need to do is replicate the UK on a one-tenth scale, as Scotland would have far fewer global ambitions. It could actually repurpose a number of assets and base them in Faslane, or the wider area – it would just need to do so coherently.

In imagining what this might look like it makes sense to start with a model given by a comparable European country, Denmark. The two states would be almost identical in population terms, with a little less than six million people in each country. Both are large peninsulas with archipelagos, and possess developed, advanced economies. Denmark also has revealed how a smaller state can play a relatively important role in NATO without spending massive amounts more in defence than its neighbours. The other reason Denmark is an interesting model for Scotland to follow is that it maintains two separate force structures in manner that would make sense for Scotland to emulate.

The Danish have divided much of their navy into two distinct forces housed at separate facilities: Frederikshavn and Korsor (Danish Defence, 2020). The division means that part of the navy – and supporting air and land units – are more focused on domestic operations and security (patrolling Danish waters, maintaining sovereignty and providing support to civilians) and the other half is focused on being deployable as part of NATO or other international missions that Denmark would wish it to undertake.

This could be replicated almost identically in an independent Scotland. There could be an internationally deployable force based at Faslane, which could interact with whatever ground forces Scotland would wish to maintain – perhaps something such as advanced military medicine and special forces. Just giving one example, UK military medicine (which could be used both in NATO operations and those of the UN or international peacekeeping, for instance) has a present force in Glasgow that could help form the basis of such a force. It is also a world leader, with vast experience around the world and a long-standing culture of excellence. If Scotland were to maintain a well-supported and internationally deployable military medicine capability based out of Faslane (using the nearby airfields of Glasgow or even Prestwick), it could offer something important to NATO and at the same time something that could contribute globally to UN or humanitarian missions. Within the domestic political world of Scotland today, that is a very attractive combination.

The domestically focused force, on the other hand, would have to be based on the East Coast. Actually, Scotland has air–sea facilities presently being used by the UK which combined could work nicely for an independent Scotland. There is the airstrip at Leuchars in Fife, originally an RAF facility but now being used by the Army, which is only minutes away from Tayside and possible base facilities in or near Dundee. Alternately there is the RAF facility at Lossiemouth, from which the UK patrols its northern airspace and runs maritime patrol. This latter facility is close enough to possible basing facilities in Inverness to work well as a hub for domestic protection operations. The structure of these forces would have to be well thought out. There would have to be a mix of surface ships capable of patrolling the waters and aircraft of some kind. Here indeed, the chance of cooperation between Scotland and rUK would be strong. It is unlikely that Scotland will want to maintain a wide mix of expensive fixed-wing aircraft. However the rUK, much larger, wealthier and with greater strategic ambitions, might indeed help patrol out of these Scottish eastern bases. Such a move would be a concrete sign of good relations between the states.

Another consideration is how to house a Scottish Ministry of Defence – this is potentially quite political. Scotland's capital, Edinburgh, is already considerably wealthier than Glasgow and the new state would be right to be careful not to base even more of its economic activity in the capital. There is already a number of large UK government facilities in the greater Glasgow area, such as Kentigern House in the city centre which houses the Army Personnel centre in Scotland. They could be repurposed as a Scottish MOD.

So all in all, while there is little European defence desire to see Scotland leave the UK, it could be made to work – if Scotland were reasonable in its requests and be willing to work co-operatively with the UK government. In that case, many existing facilities could be repurposed to provide the infrastructure needed to be a useful member of NATO, a European defence partner to other states (particularly in the High North), and a friend of the UK. It will almost certainly require compromise on the time needed to move Trident, but that is probably a price worth paying.

References

'Devo Max is no Through Road say Anti-Nuclear Campaigners (2021), *Ban the Bomb*, 9 June, https://www.banthebomb.org/

'HMNB Clyde' (n.d.), *MOD Website*, https://www.royalnavy.mod.uk/our-organisation/bases-and-stations/naval-base/clyde

'Scotland Approaches its Hour upon the Stage' (2014), *Stratfor*, 15 September, https://worldview.stratfor.com/article/scotland-approaches-its-hour-upon-stage

Scottish Government (2013), *Scotland's Future: Your Guide to an Independent Scotland*, https://www.gov.scot/publications/scotlands-future/

'SNP Members Vote to Ditch the Party's Ant-NATO Stance' (2012), *BBC*, 19 October, https://www.bbc.co.uk/news/uk-scotland-scotland-politics-19993694

'Structure of the Navy' (2020), *Danish Defence*, 1 September, https://forsvaret.dk/en/organisation/navy/structure-of-the-navy/

'Trident: 8 Things You Need to Know' (2021), *SNP*, 16 March, https://www.snp.org/tridentfacts/

'Who has the Right to Claim North Sea Oil' (2013), *BBC*, 16 April, https://www.bbc.co.uk/news/uk-scotland-scotland-politics-20042070

CHAPTER 27

Hidden in Plain Sight: The Importance of Scottish Foreign Policy
Stephen Gethins

Foreign Policy Has Shaped Scotland Through History

FROM EARLIEST TIMES Scotland has shaped and been shaped by international affairs. Foreign policy and relationships with other nations has had a profound impact on our domestic politics and provided a key part of Scotland's sense of nationhood.

Over 700 years ago, William Wallace and Andrew Moray wrote what is known as the Letter of Lübeck, just after their appointment as Guardians of Scotland. It was sent to cities in the Hanseatic League telling Scotland's trading partners that the country was once again open for business. Almost a quarter of a century later it was another letter, this time sent to the Pope, the Declaration of Arbroath, that was a critical part of Robert the Bruce's diplomatic efforts to seek recognition for his kingship and the country's independence. That statehood came to an end almost four centuries later with the Treaty of Union of 1707.

In the aftermath of the Treaty of Union Scots continued to play a role internationally – in the British Empire, the Commonwealth and many other institutions. The country's impact was global and resonates today. Scotland enjoys international brand recognition that is the envy of most fully independent states and a diaspora to be found in almost every corner of the globe numbering in the tens of millions. As Arthur Herman put it: 'A large part of the world turns out to be Scottish without even knowing it' (2002).

In recent years Scotland's international engagement has accelerated. Even before the return of the Scottish Parliament in 1999 the Conservatives had been promoting Scotland's brand opening an office in Brussels in 1992. After devolution, that international engagement was deepened by successive Labour–Lib Dem administrations, with Henry McLeish setting up a Scottish Executive office in Washington DC and Jack McConnell opening an office in Beijing in 2005, as well as establishing Scotland's own International Development Fund.

Since 2007, there has been a deepening of Scotland's international profile and footprint under the SNP. That is reflected with a greater divergence in the policy consensus between Westminster and Holyrood across a range of issues, including international development, the refugee crisis, and climate justice, among others. Nowhere has the divergence between the two Parliaments and politics in the two biggest parts of the UK been more profound than our attitudes towards the EU.

Brexit and the Material Change in Circumstances

During the EU referendum, one of the challenges faced by broadcasters north of the border was balancing debates and panels. With few exceptions, it was difficult to find speakers who thought leaving the EU was a good idea. No Scottish MPs and just one MSP out of 129 in the 2011–16 Scottish Parliament publicly backed Leave. UKIP, who had helped drive the rise in Euroscepticism in England, had made no progress in Scotland, losing its deposit in every Holyrood and Westminster constituency it had contested in its 20-year history (saving it on just one occasion when the party secured 6.3 per cent in Orkney and Shetland in 2010).

Since the 2016 referendum, the UK's decision to leave the EU has driven support for independence. John Curtice told the *BBC's Debate Night* programme in May 2021:

> It's perfectly clear from the polling evidence, the polling evidence which has now been confirmed by the result last Thursday [the Holyrood election] that the pursuit of Brexit has undermined support for the Union (Curtice, 2021).

What is more, the SNP (and other pro-independence campaigners) have put Brexit at the heart of the case for another referendum with the aim of Scotland rejoining the EU as a full member state. This background is critical – the reasons why Scots increasingly support full statehood will have consequences for how our foreign policy is defined. During the 2014 independence referendum the issue of our relationship with the EU was an important factor in the debate but Brexit ensures it sits at the epicentre.

No one can wish away the results of the EU referendum or the years of political chaos that followed. The impact will have implications beyond the opinion polls – Brexit will mean dramatic changes to the UK's relationship with its international partners and in particular our EU neighbours. Brexit is a unilateralist project that, at its core, rejects deepened cooperation that is accepted by most European states. These changes will not be limited to foreign policy, with the relationship between the constituent parts of the UK now altered by the Internal Market Act which has been criticised by a House of Lords committee as providing powers to curtail the competencies of devolved administrations and 'imposes new legal restrictions on the devolved administrations' (House of Lords, 2020).

If Scotland is to gain its independence in the coming years, it will have been driven by Brexit and the rejection of that unilateralist vision by voters. That will not be incidental to the development of Scotland's foreign policy and the associated challenges and opportunities. The nature of Scotland's independence will have a bearing on its international outlook and the foreign policy priorities and objectives that emerge.

Fresh Challenges and New Opportunities

Multilateralism will undoubtedly be at the heart of Scottish foreign policy. As a consequence, there will be much greater willingness to co-operate internationally and pool sovereignty in a way that has become politically unacceptable at Westminster.

This will place Scotland back in the European mainstream; neighbouring countries with a similar size and influence see multilateralism and the willingness to co-operate as being a corner stone of their foreign policy. Our closest EU neighbour, Ireland has seen support for its EU membership rise during the Brexit crisis, reaching an unprecedented 92 per cent support in the aftermath of the referendum. Brexit provided a unique challenge for Ireland that it met by bringing its diplomatic clout to bear in the capitals of Europe, as well as Washington DC, and was described by the Economist as a 'diplomatic superpower'.

There is a lot to learn from the Irish, and for the first time in history, Dublin has found itself more influential than London. In the opening section of the Irish Foreign Ministry Strategy document, 'Global Ireland: Ireland's Global Footprint to 2025', Foreign Minister Simon Coveney states: 'our membership of the European Union, and our close working partnership with other member states, has strengthened, rather than diminished, our independence' (Government of Ireland, 2018).

The Finnish Foreign Ministry describes its foreign and security policy as: 'based on good bilateral relations, an active role within the European Union, and effective multilateral cooperation based on respect for and strengthening of international law'.

The pooling of sovereignty is also important to the three Baltic states, with EU membership seen as strengthening their hard-fought independence. In 2018, former UK Foreign Secretary Jeremy Hunt compared the EU to the USSR, drawing a furious reaction in those countries. Lithuania's EU Commissioner Vytenis Andriukaitis who was born in a Soviet gulag offered to brief Mr Hunt on the differences. The then Latvian Ambassador to London Baiba Braže took the unusual step of criticising her hosts and wrote on her Twitter feed:

> Soviets killed, deported, exiled and imprisoned 100 thousands of Latvia's inhabitants after the illegal occupation in 1940, and ruined lives of 3 generations, while the EU has brought prosperity, equality, growth, respect (Braže, 2018).

These reactions go a long way to underlining the importance of multilateralism and the rules-based system to closest partners. Cooperation and collaboration are vital to strengthening the independence and integrity of these states and most importantly the rights and wellbeing of their citizens. With the way that Boris Johnson's government has conducted itself by failing to keep to agreements and even threatening to break international law, it is easy to see just why Brexit Britain so horrifies our neighbours.

The Mainstream Option

It is difficult to underestimate just how much Brexit has changed the political landscape in the UK and the debate about independence in Scotland. The UK Government's pursuit of a hard Brexit means that, for good or ill, this Westminster administration is one of the most radical any of us have known – it will change the UK and its place in the world for good. For those engaged in the constitutional debate, there is no longer a status quo to defend in the same way as in 2014.

The commentator Alex Massie wrote in *The Spectator* in 2021 that 'at its best the SNP is Europe's most boring nationalist movement'. He meant it as a compliment – in many ways the option of independence is the least radical future on the table. Returning to the EU as a fully independent state could be considered the more stable and mainstream (some might say boring) option. Whilst the Brexit experiment has only one adherent in Europe and precious few supporters elsewhere, there are 27 independent member states of the EU and plenty more who aspire to that status.

Pursuing a foreign policy that is anchored in multilateralism and membership of the EU is the preference of most of our similar sized neighbours such as Denmark, Finland and Ireland. Even Norway, who never joined the bloc, has chosen a relationship far closer to the EU than the UK now has.

Independence must mean enthusiastic support for and engagement in multilateralism, international institutions, and the pooling of sovereignty. That will strengthen the country's independence and place in the world. It provides the best way of reaching out to sceptics in the international community by illustrating that the country is a responsible international citizen. It will be reassuring to those 'independence curious' Scottish voters who backed No in 2014, and will be key to a future referendum. Those voters have been put off by the mayhem and isolationism of leaving the EU.

There are significant challenges: the international community and EU will treat the question of independence as an internal political matter; their views will nevertheless matter and there is still a lack of understanding about what kind of global citizen Scotland is likely to be. That requires more engagement internationally from those who seek independence.

The Scottish Government has limited diplomatic clout at its disposal. In part, this is due to the devolution settlement. Other sub-state actors such as the Faroe Islands, Flanders and the German Länder enjoy far greater resource allocation and recognition at a state level for their foreign policy outreach. There have been some appointments in recent years of former British diplomats who bring skills and contacts that will be crucial to Holyrood in the post-Brexit world. More can be done with overseas offices such as the flagship Scotland House operation in Brussels that should be expanded, greater diplomatic engagement encouraged including at the Scottish Government's offices in London, and ministers prepared to make more regular visits abroad.

At a time of tight budgets and limited resources, that will be a big ask but other sub-states actors invest far more in their foreign policy footprint. At a time when the UK's international brand is diminished, that makes good political and economic sense. Limited budgets will be a challenge and the Scottish Government will need to decide where our expertise and priorities lie. Scotland should not seek to try and make an impact on every area of foreign policy. That requires tough decisions over resource allocation.

There are clear areas of expertise, however. In the field of peace-building, many in the international community see Scotland as a safe space to host those from areas affected by conflict. Already the Scottish Government has been working with the UN on training women peacebuilders, hosting groups from around the world including Iraq, Yemen, Syria and Libya. This work is facilitated by the excellent team at Beyond Borders Scotland who, along with other Scottish-based NGOs such as Mercy Corps Europe and the HALO Trust, are helping support and increasingly active international community. This will be further helped by the establishment of a Scottish Council on Global Affairs.

Work has taken place in other areas – the Scottish Government has had a fund for climate justice for almost a decade. This is part of its efforts to tackle climate change and engage in climate diplomacy. The Scottish Government has not acted alone, and the efforts have drawn together expertise from across Scotland including its world leading offshore renewables, its higher education and its research sector. Prioritising Scotland's work in international engagement will require difficult choices. If Scotland is truly to embrace its place as a multilateralist mainstream European nation, then discussions over those choices will have to be reflected in political discourse.

Our neighbours will also be expecting Scotland to fulfil its responsibilities in terms of security. The opening up of the northern sea routes and our geographic location means that we will need to invest in our armed services and security infrastructure. Our closest allies such as the Nordic and Baltic states will expect Scotland to be a close and reliable ally when it comes to challenges such as that posed by Russia. This contribution was written before Russia's invasion of Ukraine. That has already changed the shape and nature of the EU and nowhere more so than the field of foreign and security policy. The EU will be a much more important security alliance in future and that will be important to Scotland and the UK's future relationship with the bloc. For those states who are members their security therefore hinges on the twin pillars of EU and NATO membership. In terms of increased security engagement with the EU, Ireland has made major contributions in this area with Irish General Pat Nash leading the EU's Mission in Chad, EUFOR, in 2008 for example.

Security is not limited to operations by armed forces personnel, however. The recent work by SNP MPs Stewart McDonald and Alyn Smith on disinformation has been an important part of helping facilitate a conversation about the spread of disinformation. This can often be a difficult subject area for political campaigners. It is all too easy to excuse bad faith actors who back up your political opinion or worldview, but disinformation poses a long-term threat to our democracy and that of every other European democracy.

The World is Watching

The debate about Scotland's future is being taken seriously internationally. There is a greater expectation that the country will back independence when the matter is put to the people than previously in 2014. This is an encouraging sign for those of us who believe in independence, but it comes with a greater sense of responsibility – our partners will be looking for signs of the kind of Scotland that emerges as a full member of the international community.

We must take our foreign policy and international engagement seriously – the Scottish Government should increasingly look and sound like an independent government. Building on initiatives such as the First Minister's work at the UN, engagement with European partners and continuing to work on climate change, the biggest challenge of this generation, has provided a good start.

It also means acting responsibly closer to home. Over the Brexit period, Ireland won plaudits and was able to defend its national interest most effectively when it was seen as an honest broker between itself and the UK. The country was the best friend that the UK had during this process of seeking compromise and a deal in the face of Westminster hostility and EU frustration. Scotland should seek to act as a close friend and ally to England, as a bridge to help rebuild the relationship between London and Brussels – supporting our most important bilateral and multilateral relationships.

Independence should come with a spirit of generosity towards all in these islands. The first phone call of any incoming Scottish foreign secretary should be to their counterpart in London. This is also the case with Ireland appointing the country's most senior civil servant, Martin Fraser the Secretary-General to the Government, as Ireland's new ambassador to London in July 2021.

In many ways, other countries will be looking for reassurance that the partnership between the countries in these islands remains intact. There is already a solid model next door among the Nordic states, who enjoy a good partnership between independent states with a common history and even identity, some of whom are in the EU and some not.

Where Scotland sits in the world is not a debate that can wait. Malcolm Chalmers expressed in an interview for the book *Nation to Nation*:

> New states are often defined by decisions made at the
> start so how you define yourself and getting that right
> is critical' (Gethins, 2021).

There will not be a second chance for a first impression for a newly independent Scotland. We can draw lessons from others and the legacy of being part of the UK; however, each country has its own unique set of circumstances and values that define its place in the world. It is time we discussed ours.

References

Braže, B. (2018), *Twitter*, 30 September, https://twitter.com/natobrazeb/
status/1046442294684123139?lang=en

Curtice, J. (2021), *BBC Debate Night*, 12 May, https://www.bbc.co.uk/iplayer/episode/mooow3t9/debate-night-series-3-12052021

Gethins, S. (2021), *Nation to Nation: Scotland's Place in the World*, Edinburgh: Luath Press.

Government of Ireland (2018), *Global Ireland: Ireland's Global Footprint to 2025*, Dublin: Government of Ireland.

Herman, A. (2002), *How the Scots Invented the Modern World*, London: Fourth Estate.

House of Lords Select Committee on the Constitution (2020), *United Kingdom Internal Market Bill*, 17th Report of Session 2019-2021, 16 October, HL Paper 151.

Massie, A. (2021), 'Yesterday's man in uncalled for comeback', *Times*, 25 April.

CHAPTER 28

Preparing for Negotiations on
Nuclear Weapons
Malcolm Chalmers and William Walker

ESTABLISHING CLOSE BILATERAL defence and security relations would be in the interest of both Scotland and rUK, and of the community of allied countries, if Scotland were to become a sovereign nation state; rUK's sense of security – and its power – would be diminished if Edinburgh and London failed to work together effectively. Scotland would be a small country with limited abilities to defend itself alone in a difficult and fast-evolving security environment.

Abroad, Scotland's special geography and frontier with the North Atlantic would lend it strategic significance that is expected to increase as global warming opens Arctic sea-lanes. Although Ireland-like neutrality has supporters in Scotland, and would be an option in the absence of co-operative arrangements, it is not the Scottish Government's objective. It would not be welcomed by states on whom an independent Scotland would rely for recognition as a responsible new member of the European community of states.

'Scotland's Future' observed that 'Improving the way defence is delivered in and for Scotland is one of the most pressing reasons for independence' (Scottish Government, 2013). It went on to explain the envisaged purposes of an independent Scotland's foreign and defence policies and provided a list of capabilities needed to achieve them. Some would be acquired through division or recasting of the UK's existing assets, some purchased anew and some dispensed with, subject to negotiation.

Considerable detail was provided in a ten-page section. Little was said, however, about the most significant and controversial issue – the fate of the nuclear bases at Faslane and Coulport whose closure the SNP has long sought. The paper sets out reasons for the party's objection to nuclear weapons, emphasising their 'indiscriminate and inhumane destructive power', their opportunity costs and burden on public expenditure. But the commitment to securing 'their speediest safe withdrawal' from Scotland was left vague, lacking a persuasive accompanying statement on implementation. There was an evident desire to avoid being drawn into discussion of the many complications, an evasion practised throughout the referendum campaign.

The UK government, for its part, agreed that defence 'matters in the debate about independence' (HM Government, 2013). In a detailed 88-page report, it laid out the strategic and economic reasons why it believed that Scotland's defence benefited from the union. On the nuclear question, it argued that Scotland's unwillingness 'to subscribe to the nuclear aspects of NATO's Strategic Concept ... would represent a significant complication to its membership.' It asserted that:

> The UK Government has made it clear that it is not planning for Scottish independence or to move the strategic nuclear deterrent from Her Majesty's Naval Base Clyde. If the result of the referendum were to lead to the current situation being challenged, then other options would be considered, but any alternative solution would come at huge cost. It would be an enormous exercise to reproduce the facilities elsewhere.

Despite both sides acknowledging the potentially radical consequences of Scotland's independence for the future of the UK's nuclear force, it did not figure large in a referendum campaign dominated by national aspiration, the economy and other issues that mattered more to the electorate. It would be no surprise if defence again took a back seat in a second referendum, although the UK government may try harder to impress on Scotland's voters the potential costs of defying its and NATO's interests in nuclear deterrence.

Boxed in on Trident

Had there been a Yes vote, the Scottish and UK governments – together with publics on both sides of the border – would have been woefully unprepared for the negotiations on nuclear weapons that would have swiftly followed. The difficulty of finding common ground would have been exacerbated by the manner in which governments and political parties had boxed themselves in through stances adopted and actions taken over many years. Public opinion on nuclear weapons in Scotland is not uniform, with polling answers dependent on the questions being asked. Nonetheless, commitment to the removal of all nuclear weapons from Scotland has been unwavering within the SNP and has found strong support in other political parties (especially the Greens and Labour) and in the wider population.

Besides ending Scotland's engagement with nuclear weapons, their removal has been advocated by the SNP as a means of releasing bases and surrounding areas so that Scotland could establish defence forces and infrastructures appropriate to the needs of a Nordic-like country. Faslane would 'become the main operating base for the Scottish Navy, and the headquarters for the Scottish defence forces as a whole' (Scottish Government, 2013). Throughout, there has been a tendency to downplay the immensity and complexity of the task of relocating the nuclear force from its bases in Scotland and their conversion to other uses.

Whereas the Scottish commitment to denuclearisation has been fixed in the imagination of what independence means, the UK government has been boxed in by decades of investment in weaponry and infrastructure and their associated policies and careers, and by the focusing on a single Scotland-based weapon system after the scrapping of airborne capabilities in the 1990s. Throughout – in the adoption of Polaris in the 1960s, its replacement by Trident in the 1990s, and in Trident's current renewal – no concessions have been made to Scottish demands for the weapons' removal. Since 1998, the UK government's monopoly on decision has been framed by the Scotland Act and its strict reservation of defence policy to London and ring-fencing of nuclear issues. Holyrood's views and votes on Trident have had no formal consequence and have been routinely ignored in Westminster despite the strength of Scottish interests in the outcome of decisions.

Commitment to the Scottish bases by successive UK governments has therefore been persistent, inflexible and often imperious. The 2002 decision to base the seven new Astute-class attack submarines at Faslane, which is nearing full implementation, has narrowed longer-term basing options in England. In 2016, the UK government announced that it would proceed with the manufacture of four Dreadnought Trident-missile-carrying submarines, implementing the 2007 decision on renewal, and confirmed that they would be based in Scotland.

The Responsibility to Prepare

When the referendum campaigns on Scotland's independence were launched in 2013, there was little expectation in Edinburgh or London that it would result in a yes vote. There was felt to be some justification, therefore, in postponing the day when serious contingency planning should be undertaken. Now, this no longer seems appropriate. Although uncertainty remains over timing and questions of legality are unresolved, there is a distinct possibility that a second referendum will be held in the next few years, with an outcome that might well be fatal to the union. A recent press report has suggested that contingency planning for a scenario in which Scotland gained independence, looking at various options for the future of the nuclear bases, was undertaken by Whitehall recently. This indicates the seriousness with which Scotland's departure from the union is now being viewed in London (Dickie, Payne and Warrell, 2021).

Each side has a responsibility to consider what a Yes vote would entail in advance of the negotiations that would swiftly follow. This applies especially to nuclear weapons in the defence field given the difficulties that they present and their great domestic and international significance. Brexit has vividly demonstrated the dangers of engaging in complex negotiations without sufficient prior thought and preparation, and of room for manoeuvre immediately being constrained by the painting of the reddest of red lines.

Of course, neither side would wish fully to display its hand in advance, and much would remain to be worked out and decided through negotiation. However, inhibition of private and public discussion of these nuclear affairs is unhealthy. It should not be allowed to persist in the run-up to another referendum. In the remaining paragraphs we suggest the assumptions that should shape approaches to negotiations, and the issues and questions that will demand attention. We can only sketch them given the need for brevity.

Guiding Assumptions

Contemplation of the post-vote nuclear negotiations should rest on four particular assumptions, irrespective of the referendum's timing. Firstly, they would be conducted against the background of rivalry among great powers, involving the US, China and Russia in particular, all of whom continue to attach a high value to their nuclear deterrent forces. Europe will be affected and concerned about its own protection. At the same time, dramatic technological changes (cyber, space weapons, etc) will be posing fundamental questions (already being asked) about the future safety and reliability of nuclear deterrence, about conventional and nuclear force structures, and about the opportunity costs of heavy nuclear investment. The changes may be particularly unsettling for the UK, France and other states possessing small and relatively vulnerable nuclear arsenals. Although rUK's support for nuclear deterrence within NATO would be unlikely to waver, its desire and ability to maintain nuclear forces over the medium and long terms cannot be taken for granted.

Secondly, Scotland would choose and be expected to become a non-nuclear weapon state under international law – notably the Nuclear Non-Proliferation Treaty (NPT) – and would seek membership of other pertinent multilateral treaties and agreements when it attained sovereignty. Although elements of a post-independence government might well be sympathetic towards the 2021 Treaty on the Prohibition of Nuclear Weapons (TPNW), it would only consider joining it if NATO's current bar on membership had been lifted. rUK's right to be regarded as the UK's continuator state under the NPT, inheriting its legal rights to possess nuclear weapons along with obligations to pursue nuclear disarmament, would be accepted internationally. A nuclear weapon state's operation of its entire nuclear force out of the territory of a (truculent) non-nuclear weapon state would nevertheless be unprecedented and attract much international attention, possibly causing division among governments.

Thirdly, nuclear agreement(s) between Scotland and rUK, as sovereign states, would take the form of an international treaty or treaties, in conformity with international law and practice. They would require ratification by both Holyrood and Westminster Parliaments.

Fourthly, neither quick removal of nuclear weapons from Scotland nor acquiescence to their indefinite stay there would be politically acceptable and feasible and could therefore provide basis for an agreement. How to conceive and manage transition to a situation in which nuclear weapons are absent from Scotland, without undermining the security of either party, would therefore be the question. The four submarines under construction at Barrow-in-Furness are due to enter service in the early to mid-2030s. Even if an independent Scotland conceded to their stay over their projected lifetimes (into the 2060s), which is hard to imagine, planning for the phasing in of alternative arrangements would have to begin decades in advance – as early as the 2030s – given lengthy procurement lead-times. As a negotiated phase-out would be consistent with each country's non-proliferation and disarmament obligations under the NPT, it would surely be regarded as a reasonable outcome in most capitals and would be hard for NATO states to oppose, despite any misgivings about risks to the alliance. The US attitude and role would be vital. It would expect each side to compromise, the onus falling especially on Scotland which would depend on US – and rUK – sponsorship to become a new member of NATO.

This fourth assumption implies that agreement between London and Edinburgh would be required on two sets of issues, possibly requiring separate albeit interrelated treaties: one regarding rUK's nuclear force's operation out of Faslane and Coulport prior to phase-out, the other the phase-out's implementation and timetable. Another agreement, not discussed here, would be required between Scotland and the International Atomic Energy Agency in Vienna on the safeguarding of civil nuclear materials and facilities, a necessary step in its passage to becoming a non-nuclear weapon state under the NPT.

Issues Requiring Attention in Regard to Continuation

Nuclear submarines would continue operating, it may be conjectured, out of the Scottish bases into the 2030s or 2040s. The terms under which this occurred would require negotiation and settlement. In broad brush, significant issues needing address and questions needing answers would include the legal status of nuclear bases in Scotland; rights of consultation and decision; the control and management of waterways; transport of nuclear warheads to Coulport; and intelligence gathering.

In terms of legal status, decisions would be required on whether Faslane and Coulport's lands would be leased by rUK or maintained as its sovereign base areas. Whichever was chosen – the former seems much more likely – a number of familiar questions would require attention, including the bases' usage, territorial boundaries, responsibility for their security, provision of services and utilities, overflight, criminal jurisdiction, and grounds for termination (Woodliffe, 1992).

What rights would the Scottish Government and Parliament possess to be consulted, and to decide, on matters pertaining to the nuclear force's development, operation and regulation when it is still located in the Clyde? What obligations would be placed upon them? Those rights and obligations would require delineation. Some lessons might be drawn from the basing of US nuclear forces, including Polaris submarines in the Holy Loch, in the UK and elsewhere, including NATO's nuclear sharing agreements and consultation and planning mechanisms. However, a non-nuclear weapon state's hosting of a nuclear weapon state's *entire* nuclear force, and a submarine force to boot, would be unprecedented in several respects. How to reconcile Scotland's felt right of influence over the usage of nuclear forces operated from its territory with the UK's demand for freedom from constraint in its exercise of deterrence, all subject to the NPT's stipulations, would be a tough question on which innovation may be required. One can anticipate that rights, or their absence, to participate in decisions on the use of nuclear weapons based in the Clyde would be an especially sensitive and controversial matter in Scottish politics, since it touches on fundamental aspects of a state's and people's sovereignty and survival.

As regards the control and management of waterways, under the Law of the Sea, the Gareloch (Faslane) and Loch Long (Coulport) would become Scotland's internal waters, with stretches of the Firth of Clyde and down the coast becoming its territorial waters. How would traffic involving submarines and other craft in these areas be managed and by whom, and what rights would rUK retain to operate sensors and other equipment and forces to ensure the submarines' protection?

In terms of transport of nuclear warheads, there would be a need for joint oversight and physical protection, with carefully assigned roles to police and other authorities, of the transport of warheads to and from Coulport across Scotland's roads.

Finally, what role would be ascribed to Scotland and its fledgling intelligence agency in the gathering and processing of information relevant to the nuclear force's stationing and operation?

Issues Requiring Attention in Regard to Phase-Out

Almost from day one, rUK would need to embark on a search for alternative sites for basing its nuclear submarine force. This matter was discussed at length in the book that we published twenty years ago, since when it has often been assumed that relocation in the UK (for instance to sites in Devon and Cornwall) would face severe practical and political difficulties, as would the submarine force's operation out of bases in France or the US that has also been mooted (Chalmers and Walker, 2001). A more recent study by the Royal United Services Institute suggested that relocation in England might be possible given enough time, financial investment and political commitment (Chalmers and Chalmers, 2014). These claims would now have to be put to the test. If it were concluded that no other sites were viable, the development of alternative nuclear weapon systems or the eventual abandonment of rUK's nuclear deterrent would come into play. Come what may, a decision to establish Scotland as an independent state would trigger, inevitably, a great debate on rUK's nuclear future for which there has been no preparation hitherto.

Timing, cost and compliance – and their uncertainties – would haunt the inquiries and negotiations. How much time would be required, and should be allowed, to decide on new sites and their plausibility? What would relocation or development of alternative systems cost and could it be borne within a diminished defence budget? How much uncertainty could and should be tolerated? Would governments be drawn towards a step-by-step evolutionary approach, or would actions have to be time-limited or some mixture of the two (this is reminiscent of debates about nuclear disarmament)? How could agreements on phase-out be made binding, and how should compliance be overseen and ensured?

The phasing out of rUK's nuclear activities and capabilities in the Clyde, and subsequent transfer of bases to Scottish usage, would require close cooperation between the rUK and Scottish Governments. Issues requiring attention would include the scale and timing of decommissioning, decontamination and dismantlement of nuclear facilities and assets; disposal of residues; allocation of responsibilities; and sharing of costs. Although agreement on principles, obligations and processes would be required early on, details could be worked out over a longer timeframe.

Conclusion

Agreement on nuclear weaponry is a necessary condition for a wider agreement between Edinburgh and London on the terms of separation. Negotiations are likely to be hard-fought, but the broad parameters of the landing zone seem clear – basing for some time, but not indefinitely.

Such a settlement is likely to reflect an equilibrium of discomfort between the two parties. Scotland's negotiators will have to explain to impatient disarmers why they are prepared to accept the basing of nuclear weapons on the Clyde for a decade and possibly longer. rUK's negotiators will have to explain at home and abroad how the running of its nuclear deterrent out of foreign territory can be made to work, albeit temporarily, why the submarine force's relocation or development of an alternative system will be necessary, and how it might be achieved with scarcer defence resources.

Whilst agreement on main parameters should be attainable, negotiations on detailed content are likely to be difficult and fractious, especially if issues have not been analysed and solutions explored in advance. It is incumbent on each side to prepare the ground. If a referendum delivered a vote for independence, Edinburgh and London would be impelled, we have argued, to negotiate treaty-based agreements on, firstly, terms of the nuclear force's operation out of the Scottish bases in a transitional period and, secondly, the nuclear bases' phasing out and conversion to other use.

Yet the nuclear issue could also be a powerful force for moderation in the wider relationship. It would be hard to see rUK signing up to a broad agreement on close economic cooperation if Scotland insisted on rapid removal of the nuclear force. It is also hard to see Scotland accepting long-term basing if rUK played hard-ball on the wider settlement. A spirit of compromise on the nuclear issue will require a similar spirit in other fields. If there is intransigence, a more radical break in relations could result, doing harm to the countries' and their allies' security and to their international relations.

Postscript on nuclear weapons and the Russia-Ukraine crisis

Russia's war against Ukraine is a crisis for the international nuclear order as well as for so much else. There is widespread shock that a nuclear weapon state has launched a brutal war of aggression against a sovereign non-nuclear weapon state, in violation of the security assurances provided to it in the 1994 Budapest Memorandum. Russia is in grave breach of the post-1945 order's most basic norms and rules, and is using the threat of nuclear escalation to inhibit the response of NATO and other states. The Russia–Ukraine crisis is both strengthening attachment to nuclear deterrence and heightening public and governmental awareness of its perils and grave injustices. How this plays out here and abroad remains to be seen. Although debates may sharpen, our surmise is that the fundaments of the politics of nuclear weapons in the Scottish/UK context will be unchanged. We stand by the line of argument above, while acknowledging that there is much uncertainty.

References

Cabinet Office (2021), *Global Britain in a Competitive Age: The Integrated Review of Security, Defence, Development and Foreign Policy*.

Chalmers, M. and Walker, W. (2001), *Uncharted Waters: The UK, Nuclear Weapons and the Scottish Question*, East Linton: Tuckwell Press.

Chalmers, H. and Chalmers, M. (2014), *Relocation, Relocation, Relocation: could the UK's Nuclear Force Be Moved After Independence?*, London: Royal United Services Institute.

Dickie, M., Payne, S. and Warrell, H. (2021), 'UK draws up plan to shift Trident subs abroad if Scotland secedes', *Financial Times*, 2 September.

HM Government (2013), *Scotland Analysis: Defence*.

Scottish Government (2013), *Scotland's Future: Your Guide to an Independent Scotland*.

Woodliffe, J. (1992), *The Peacetime Use of Foreign Military Installations under Modern International Law*, Leiden: Martinus Nijhoff.

CHAPTER 29

Does Scotland Already Have a
Feminist Foreign Policy?
Caron E. Gentry

CONTAINED WITHIN THE SNP's manifesto for the May 2021 election was a small line about pursuing a feminist foreign policy. This line came without much context but spurred a great deal of interest. Much of the interest has centred around two questions: what is a feminist foreign policy (henceforth FFP); and can Scotland adopt one? This chapter sets out to answer those two questions by looking at the origins of FFP and what scholars and policy makers see as fundamental to building a successful one. Also, many of Scotland's internal policies are already feminist, reassuring the reader that a FFP is well within reach.

Before answering these questions, though, it is helpful to establish a baseline about the use of 'feminism.' As a feminist scholar of almost twenty years, I have always been struck by either the resistance to, confusion over, or concern about using the word 'feminism.' In recent years, I have also adopted the use of 'patriarchy,' 'misogyny,' and 'white supremacy' and these are also met with discomfort. Adoption of a FFP requires both using these words, unashamedly, and helping others understand why they are necessary. They are necessary because they accurately and clearly identify the misuse of power, or injustice. Fundamentally, feminism aims to dismantle power because power very often leads to harm. Patriarchy, or a socio-political system led by men, misogyny, or the hatred of women, and white supremacy, where most power is held by white people, are all abuses of power; they are also known as power structures. These power structures do harm: they keep certain people in power with control over economic and material resources, while others are left out without, or with little access to, power. In many regards, the maintenance of power as the ability to access it falls along gender, race, class, and sexual lines. Feminism aims to empower those who are marginalised – not just women, but racial, ethnic, and sexual minorities, and people from different class backgrounds.

Feminism may be concerned with gender but it is incredibly important to recognise that gender is not synonymous with women. Gender is a social construct, meaning the differences between the sexes is neither natural nor unchanging. Instead, society determines what characteristics pertain to masculinity and femininity, and thereby men and women respectively, as well as organisations, institutions, and actions associated with masculinity and femininity. For instance, masculinity is associated with rationality, logic, assertiveness if not aggression, and autonomy. Society has often constructed masculinity/femininity as complete opposites; thus, femininity is associated with indecisiveness, nurturing nature, peacefulness and/or submissiveness, and illogic (Runyan and Peterson, 2018). Gendered characteristics associated with men and masculinity are often valued above feminine ones, particularly when it comes to public life (politics, governance, business), which is why there has been a historic resistance to female leadership or to values equated with femininity in the public (Elshtain, 2020; Pateman, 1980).

Patriarchal societies prioritise masculinity, making masculine characteristics the norm and the desired way of being, such as accepting war and/or the threat of violence as a solution or prioritising competition and self-sufficiency in the neo-liberal economic order. Domestic and global politics, international relations, and foreign policy have also been criticised for masculinist priorities (Sjoberg, 2013). In contrast, feminism emphasises a different approach, one that seeks to dismantle power structures, reducing socio-economic, gendered, and racialised harms, amongst others, via empathy, cooperation, dialogue, diplomacy, and the recognition of interdependency between states (Tickner, 1992). Thus, a feminist foreign policy takes these ethical requirements to heart and begins to articulate a deviation from the status quo.

The Beginning Point: UNSC 1325 and Feminist Foreign Policy

A feminist foreign policy requires a fundamental shift in thinking. Where masculinist thinking too easily falls to militaristic and aggressive solutions to international challenges, FFP demands policy visionaries hold different priorities: of (social) justice and human rights, devolved power, cooperation, and cosmopolitan ideals. Its roots are found in the early 2000s, when there was growing global promotion of women's rights. Beginning in 2000 with the adoption of UNSC 1325, which focused on mainstreaming women and gender into all areas of the UN (Aggestam and Bergman-Rosamond, 2016, 323). Other, state-led initiatives also focused on gender. William Hague, when serving as the UK's foreign secretary, worked with Angelina Jolie on the ending of sexual violence in war. In the US, Secretary of State Hillary Clinton articulated her own Clinton Doctrine that argued for humanitarian intervention on the grounds of women's insecurity (see for instance Hudson et al., 2012). Yet, FFP really came into force in 2015, when the Swedish Social Democratic Party and the Green Party formed a coalition government, declaring it to be a feminist government with a FFP. Accordingly, the Swedish government's FFP was 'to become the strongest voice for gender equality and full employment of human rights for all women and girls.' They included in their 'toolbox' the '3 Rs': women's *representation* in governments and places of power, human *rights* for women, and *reallocation*, or equitable distribution, of global income and natural resources (Aggestam and Bergman-Rosamund 2016, 325).

Still, FFP, to be more holistic and cognisant of how gender impacts everyone, should look beyond women. A more comprehensive FFP does not just address women's material positions around the world but also embraces a 'reorientation' of foreign policy based upon cosmopolitan ideals of justice, peace, and pragmatic security. It is interested in upending current (masculine) power structures by redistributing power to more, if not all people, thereby raising the status of historically disempowered people, not just women. Thus, scholars of FFP (Aggestam and Bergman-Rosamund, 2016, 323; Aggestam, Bergman-Rosamund, and Kronsell, 2019; Aggestam and Bergman-Rosamond, 2018) believe that FFP should 'explicitly seek to renegotiate and challenge power hierarchies and gendered institutions,' which are often intersectional, involving to various and unknowable degrees gender, race, class, heteronormativity, and religious bias. Without understanding these more complex hierarchies, they will only be replicated.

More specifically, FFP is an ethical, cosmopolitan framework; intersectional, by paying attention to gender, race, class, etc; resistant/in direct opposition to militarisation; attentive to different forms and levels of power: international, national, local, and domestic; And it is self-reflective in that those who run the state or nation are aware of their own power and privilege, the power and privilege of the state/nation, and are aware of past (and present) injustices, such as colonialism and imperialism.

More importantly, it should be disruptive. By simply using language like misogyny and white supremacy, FFP begins to interrogate questions about power and wealth – wherever they are based (Thomson, 2020; Aggestam and Bergman-Rosamund, 2016; Aggestam, Bergman-Rosamund, and Kronsell, 2019; Aggestam and Bergman-Rosamond, 2018).

Resistance to, or just simply failure to understand, FFP's sweeping, system-wide changes should be expected. Adopters and supporters of FFP must recognise that it is a policy framework that does more than set policy. It challenges 'deeply ingrained patriarchal [and racial] structures, gender bias, and international institutions' (Aggestam and Bergman-Rosamund 2016, 329). With its focus on rights and ethics, FFP makes us ask different questions about security: it shifts focus from hard security to soft, from military security to health, human, and environmental security. Thus, what started with a specific group of underrepresented and disempowered people becomes about transforming the lives of the many who are underrepresented and without power. It becomes about setting new and different priorities. This is the hitch: FFP, as a concept, will become a target because it challenges the patriarchy, misogyny, the white supremacist system, the status quo of militarised policies, common understandings of defence and security. Above all, it requires bravery.

Scotland the Brave

This is where Scotland enters the picture: contemporary Scottish politics are inherently feminist ones. They may not be known as such potentially for the same reasons that were noted in the introduction. Since devolution, Scottish voters have noted their interest in politics and policies that emphasise equality of all kinds, parity, justice, and fairness. Policies like these will, eventually, inherently upend masculinist power structures. The combined strength of the SNP, Labour, Greens, and Lib Dems in Scotland demonstrates a population interested in social, economic, and climate justice. Scotland is a 'a vibrant, inclusive democracy with ... power devolved to local levels' (SNP, 2021, 40) – it has built, already, many of the indicated tools necessary for the implementation of a successful FFP.

If feminist politics and policies are ethical, caring, people-centric, power and hierarchy dismantling systems, then quite a bit of Scottish domestic policies since devolution fit this agenda. Domestically, this is seen in Scotland's 'National Performance Framework' with its national outcomes that aim to 'give opportunities to all people' (Scottish Government, 2020) by increasing the wellbeing of people by addressing child poverty and ending homelessness, amongst other goals; creating sustainable and inclusive growth through a net-zero society and the continued implementation of UN Sustainable Development Goals; and, finally, by reducing inequalities and placing equal importance on economic, environmental and social progress.

These aims, which would ensure that all people can prosper, are demonstrative of a national commitment to equality and inclusivity. These commitments have borne out in various policies, including a more progressive tax structure; a more inclusive benefits system; commitment to power devolution; commitment to peaceful resolutions; the 'baby box'; no prescription charges; more NHS spending; community policing; free sanitary products to pupils and students; and affordable housing.

The SNP manifesto states that the values of compassion and solidarity have guided the party, and Scotland as a nation, and will continue to guide the approach to further pledges (SNP, 2021, 2). As noted above, these are values that feminism carries at its very core and can be the very words that guide a Scottish FFP.

As a nation moves its political agenda beyond its borders, it does so only based upon the issues and politics that are cared about internally. The Scottish vote to Remain in the EU demonstrates the population's desire to be part of cosmopolitan intergovernmental organisations. Scotland's request for special consideration in the Brexit negotiations, maintaining an office in Brussels, alongside six other international offices, indicates that Scotland already has a foreign policy. Arguably, it is a feminist one. Given the Scottish resistance to nuclear weapons and to the enormous costs of a building a military, it is in its best interest to build a security system built around soft security, to become, as noted in the 2021 manifesto, a place to build peace (SNP, 2021, 72–74). This would be to position Scotland, like Sweden, as a 'humanitarian superpower'.

Thus, examining the SNP's 2021 manifesto begins to illuminate the current Scottish Government's global aspirations, specifically discussed in the manifesto's last section, 'Scotland In the World' (SNP, 2021, 71–74). This section is divided into three sub-sections, all containing a number of initiatives and points that define Scotland's international engagement. Within the manifesto, it would appear that FFP is just one element. Yet, what I would urge the Scottish Government to realise is that all elements contained in this last section could be contained within the FFP umbrella.

Specifically, the manifesto sets out goals to rejoin the EU, establishing Scotland's cosmopolitan vision and co-operative ideals; criticises the UK's migration policy as inhuman and unfair; and introduces the creation of the Scottish Council for Global Affairs and the adoption of a FFP. From there it specifies a desire for a wellbeing economy government network. It elaborates on international, co-operative ideals by 'being a good citizen,' increasing the International Development Fund, supporting the Humanitarian Emergency Fund, establishing an International Development Women and Girls Empowerment Fund, and a Global Renewable Centre. Its commitment to the UN Sustainable Development Goals parallels the aforementioned National Performance Framework with Wellbeing and Sustainable Development Bill, which makes it a statutory requirement for all public bodies and local authorities to consider the long-term consequences of their policy decisions, which tracks with the wellbeing economy network. Finally, along with confirming the opposition to nuclear weapons, the Institute for Peacekeeping, Peace Institute, and Scottish Cities of Refuge will be created and also used to support UN1325.

Combined, these elements all speak to the values, ethics, and goals of FFP. They are cosmopolitan in their commitment to rejoining the EU, welcoming migrants and people of all nationalities as 'new Scots,' addressing climate change and justice, and to collaborative efforts such as the Global Renewable Centre, the International Development Fund, the Humanitarian Emergency Fund, and the

International Development Women and Girls Empowerment Fund. These are also caring, people-centric goals – all of them emphasise the humanity of citizens and non-citizens alike and all of them invest in an international form of devolution by looking to empower the local level over the international and a more supportive approach to development, for instance, the emphasis on a wellbeing economy. Furthermore, these are as far from militaristic and aggressive solutions as possible. The decision to create two institutes committed to peace and peacekeeping, the continued opposition to nuclear weapons, and the founding of the Scottish Council for Global Affairs all speak to an investment in other forms of power. Thus, the FFP agenda set out in the SNP manifesto is *already* inherently feminist, and therefore is *already* an articulation of what a Scottish feminist foreign policy (can) look(s) like.

References

Aggestam, K. and Bergman-Rosamund, A. (2016), 'Swedish Feminist Foreign Policy in the Making: Ethics, Politics, and Gender', *Ethics and International Affairs*, 30(3), 323-334.

Aggestam, K. and Bergman-Rosamund, A. (2018), 'Re-Politicising the Gender-Security Nexus: Sweden's Feminist Foreign Policy', *European Review of International Studies*, 5(3), 30-48.

Aggestam, K., Bergman-Rosamund, A. and Kronsell, A. (2019), 'Theorising Feminist Foreign Policy', *International Relations*, 33(1): 29-39

Elshtain, J.B. (2020), *Public Man, Private Woman: Women in Social and Political Thought*, Princeton: Princeton University Press.

Hudson, V. M., Ballif-Spanvill, B., Caprioli, M. and Emmett, C.F. (2012), *Sex and World Peace*, New York: Columbia University Press.

Scottish Government (2020), National Performance Framework, https://nationalperformance.gov.scot/, accessed 1 September.

Pateman, C., (1980), "The Disorder of Women': Women, Love, and the Sense of Justice', *Ethics*, 91(1): 20-34.

Runyan, A.S., and Peterson, V.S. (2018), *Global Gender Issues in the New Millennium*, London: Routledge.

SNP (2021), *Scotland's Future*, https://www.snp.org/manifesto/, accessed 1 September.

Sjoberg, L., (2013), *Gendering Global Conflict: Toward a Feminist Theory of War*, New York: Columbia University Press.

Thomson, J., (2020), 'What's Feminist about Feminist Foreign Policy? Sweden's and Canada's Foreign Policy Agendas', *International Studies Perspectives*, 21(4), 424-437.

Tickner, J. A., (1992), *Gender in International Relations*, New York: Columbia University Press.

CHAPTER 30

Scotland and International Peacemaking
Mark Muller Stuart

WITH THE UK leaving the EU and repatriating powers back to itself, an important debate has opened up about Scotland's role both in the British Isles and in the world. Here this debate is explored through Scotland's recent attempts to support international peacemaking, setting out why it has a potentially unique contribution to make in the field of conflict resolution. That is something which may of course come into even sharper focus as wider lessons are drawn over time from the Russia–Ukraine crisis.

This chapter touches upon Scotland's growing desire to have a greater voice in international affairs as a global citizen. It also considers whether the 'reserved powers' dichotomy of the current devolved settlement is fit for purpose. Particularly given the emergence of a set of global issues that transcend borders and traditional constructs of foreign policy.

It remains to be determined whether Scotland's desire for a greater voice at the international level can be accommodated through existing devolved arrangements or a new, post-Brexit, internal settlement within the UK or only through the creation of a separate sovereign state – but two matters, in my judgement, already appear beyond contention.

Firstly, people in Scotland are no longer content to let non-devolved institutions at Westminster speak exclusively on their behalf when it comes to foreign or global affairs. Nor are they content for Scotland to be projected abroad through just its sporting and Walter Scott type heritage – they also want Scotland's contemporary values to be projected.

Secondly, both Scotland and the world have fundamentally changed since the UK joined the EU and pooled certain diplomatic and policy powers. The UK cannot simply return to the status quo ante that existed before it joined the EU, nor can it undo the gains made under the devolution settlement. It therefore looks likely that we are heading for some sort constitutional reorganisation of the governance structures in these Isles, whatever happens.

It follows that a debate about Scotland's future will emerge irrespective of whether Boris Johnson grants a Section 30 Order to enable an independence referendum to take place or not. Thus, the debate about Scotland's global footprint in the world cannot be ducked, whatever some politicians might have us believe. Furthermore, Scotland wants to know what 'Global Britain,' and its impact on it as a global citizen, actually means.

A review into the efficacy of the UK's foreign policies and institutions is both timely and necessary. Particularly, given Scotland's desire to act in support of the global rules-based order, including in relation to international peacemaking. At the heart of this debate lies the question as to what type of country Scotland wants to be. In a recent interview Douglas Alexander, the former Labour minister, described how he conceived of devolution as essentially an experiment in 'social justice.' The people of Scotland have moved on from that more limited vision.

Since 1999, Scotland's values have become more social democratic, pluralist, internationalist and rules-based in tone. They are more in keeping with the soft power, multilateral values of Northern European countries, including the Nordic Council. Such values have led to a new civic and inclusive form of Scottish national identity, based not on ethnicity but a sense of belonging to Scotland and Europe. Hence the 62 per cent vote in favour of remaining in the EU.

Boris Johnson's 'Global Britain,' on the other hand, seemingly offers a different vision. Whether both visions can exist simultaneously within a reformed unionist structure will depend upon what notions of sovereignty and 'reserved powers' prevail. Many of the issues we face are no longer 'foreign' but global. They are, as Kofi Annan reminded us, 'problems without passports,' such as climate change and conflict. They require action not only on the international level but simultaneously on the national and devolved level as well. In short, they require sovereignty to be pooled rather than just repatriated. The emergence of these global issues has real consequences for how the UK is to be governed.

More to the point, since 1999, the Scottish administration (first as an executive then government) has demonstrated its capacity to act on the international stage, both in relation to development assistance and its support of the global rules-based order. A succession of first ministers of different political hues have not only promoted Scotland economically and culturally within the EU and elsewhere through the setting up of Hubs and Scotland Houses. They have also expressed its commitment towards protecting the rule of law, combatting climate change and helping to promote peace as a global citizen of the world.

Take, for example, my own field – peacemaking, which has itself transformed over the last twenty years. Today, best practice suggests the most sustainable peace processes are those which are most inclusive and based upon respect for international norms. Research demonstrates that hard power elite bargains between diplomats and 'men with guns' have failed to transform conflict situations. It is why recent UN peace processes have developed innovative new mechanisms to include the voice of civil society, women, business, local communities and youth. The move toward more transparent peace processes favours peace support from small nation countries like Scotland.

That there is a need for such new approaches is self-evident. Western stabilisation efforts in Afghanistan, Iraq and Libya have demonstrated that hard power, by itself, cannot transform or ameliorate the impact of long-term societal violence and historical injustice. What is needed is a much more multi-layered, full-spectrum approach. Where hard power is married to soft power, and the dynamic energy of small nations and other sub-state actors – from non-state mediators, INGO's, civil society, cultural institutions, religious, business and local communities – are all harnessed in the service of peacemaking.

Now, I recognise that this analysis may sit uneasily with those who believe states and multilateral bodies should monopolise rather than share power with the sub-state and the non-state sector. But the recent failures to quell terrorism since 9/11, or predict events such as the Arab Spring or the rise of ISIS or the migrant crisis, raise serious questions about the UK's institutional ability to spot, prevent and deal with conflict in this new 21st century conflict environment.

That is because conflicts in the 21st Century are no longer interstate in nature. Like Syria, they are beset by disruption and involve an array of non-state actors, backed by shadowy spon-sors, who pay little respect to territorial boundaries, the sovereign rights of states or the law of armed conflict. In this environment the distinctions between foreign, domestic and security policy, hard and soft power, state, sub-state and non-state mediators and actors, are fast disappearing.

If my experience as a UN mediator has demonstrated anything, it is that government should not exercise a total monopoly over peace-making. Societies, rather than governments, ultimately make peace and rebuild shattered communities and if a government wants to help stabilise a country, it has to reach out and understand its culture and people first. This requires an altogether more radical, innovative, asymmetrical approach towards international peacemaking. Let me then set out why Scotland has already made a unique contribution in this new field of peacemaking and should be allowed to do so in any constitutional arrangement going forward.

Unique Branding

Over the course of the last twenty years, I have been struck by how emerging leaders from around the world embrace Scotland as a small, distinct, but vibrant, soft power nation, with an extraordinary histor-ical brand, that somehow speaks to their own experiences. Whether deserved or not, it is perceived as a proud, independent nation which has managed to preserve its culture and identity, despite the presence of a much more powerful neighbour. As such it appears to exercise a powerful hold over the world's collective imagination, particularly with small nations and groups.

Neutral Platform

Scotland is well placed to provide a safe space and platform to many groups involved in conflict so that they might discuss dif-ferences in an atmosphere of trust, away from the hothouse of the conflict. Scotland can do this because it is viewed as neutral host, despite being part of a P5 state. For better or worse, it is not associated with votes in favour of military intervention in Iraq or Afghanistan or Libya and is seen and treated differently from that of 'England' or 'Britain.' This gives it a unique perch in interna-tional peacemaking.

History of Dialogue

That Scotland can be a platform for dialogue in the service of peace-making is not a new idea. The Edinburgh International Festival was founded in 1948 in an effort to bring a shattered world together in the aftermath of WWII. The Edinburgh Dialogues, that took place during the Cold War, saw foes from across the capitalist and communist divide come together to unpack and explore seminal geopolitical issues. More recently in the 1990s, Angus Robertson chose a small Speyside town, Craigellachie, in Scotland for reconciliation talks between two former Soviet allies in association with the NGO links.

Beyond Borders

In 2010, with the help of elder statespeople from across the political divide, I established Beyond Borders Scotland, a Scottish organisation dedicated to promoting mutual understanding between different nations, groups and cultures through international dialogue and cultural exchange. Since 2010 Beyond Borders has built upon this legacy of dialogue through its festivals and dialogue platforms.

For example in 2011, together with the Democratic Progress Institute, it brought parliamentarians and opinion formers from across the Turkish and Kurdish political divide to Scotland to broaden the basis for peace in Turkey in respect of its 2011–13 peace process. A similar space was provided in 2012 to Bahraini representatives involved in an effort to support national dialogue, with the help of Chatham House (London) and Beyond Conflict (Boston).

It is also why members of the Ukrainian Government Party of the Regions came to Scotland in late 2013 when deciding whether to sign an EU association agreement. The decision not to join the EU led to revolution. However, in a fitting postscript, we were able to build a dialogue process in the east of the country for the Geneva-based Centre of Humanitarian Dialogue because of the trust and goodwill built up by Beyond Borders and the John Smith Memorial Trust, which over the last 21 years has brought emerging young leaders from all the former Soviet republics to Scotland to learn lessons about good governance.

UN *Ties*

Scotland's ties with the UN system are increasing. Its capacity to facilitate dialogue was graphically illustrated when the UN Special Envoy to Syria Staffan de Mistura deployed Scottish resources in support of the UN-facilitated Syrian Peace Process. This was after the UN Security Council came together over Syria in December 2015 to pass SC Resolution 2254, which called for peace talks and a negotiated political transition.

De Mistura was keen to show Syrians it was possible to affect a political transition and create a new Parliament in relatively short order, provided the requisite political will was there. He also wanted to build a new, inclusive, gender-sensitive, peace process that provided for the participation of women and broader civil society. That is why in October 2015, in the run-up to negotiations, de Mistura and I stopped off between Moscow and Washington to meet with Nicola Sturgeon to explore Scotland's gender parity cabinet and how its Parliament came about.

At that time, Scotland boasted three female party political leaders and a speaker of Parliament. De Mistura was so impressed he took the Syrian Women Advisory Board to Scotland the day after the Scottish Parliamentary elections of 2016. There they met with all party leaders from the Parliament. They then spent a week in the Scottish Borders establishing their objectives and working procedures with the Special Envoy for the peace process.

The neutral, calm space was important as the Board consisted of representatives from both sides, many of whom had lost sons and husbands. It would have been impossible to send such a delegation to London due to the UK's P5 status and general hostility towards the Syrian government; yet, somehow Scotland was seen as different. Even the First Minister noticed how the Board visibly relaxed over the week as they bonded and established important working relationships. A similar safe space and technical expertise was later provided to the Women's Technical Group of the UN Special Envoy to Yemen, Martin Griffiths, when he came to Edinburgh in 2019 and met with Nicola Sturgeon and the staff of Yemeni Voices, a digital peace initiative which he sponsored.

Experience of Political Transition

Scotland can also offer unique insights into a critical issue that international peacemakers have to deal with – namely how to negotiate and effect a political transition and/or a devolution and transfer of power away from the centre to the periphery, without recourse to violence. Both of the Special Envoys cited above recognised Scotland had a phenomenal story to tell in relation to these critical issues.

They understood that its political and constitutional transition offers one of the best examples of how smaller nations within larger states can transition towards greater democracy in a peaceful and consensual manner. It provides both a template and point of discussion for others confronted by a similar need for change. Thus, the 2012 Edinburgh Agreement is often regarded as a conflict resolution instrument in all but name. That is to say nothing of Scotland's practical experience of holding referenda and national dialogues.

Scotland can also help others to think through how to assert and exercise the right to self-determination in a non-violent, consensual manner. One need only look at Catalonia to see what might happen when such processes are not agreed, properly mediated or thought out. This gives Scotland a particular traction with small nations and groups in the EU as well as with those embarking on political transitions or seeking to assert the right to self-determination elsewhere.

Devolution

Scotland's practical experience of devolution is also important. Since 1998, I have worked on a myriad of conflicts in places such as Turkey, Iraq, Sri Lanka, Libya, Syria, Ukraine, Zimbabwe, and Spain. All of them feature disputes over the devolution of power within the context of a negotiated political transition. Virtually all of the conflict players I dealt with were interested in Scotland's story from one perspective or another.

Thus, in 2012 the Scottish Borders played host to a number of Basque politicians and thinkers, intent on finding a solution to the Basque problem – their work helped end the violence between the Spanish State and Euskadi Ta Askatasuna (ETA). In 2017, members of Edinburgh University law department worked in tandem with Beyond Borders and the Swiss Ministry of Foreign Affairs, to provide space and technical support at Traquair House in the Scottish Borders to lawyers and judges from the Sinhalese and Tamil communities, in an effort to agree a new devolved settlement in Sri Lanka, following the election of a new president.

Cultural Platforms

Scotland also helps peacemakers through its world famous cultural festivals. They can be used to explore and ameliorate conflict, as well promote reconciliation and forgiveness. In fact, such capacities have been tested out over the last ten years through the Beyond Borders International Festival of Literature and Thought. It has brought together a multitude of artists, thought and civic leaders from numerous conflict zones around the world to express and share their experiences. The demand for this type of peace engagement has grown exponentially – it is noticeably how other book festivals and mediums are increasingly promoting these types of exchanges.

Such platforms not only promote mutual understanding, but they also help engender healing and provide civil society with alternative mechanisms to make interventions into peace processes. For example, when the exiled President of Catalonia came to the Beyond Borders Festival in 2018, he came with a message of unconditional dialogue for the new Spanish socialist prime minister. It began a process that, in time, led to the pardoning of all Catalonian politicians convicted of alleged sedition for the holding of an alleged unconstitutional referendum.

Conflict Expertise

Scotland also has at its disposal a wide variety of expert and educational resources to deploy in the service of peacemaking. Its international relations, law and conflict resolution departments at Edinburgh, Glasgow, St Andrews, Aberdeen and Dundee Universities have enormous experience in conflict analysis and policy programming. The Political Settlements Programme run by Professor Christine Bell at Edinburgh University gives regular support to conflict parties and peacemakers tasked with drafting peace agreements. This is to say nothing of the work of Scotland's civil society institutions, development charities and community organisations who work closely with local communities in conflict zones across the globe.

Digital Capacity

Scotland's digital and infographics communities are leading the way in supporting digital peace work. In 2018 Beyond Borders Scotland and Edinburgh University teamed up with the London School of

Economics to develop Yemeni Voices, sponsored by the Office of
the UN Special Envoy to Yemen. It developed a number of proto-
type digital tools and participatory forms of inclusive participation
for peace processes. Some of its dialogue apps and approaches were
later taken up by the UN Department of Political and Peacebuilding Affair's Innovation Unit, which ran the first, large-scale, inclusive digital dialogue with communities across Yemen in 2019. The
development of the app PeaceFem by Bell's Settlement Programme is
another such example.

Diplomatic Experience

Scotland can also deploy a unique collection of Scottish elder statespeople with real experience of government and multilateral diplomacy at the highest level within the EU, NATO and the UN Security
Council, unlike other smaller nations involved in international
peacemaking. Beyond Borders and other consultancies in Scotland
have deployed such experience in their work, including helping other
parliamentarians and legal institutions to reform and improve their
parliamentary processes in places such as in Oman and Iraq, often
with the help of the FCO.

Global Citizen

Scotland has its own obligations to discharge as a global citizen in
its own right. Numerous recent international instruments now place
duties on sub-state and non-state actors, including in relation to climate
change, human rights, poverty alleviation, development and peacemaking. For example, UN Security Council Resolution 1325 calls upon
all parties and institutions to promote women's inclusion in peacemaking processes. Elsewhere, the Scottish Government has developed relations with UN Women and other UN bodies involved in climate change.
This emerging new international architecture makes a mockery of the
current rigid 'reserved powers' arrangement in which global issues are
seemingly characterised as exclusively foreign policy ones.

Women and Gender

It is within this broader context that the Scottish Government's commitment to the international Women, Peace and Security Agenda

should be seen. In 2015, Beyond Borders Scotland ran a women's peacemaking fellowship pilot with help of the Brussels-based European Institute of Peace to test Scotland's capacity. This, together with the UN's experience of Scotland cited earlier, convinced the Scottish Government in 2016 to fund the BB 1325 Women in Conflict Peacemaking Fellowship Programme for one year, aided by the expertise of the UN's Mediation Support Unit. Its success led to the First Minister committing a further four years of funding when visiting the UN Headquarters in New York in 2017. Since then, the Fellowship Programme has brought 250 women peacemakers to Scotland to create a unique 'community of practice', promoting women's participation in peacemaking across the world.

This is but one of a growing set of examples as to how Scotland can, and should, be allowed to play a greater role in international affairs: today its 1325 Alumnae Programme is actively involved in supporting peace efforts in places like Syria, Yemen and Afghanistan, where it helped to establish the Afghan Mechanism of Inclusive Peace, which is linked into the Doha Process; it is working on peace research programmes, such as Yemeni Voices and the International Norms Project run by the LSE; and it is also helping to devise a new climate change, gender and conflict resolution framework, discussed at The New York Times Climate Hub at COP26 in Glasgow.

In short, the Scottish Government funded 1325 Fellowship and Alumnae Programmes to bring together all the strengths that Scotland has at its disposal, to help the international community to promote peace. Quite why Westminster would see it in the public interest to cull such activities is beyond my comprehension. People in Scotland want to see their government project their values onto the international stage in support of Scotland's global obligations. If they are estopped from doing so, the clamour for independence will only grow ever stronger.

Thus, as the four nations of the UK, and indeed Europe and the wider world, digest and come to terms with the full implications of the UK leaving the EU, it ill behoves any policymaker serious about peacemaking not to recognise Scotland's growing desire and capacity to act on the international stage in support of it and the global rules-based order.

Whether this should be conducted through a devolved arrangement or an independent state is for the people of Scotland to ultimately decide. But the positive values that underpin Scotland's internationalism and humanitarianism, as demonstrated through its commitment to peacemaking, can only make it a greater force for good in the world, whatever its constitutional future turns out to be.

That is why this book is so timely and important. It sets the scene for one of the most important political debates and dialogues that Scotland is likely to face for generations.

Last Words

A Different Kind of Campaign and Debate?
Hannah Graham, Maike Dinger, Paul Sweeney, Allan Whyte and Fatima Zahra Joji, with Simon Barrow and Gerry Hassan

In the process of drawing together our own reflections on the varied and thoughtful contributions to this book, the co-editors convened a roundtable discussion involving two people who had campaigned on different sides in the 2014 referendum, two academics (special thanks to Hannah Graham for acting as chair), and one person involved in a civic independence campaign seeking to communicate with hesitant or undecided people. The purpose was to ask whether a different kind of campaign and debate is possible around constitutional questions, and looking at their relation to Scottish society and politics more broadly.

The participants all share a common concern for achieving a more equal and just Scotland, for eliminating poverty, promoting inclusion, and tackling the climate emergency through a genuinely just transition away from a fossil fuel economy. Yet they have held (and continue to hold) different views on Scotland's future away from, or as part of, the United Kingdom. Our conversation did not dwell on details concerning the range of constitutional possibilities, but looked instead at how they are framed and developed within a wider set of political concerns. We began, importantly and unsurprisingly, with the impact of the pandemic.

Allan (Voices for Scotland): 'We have been through a lot of changes personally. COVID-19 has impacted how we engage with people generally, as well as our family and friends – and that effects how we engage with political and social issues, and with the question of independence. It's only as we have our sense of freedom returning that we might actually start to process what we've all been through, and what impact that's had on us individually and collectively.'

Fatima (Aberdeen Independence Movement): 'I agree with Allan. The pandemic has forced us to rethink things, to look more deeply at issues such as health, wellbeing and the environment. Practically it has made campaign groups such as ourselves look at how we deliver our message across different platforms, too. We've been forced to be creative, and it has made us try to be more accessible. So I feel we're reaching a wider audience now.'

Maike (researcher): 'There's certainly more awareness of how neglected health issues and the NHS has been. Now we're seeing similar thing with the climate crisis. But, without wanting to be negative, I don't know if that really changes things. Because we have been aware of these issues for some time. From a research perspective, I have observed both nationalists and unionists trying to position themselves as positively as possible in relation to these questions, but it's not clear how much difference this has really made to the debate.'

Paul (Labour MSP): 'My experience has been that Scottish politics has been in paralysis for a while, because there are entrenched positions and bad faith is assumed as well. So you're defined in terms of one side or other of a binary constitutional position, and that colours everyone else's opinion of your situation. The pandemic has further entrenched that position in some quarters. But what we're also seeing is an increasing amount of interaction about practical policies that will drive public debate forward and help it to be less defined by constitutional politics. One example I've been involved in has been the drug reform debate. It's an urgent crisis, and people of goodwill can come together to fix this problem. I think that's actually quite an encouraging sign – while on the margins you've seen an aggressive kind of identity politics in the form of Alba, perhaps, and also a very violent sort of Ulster-style unionism. So that's bubbling away at the extremes of the debate.'

Allan: 'I wonder if that's a general malaise, or if there are, in fact, a growing number of people who are tired of that divisive style, who want to get to the real issues, and who are not willing to engage with extremes posed in that way? We are certainly finding conversations which are far better than that.'

Fatima: 'Whether we like it or not, our identity affects the outcome of our life experience. That has certainly been shown through the pandemic. If you're a woman it's real. If you're trans, it's real. If you're disabled, it's real. All of this does affect how you navigate Scottish society, and it certainly shapes how you fear the outcome of the independence debate one way or another, too. If I saw certain groups leading our charge to the independence, I'd be scared about my place as a Muslim woman. But equally, what's going on in the UK in terms of migration and racism, say, is scary.'

Simon (co-editor): 'It feels like we all agree, from different starting positions, that any debate about Scotland's future needs to be shaped by the big issues – COVID, climate, poverty, migration – their impact on people's lives, and what can be done about them?'

Allan: 'Yes, but it's a question of what choices those issues require. The pandemic has illustrated that we are all vulnerable, but also that our systems are failing the *most* vulnerable. It's about which systems, where, and how to change them.'

Paul: 'I think there can be a red herring in all of this. The independence debate seems to be stuck on the referendum, rather than the actual pros and cons of a separate state and other constitutional possibilities, and what lies within and beyond all that. Is the question a repeat, essentially, of 2014? Or does it need to evolve beyond that to something else? Virtue in pronouncements or wishes is one thing, but practical delivery is another. Take energy politics in Scotland. Yes, indeed, there is great potential for renewables, but basically all of the infrastructure for renewable energy is foreign owned and imported. So in terms of delivering an industrial supply chain in Scotland, there's not really a policy to do that. Is that an issue of constitutional politics? Or is it a failure of political economy?'

Fatima: 'I think it's partly down to the fact that politics isn't really accessible. A lot of people who are marginalised from the debate are the people who are most directly impacted by the policy decisions that happen in this country – whether its migration, poverty, climate or something else. These are the people who don't really have a voice. So how are we supposed to be able to ensure that we move forward with our politics when these people are pushed to the sidelines? Politics is often seen as something for the rich, for people with connections. We need to move away from exclusionary politics.'

Maike: 'For many, 2014 provided what looked like a choice and an alternative. Rightly or wrongly, people felt that something could change...'

Allan: 'That's a lot of what we try to do in Voices for Scotland – to take party politics, big personalities and labels out of it, to try to move away from this idea that it's a binary question. We need to recognise that a simple Yes or No isn't where many people are, or where the political movement is. People are on a spectrum. We need new and innovative ways to reach a fresh audience for the issues that matter. What we can do together is to create positive ideas for the new country we want to be: but that only comes from speaking to people, engagement. Otherwise the whole idea of independence becomes meaningless. If you get the same people at the table time and time again, telling other people what they need, that isn't real change. You need to talk to people to find out what they need, what they want. And that's the basis of the blueprint for a better Scotland, that's how to shape the country that we need and the powers that we need to be that country.'

Fatima: 'I agree strongly about engagement being the key to tackling the causes of poverty and much else...'

It was interesting to note at this point in the conversation that people with different constitutional positions were agreeing that the current framing of the debate could easily become cosmetic, avoiding tough issues of power and the need for a popular politics that challenges who decides what, and how.

Maike: 'While there are disagreements about where powers do or should lie, and while that effects outcomes, people on all sides sense that there's a need to explore opportunities for what we can do right now, rather than endlessly deferring to what might be possible in some changed future.'

Paul: 'I found it really interesting going to the Batley and Spen by election, and getting there a feeling for the same sense of alienation that I encountered in 2014 in the north of Glasgow. This idea that the political system doesn't respond to my material situation. The debate doesn't engage with me, therefore the disruptive option becomes attractive. People thinking or feeling that 'this current system is actually oppressive. This is an option for me to liberate myself somehow. Even though what we are going towards is unclear, at least it's going to shatter the status quo. That's a really interesting impetus which, I think, was definitely a feature of the 2014 referendum – and probably, to an extent, in England with the Brexit situation as well. It was definitely the eruption of a sense of rebellion against the establishment. But that's where we need to pay attention to what's really on offer, such as an economic prospectus written by Charlotte Street Partners. This has started to create tension within the debate in Scotland. Beyond the idea of the independence movement being a big coalition based around some very broad principles of improvement, liberation and democracy lies the question of who is really in control. The risk is that if you achieve this outcome then people are going to end up feeling disappointed that the power structures haven't really changed. That the class system still operates, along with the international dimension of the oppression of the Global South. I don't think that necessarily featured in the debate among people in Glasgow who wanted change because it was something that would upset the status quo. Would it ultimately deliver?'

Simon: 'That question about who owns and runs Scotland, for and with whom, is obviously fundamental – and it applies both to the current devolved situation within a divided and unequal UK, and also to how independence would be shaped, and who would have power to do the shaping.'

Fatima: 'My thinking and activism – in relation to violence against women, to independence, and to other political issues – comes from the foundations of poverty and inequality. That's the biggest issue making or breaking people's ability to speak and be heard. That's why I keep coming back to the issue of accessibility in politics as being really crucial.'

Allan: 'I think we need to organise more and mobilise less. What I mean by that is that a traditional political campaign is based around mobilisation: you have a central organisation, and as a political party, or as a single issue campaign, that you have a particular viewpoint and you mobilise people to support that viewpoint. What we need to do more of, however, is help people to organise themselves to have more power, to make the changes they need for their communities, for society and in their lives. That ought to reshape the agenda of parties and campaigns. It's about independence and interdependence starting from where people are.'

Maike: 'I think it's very important to recognise that we live in a neo-liberal capitalist society marked by classism, by racism, and by division over the social issues that shape our experience. So, yes, reconnecting politics through the lived experiences of people with different beliefs and backgrounds is crucial. Recognising this as a first step is so important, because then you recognise your own privilege in relation to others – and also the way we communicate, who has access to education, and so on. How we depict issues and how we relate to other people makes a real difference: communicating that people can make change, that they are important, their experiences matter. If we want to address bigger issues effectively we have to encourage activism on a smaller scale, to see the deep connections between the two.'

Paul: 'Talking of connections and disconnections, although I voted No in 2014, most of the people I'm working with in my office voted Yes. So it's an interesting discussion to look at how we arrived at those different positions, even though we share a lot of the same ideas, the same analysis of society class, and want to see the same policies implemented. I think what we ended up doing was almost rounding up or rounding down to what we thought was the best and arriving at a junction point – one where you have to decide which fork in road to take. It's not that we thought all would be perfect, it was about the way to go to best effect the outcome we all wish to see.

So it's not about flags but what's best for my community and to achieve change. I think that's really fertile ground to have a more interesting discussion about Scottish politics, the power structures that operate in Scotland, ideas about how the economy and land is owned and run – not just within the context of devolution, and the Scottish Parliament, but locally too. We have to get beyond this idea that everybody holds back and then we explode into an outcome, which is either an independent state or not. For me it's about evolving a new system that people are building anyway. That's historically what the Labour Party has been about – building that kind of power structure that gives working-class people representation and power. In 2014 we were seen as agent of denying change, aligned with the Tories. That destroyed a lot of the credibility we had with people and it's a big challenge for the party. We can't be unconditionally supportive of the status quo. The British state as it is now in unsustainable. So we have to have an ultimatum, if you like, for change, based on engagement with the issues of power.'

Allan: 'I wonder if there is a shift or an evolution in politics moving away from what was traditionally viewed as left and right – that people are more focused on issues that affect their lives, on single issues, and they don't relate to political parties in the way that they once did. So maybe the things people really care about and can get involved in are more community based, and perhaps that is the future, and that the answer about how to achieve better engagement is getting people together to coalesce around particular issues, but collectively, so that it points towards that better society?'

Fatima: 'Yes, but left and right are lenses through which we look at different political and economic questions, coming with different assumptions, interests and aims in terms of what we want to achieve. Also issues are not single, they are part of a whole. We need multiple lenses.'

Simon: 'I'd suggest that although divisions have opened up – stoked by those who fear change, perhaps – over so-called 'culture wars', and although people on the left (more than the right) find themselves in different positions when it comes to an issue like independence, left and right are still real when it comes to the analysis of power, who holds it and how it is used. What is being challenged, rightly, are the cultures of tribalism that continue to infuse our politics – the structures and attitudes that stop as coming together when we need to.'

Maike: 'I think it's also so important to mention the media, which we haven't talked about so far. Because that obviously is a huge factor in the public debate, how we frame issues, and how we relate to them. Maybe there isn't time to go into detail about that, but we need to acknowledge it.'

Allan: 'I think in terms of engagement, and getting people connected to the issues that matter, it's important that we find ways to bypass the mainstream media, and social media as well, in a certain sense. Also to become the media ourselves. Because they are such an arena for partisan politics. Yeah, I mean, if you want an argument, everyone knows that you go to Twitter. And that's not helpful. But that doesn't automatically mean that we can't do better. Because we can.'

Gerry: 'Yes, both the media – and its incredibly unequal ownership – and the wider sense of how we platform and frame public conversations at national and community level is incredibly important. That includes social media, and conversations within neighbourhoods and families where people are starting with the kind of tiredness and anxiety we have all been through, in different ways, in the last couple of years with COVID. All this touches the human issues of people's sense of loss, uncertainty and doubt. We have been brave enough to acknowledge that in terms of how we have been talking together, which has been good. Being prepared to face difficulty and doubt within our own positions.

So although we will all still probably walk away from this engaging roundtable conversation with different intentions towards any future referendum, we all seem to be agreed that politics is not and should not be reducible to a top-down, binary constitutional question – independence versus the union as the be all and end all. That isn't helpful, either to the issues we've kept coming back to, or to a way of framing constitutional choices actually. The Scotland that people want to live in involves dealing with the real issues at hand, so that we don't end up having a debate which, is in reality, a phoney war, based on binary thinking all round.'

Hannah: 'As a final thought here, we are interacting with difference all the time within our families, at work, and in our communities. That can be difficult. But it can also be a really important arena to learn to communicate better, to make decisions, to hear one another, to find out when and how to engage and when and how not to engage. So although we have been talking about big questions and how they are framed, we can also recognise that crossing the divide is not impossible.'

―――――

Our thanks to all who took part in this conversation. This partial and heavily edited transcript only captures part of what we were able to share. But we hope it highlights the interconnection of some of the issues discussed in this book in a human way.

The Shape of Things to Come
Simon Barrow and Gerry Hassan

IT FEELS SALUTARY that this book was entering its final stages while the Russia–Ukraine crisis was emerging. That puts into sharp perspective the future of Europe, and the role Scotland may have in that – either as an independent nation, or as a continuing part of a United Kingdom which is still in post-Brexit turmoil. The preceding chapters looking at defence, security and international policy touch on these issues, but snap judgements are neither possible nor advisable. In some cases, the pace of events outstrips political process. In the case of Russia and Europe there will be no quick answers.

More salient for the overall focus of this book is the week that marked the seventh anniversary of the 2014 independence referendum. That was a day of mixed emotions: relief and rejoicing for some, and deep disappointment for others. But, as has been signalled throughout this book, the Scotland of 2021 is a very different proposition to that of 2014, and we can rest assured that the Scotland of 2022 and beyond will change still further. Brexit, dramatically divergent political trajectories among the four nations of the UK, Boris Johnson occupying Downing Street, the SNP-Green agreement at Holyrood, a life-changing COVID pandemic, and the global-local threat of the climate emergency are among the significant changes which have seen to that.

This ought to mean that the future independence debate and independence referendum will look and feel very different to previous experience. Not all of this is positive. First the UK government will do everything it can to resist new a poll on independence, throwing up delaying tactics and questioning the extent of a Scottish mandate. Second, independence supporters rightly cite the successive victories in the 2016 and 2021 Scottish elections and pro-independence parliamentary majorities, and assert that this cannot forever be denied.

Yet the picture is more complex for both sides. A UK government that continually thwarts Scottish demands for a referendum based on parliamentary and popular votes, as Ciaran Martin set out in his 2021 lecture and contribution to this book, fundamentally alters the nature of the union and issues of power, legitimacy and consent (Martin, 2021). Such a move would have a lasting impact in undermining the basis of the union. But it is equally true that mandates for far-reaching change are about more than winning a parliamentary election in seats and being the largest party. Mandates are not legally binding concepts but won and rewon in the shifting sands of public opinion, and in an environment defined by uncertainty and COVID concerns it is clear that Scottish public opinion is, for now, in flux.

The independence debate cannot become stuck in the quagmire of process without substance. Focusing on who has the right to call and not call a referendum has its point, but aids a politics of stand-offs and gridlock which, as we have seen, can reinforce the hold of the Conservatives and uber-partisans on the pro-independence and pro-union sides, and reinforce the interplay between rival nationalisms. It is something that has to be resisted, and space needs to be made – to which this volume contributes – to address wider issues of policy, ideas and thinking; centred on the challenges that Scotland faces and the kind of future our society would like to embrace. In this, a politics about the *abstracts* of independence versus the union, while attractive to some of the most passionate believers, does not get us far down this road, instead reinforcing a culture of *absolutes* among the true believers.

One mediating issue will be the attitudes and resources mustered in public life, and whether there can be progress towards a politics closer to people's daily lives and experiences. This will require marshalling the skills and talents of a myriad array of organisations, NGOs and civil society groups in raising questions about pluralism and diversity and their relationship to the media and public sphere. As several of the contributions make clear the voices of voters beyond the trench lines has to be heard: those who are in flux, undecided and uncommitted – including the 'missing Scotland' that is always with us in the continual conversation that is democracy.

Who then will resource and support these critical activities? To offer one example which could readily be replicated in the future: in the run-up to the 2014 vote, the Church of Scotland pioneered 'respectful dialogue' with a number of communities and faith groups through a programme called Imagining Scotland's Future. This brought people from across the spectrum of constitutional views together to look into 'Future Scotland', not starting from pro- or anti-independence positions, but addressing issues of substance. The participation was street level, and most who took part were not advocates for Yes or No, but were non-partisan. This listening-based programme principally ran pre-vote, but there were also public events post-vote (Church of Scotland, 2014). The process involved getting people to prioritise concerns and actions, and poverty and equality were among the issues ranked high. Many of the issues discussed as part of this programme, modelled around public and participatory deliberations about a model constitution in Iceland, resonated with the 'life-choice' concerns explored below.

Scotland's Crucial Life-Choices

For some, the supposed chilling prospects of a 'divisive' second referendum makes them wary of another such debate. But to succumb to fears is to diminish democracy itself – and to sideline the issue of who should decide some of the most life-changing questions Scotland faces. These include, as a matter of some urgency over the coming few years and beyond, seven fundamental challenges: the transition from a planet-consuming carbon economy to a sustainable post- fossil fuel one; reordering society and the world of work in relation to the new post-industrial revolution of automation, robotification and AI; the urgent need to tackle poverty, ill-health, drug abuse, and inequality; creating wellbeing social/economic security for all; our future within Europe and the world; the need to change a distorted relationship with the land and our natural environment – something which has pushed us all towards the threatening new dawn of a pandemic-ridden future; and issues of defence and security, including the choice about nuclear weapons.

It is interesting to compare these seven life-choice challenges with the fabric of the seven core arguments for, and seven core arguments against, independence as set out in our introductory chapter. It is worth asking: do the predominant political arguments which presently drive support and opposition for Scottish self-government (which ought to be a positive case for independence versus a positive case for the union) effectively map and respond to these life-choice challenges, at least four of which could be deemed truly 'existential'? Do the cases for and against an independent Scotland help us see who should be tackling such fundamental issues, with accountability to whom, and how? If they don't, what does that say about the kind of debates we are currently caught up in, how they need to be recast, and how can we realistically aid these activities now?

Equally, if the seven crucial challenges listed above really do condition Scotland's prospects for the rest of this century at least – how do we get them to the top of the political and media agenda in relation to constitutional and other public issues? And who is the 'we' that can do this? What kind of agency beyond political parties can address these concerns, with the decline of old forms of mobilising such as trade unions and churches, professionalisation of NGOs and incorporation of much of the voluntary sector?

The seven key issues set out cannot be solved by isolationism. Rather, they require common will and purpose, within and across national boundaries. That poses the question, implicit and explicit in the preceding pages, about the possible shape of an independence which demonstrably takes interdependence and internationalism seriously. Or, equally, a new dispensation of the nations, regions and people of the UK which challenges the current status quo and power dispensation, does not see devolution or the chimera of federalism as the answer, and transcends the claims of any nationalism.

This requires the Scottish constitutional debate to address the issue of the nation having 25–35 per cent of Europe's on and offshore renewable potential. The different economic and social approach is there to be championed, but has to involve more than the standard citing of 'just transition' and being 'carbon neutral'. Rather, it has to address issues of economic ownership and autonomy and the degree of economic independence and choice a self-governing Scotland can expect to exercise in a world defined by capitalist relations. And that is before we get to the continued influence of neo-liberalism in political elites including Scotland, and the problem of the British state and the fact that it is at its political centre a neo-liberal state. As Paul Mason explores in his contribution, Scottish independence has to address a series of interconnected crises – including the climate crisis, a bust economic model, breaking free from neo-liberalism and breaking out from the British state – which will require progressive allies across rUK and is in the interests of a 'progressive alliance' involving Labour and Greens outside Scotland.

The Importance of Political Community

Who then do we put our political faith in to make key decisions about our collective future? Who will engage with us as citizens rather than subjects? Those central matters of trust, engagement, proximity and legitimacy can be regarded as the key elements in constituting a 'political community' based on a set of mediating structures and relationships. Political community developed along these lines becomes strong and sustainable when people with different views, resources and investments tangibly experience commonality and shared interest across, and in spite of, their differences. That requires hard work, imagination and the structures to bring people together, facilitate deliberation, and establish connections.

It is exactly this shared political community that many believe to have been breaking down so palpably across the increasingly ill-named United Kingdom in recent years. It is part of what has maintained strong support for independence in Scotland, and a growing Yes Cymru movement in Wales. Its concomitant erosion in parts of England and Wales, especially, is arguably what led to the narrow Brexit vote in 2016, and to further divisions which have continued to flow from that. Some will of course see another independence referendum in Scotland as a further example of a deepening fissure of the 'ties that bind' across the UK. A possible Yes vote for independence will mean further fracture from their point of view.

Scottish independence can be characterised in various ways by a range of communities. It can be argued that it offers a very different dynamic to the cause and effect of Brexit, because it is about rejoining the EU and forging a partnership with rUK, in place of the current unequal union. The 'Scexit' designation of Scottish self-government seems deliberately politically charged from that perspective, ignoring as it does the fact that most arguments for independence involve pooling sovereignty in the search for a self-directed national model, whereas the 'hard Brexit' that leading Leavers wrestled out of a much vaguer 2016 referendum result led to an absolutist understanding of sovereignty as something singular and inviolable.

For these reason and others, it is surely of the utmost importance to reconsider independence, and the arguments for and against it, precisely in the light of the sustenance and nourishing of political community within Scotland. One that begs questions of what a lived political community is and what membership of that bestows on people in terms of rights and responsibilities, formal and informal.

An additional challenge is that differences within Scotland underline that existence of multiple political communities within the nation rather than one over-arching community and set of identities. Switching governance from London to Edinburgh may not be seen to be a significant enough change to persuade those living in rural communities of independence, for example. As Benedict Anderson has observed, nations and the nationalisms of various kinds are in part 'imagined communities' (Anderson, 1983). But the imagining and realising of community does not happen at this level alone. This is another potential gap between political rhetoric on the one hand, and the practical politics of performance on the other – something which has continued to push many people away from feeling that they can really vote and make a difference. The independence/union debate provides an opportunity to re-address that concern, and will be found wanting if it does not. While detailed decisions about further decentralisation might be considered post-independence, they may also indicate whether what is at stake is about sharing power or another kind of power grab.

One and Many Scotlands: The Making of a Modern Political Community

One question that persists around independence is what constitutes a defining and acceptable majority to both Yes and No and which brings forth 'loser's consent' after a future vote. Many on the No side feel that the Yes side never accepted the validity of the 2014 vote, or paid lip service to it, and then as soon as they could, in light of the 2016 Brexit vote, sought to overturn and reverse 2014. This brings forth charge and counter-charge of No saying that Yes claimed 2014 was a 'once in a generation' vote, and Yes pointing out that No had said the way to guarantee Scotland leaving the EU in 2014 was to vote Yes. Somehow we have to be able to transcend such a politics of whataboutery, and aspire to create an environment where a future vote and result is widely accepted. That brings forth questions about the size of the majority in percent and numbers, turnout, and period between referendums – all of which relate to the real, lived 'political community' we invoked earlier.

This requires a political mindset and intelligence comfortable with multiple Scotlands and multiple political identities – something regularly given credence to but which many oppose in their actions. This is why language like 'Are You Yes Yet?', 'independence is inevitable', and the 'why not?' argument (which says that Scotland is a nation and therefore should automatically be independent) – while appealing to some – can often seem unhelpful, alienating and presumptuous to those who are not yet persuaded, who do not see Scotland outside the UK as inevitable. In order to shift, people need to feel respected and secure. Reassurance is not always taken seriously enough in political campaigning. But when it is about shifting people towards a change in the status of their nation and of their identity, the need for it is central.

Any independence referendum will have 'winners' and 'losers' – that is an inevitable outcome of such a process. How to move from division to inclusion in the aftermath of the result is not just about how to win but about how to persuade, dispel fear, and encourage doubters and switchers in the process of winning, and how to move quickly from victory for just some to what looks more like a winnable position for all (or as many as possible). The extent that the independence debate has become to some a 'culture war', especially on social media, needs to be reversed. We are not more or less 'Scottish' according to how we vote, for example. 'Othering' has the effect of hardening divisions rather than resolving or dissolving them, and ramping up fear about what a move to for independence would mean, is likely to dissuade rather than convince. Making what you are offering attractive to more than just your own group is a key skill in extending the political table and getting people to gather around it.

People, Purpose and Persuasion

What it is that motivates people to change or resist change – by which we mean a majority of people in everyday life, not simply the representatives of contending political classes? The three key issues here seem to be that all-important sense of security (in which economy will play a key role); narratives of possibility that either connect with people or leave them cold; and the issue of overall framing – how it is done, who it is done by, and whose strengths and weaknesses it embodies.

The security factor is one that the No campaign played in 2014 – with worries about currency, pensions and economic viability large factors in the 55 per cent No majority. In the light of Brexit, the handling of the COVID pandemic, sleaze and corruption questions around Westminster, and its general disregard for Scotland's interests, the opportunity will exist for the Yes side to talk about risk the other way round. The status quo is not in fact a stasis. It is dynamic and the huge shift away from the EU that took place in 2016 illustrates that with considerable force.

But the ecology of defensiveness, as we observed in our introduction, is not nearly enough in itself – especially for a No campaign that relied heavily on it in 2014, and which will now be on the backfoot over both the credibility of its previous claims, and the record of the UK government since then. If Labour inch ahead in the Westminster polls ahead of the next Scottish referendum, that will allow centre-left anti-independence advocates to open the door to a 'change is possible' narrative. This is where the question of framing becomes particularly crucial. In 2014 the territory on which key arguments were deployed was substantially the home turf of the union. This time, it may swing in a different direction. That is a proactive task. It is also not certain that the Exocets of economic anxiety towards Yes which were so effective in 2014 will be quite so effective in a future vote: being repeated but at higher amplification and shorn of any positive appeal and agenda. Then again that is a challenge for a future No campaign to undertake serious work on, which has to entail yet more claims from Gordon Brown and others that the UK is somehow inching 'towards federalism', when all the evidence is the opposite and the political centre of the UK being in denial that it is the part of the problem.

The turning point becomes how an independent Scotland might offer a better and more hopeful future in realistic terms, and how it can contribute to the healing of political wounds more widely, rather than simply remaining the key point of contention. Likewise, if the union is to be sustained, it faces the serious question of how it will need to change and be reformed in relation to those wider-than-simply-political issues in Scotland (trust, respect, the desire for security and prosperity) so that it is credible and workable, and not simply the default position one returns to out of fear about the alternative.

A key issue in all this is the matter of emotional intelligence in relation to politics, to which several contributors explicitly refer. This is a challenge to both campaigns, because most advocates for and against independence are deeply immersed in politics, whereas many voters are not. It is not just better arguments which will be needed, but more human connection, honesty and empathy. As we argue in the introduction, in uncertain times people are turned off by the kind of brash certainty that appears over-confident and prone to displays of condescension or superiority. A sense of honest realism, matched by evidence of competence and authority, is more persuasive. But on the independence side especially, it has to be accompanied by an offer of a future worth having – and worth the risks that cannot be disguised or simply wished away.

Much of the foregoing is deeply enmeshed in political calculation, argumentative guile, and personal persuasiveness of course. That – plus the deployment of narratives which link everyday experience with the larger questions of purpose and possibility for Scotland, and the opportunities that being an independent nation affords. Aside from that, and the role a range of agencies can play in strengthening and repairing the quality of public discourse, is there anything else that could help the debate to become more grounded and connected, while illuminated by the prospect of change?

Is There A Game Changer?

This book has been completed without a date for an imminent Scottish independence referendum, meaning a vote is unlikely in the next year to two. The watchword at the moment is 'after the COVID pandemic subsides'; but when this is an extremely moot question (Hassan and Barrow, 2020). The shift in Scotland from containment and suppression towards 'living with the virus' is incredibly risky. Moreover, this is unlikely to be the last pandemic we face – a point made by the global historian Adam Tooze in his study of the impact of COVID. He notes that while the state has come back and shown what it can do when there is a political will across the developed world, the right will try to put it back in the box. And this will have huge implications for the future pandemics and seismic crises humanity will face. Tooze writes: 'the coronavirus marks the end of an arc whose origin is to be found in the 1970s. It might also be seen as the first comprehensive crisis of the Anthropocene to come' – the epoch of significant human impact on earth – 'an era defined by the blowback from our unbalanced relationship to nature' (2021: 22).

We would posit that Scotland's natural environment and extensive natural resources should be far more central to any debate about our political future than has been the case so far. Indeed, they could end up being a game changer. This is because the capacity to respond to the climate crisis is an existential one in a wider than purely political sense, and because the reluctance of the UK establishment on the defining issue of our time imperils all of us and future generations. More and more, as people see and experience flooding, fires and the other consequences of too-slow climate action, the issue comes home to roost personally; it is not just something out there, beyond us.

Following the arguments around COP26 in Glasgow, more people in Scotland recognise that the global warming challenge cannot be avoided and requires action. It is about safeguarding jobs and protecting communities, not simply gesturing towards something abstract called 'the environment'. Trust, leadership, security, personal interests and the commons are things we all share. These converge together around the question of what links our future and the world's future – but with an added 'local' twist. On account of its abundant natural resources, Scotland can take the generous green future it needs in its hands – but only if the necessary economic powers are available to own, reclaim and make the most of our very substantial on and offshore wind, tidal and hydro, solar PV (Photovoltaic materials), and geothermal renewables.

That means that a fresh offer of independence can and should be framed in relation to tackling climate change, recovering from the pandemic, prioritising wellbeing and human security, strengthening our place in European and global markets, tacking poverty and inequality, and putting Scotland to work in ways that benefit our economy and communities. These are issues on which bold, innovative thinking can put a negatively-framed politics on the back foot. They are about answering the key question (for many), 'Yes, but what is this independence *for*?' However, once again, the key issue resolves back to 'who gets to decide and who do I trust most?'

This brings us right back to that earlier question about the kind of political community we need to build, and its deep connection both to the human relationships we cherish daily, the relations we enjoy or suffer with the natural world, and the prosperous country

Scotland can be as part of a wider European and global family. In that way, the next independence decision becomes a matter of both of personal and political possibility – without avoiding either the difficult questions outlined throughout this book, or the challenging task of transitioning to greater self-government over several years.

Five Challenges for the Next Debate

Finally, to conclude we offer five observations on independence drawn from this book. First, there has to be a nurturing of depth and detail – not falling back onto abstracts and general principles. In a world of contested facts that poses big questions including asking who will do the serious work. For all the energies and talents on the pro-independence side, it is salutary to note that it is the anti-independence side that since 2014 have created a range of organisations intervening in the debate – Scotland in Union, Our Scottish Future. Independence has to raise its game and create and resource a range of initiatives and expertises: the setting up of Believe in Scotland being one such example.

Second, while detail matters what is even more critical is the impressionistic, instinctual way people feel about the world and their lived, everyday experiences. In this the incremental evolution of Scottish self-government over the past 20 years and the cumulative impact of Scotland making domestic decisions different from the UK has an impact. Much commentary has been made about the different approaches of Nicola Sturgeon and Boris Johnson in the pandemic, but seldom emphasised is that it builds on this backstory and strengthens existing perceptions – not just about individuals, but institutions and political communities. These general impressions connect to everyday experience and a wider collective feeling that the UK doesn't work for the vast majority and that Scotland increasingly has the capacity to govern itself. These fundamental shifts matter and frame much of the background.

Third, the politics of hope informed much of the messaging and momentum of 2014. It is not the place to explore the relationship between hope, optimism and positive psychology – all of which are different and which Yes drew from in 2014. Suffice to say that when either the SNP or independence has drawn from a politics of hope: 2007 and 2011 in the former's case, and the latter stages of 2014 in the referendum, they have made the political weather and won support. And when they have forgotten the politics of hope, whether by default or design, they have tended to be less successful.

Many of the challenges of our politics – Brexit, Tory austerity, COVID, UK governments most Scots don't vote for – have understandably at times led some senior SNP politicians and independence supporters to lapse into a negative mindset railing against Westminster. However, this cumulatively can sound like grudge and grievance politics and be framed by opponents as the caricature of Scottish nationalism they continually want to present. Such an approach from independence supporters is self-defeating and lacks strategic nous, a point underlined by Jim Sillars in his recent autobiography:

> Grudge and grievance complaints against Westminster, combined with vitriolic attacks against unionists via social media, make for a stupid policy. If Yes is to win next time, it will be on the basis of persuasion and that will require a better understanding as to why so many No voters held to the union last time and still do (2021: 263).

Fourth, independence is about many things, but at its core it is about democracy and accountability, and Scotland having the maturity, confidence and capacity to take the big decisions. Two observations will suffice on this. On the realities of public life in Scotland no one who wants to live in a dynamic, thriving Scotland should fall into the mistake of defending the domestic status quo, no what their view on the constitution. Some SNP supporters now make the error of defending every aspect of the Scottish Government; an approach some in Labour did when it was in power and hence became the out of touch political establishment.

Related to this is how power is held to account with a hollowed out mainstream media – a point underlined by David Clegg and Kieran Andrews where they talk of 'a largely understaffed and under-resourced newspaper industry' which has 'often failed to interrogate the spin being put to it', alongside 'hyper-partisan bloggers' who have tried 'to plug the gap' (2021: 321). But a bigger take from the above is the way power is shifting across Scotland and the Western world, becoming more fluid, contingent and continually challenged, which the elites both here and elsewhere find difficult to adjust to.

Hence, Scotland's 2014 independence referendum was itself an expression of these wider changes and what is an international phenomenon: 'bottom-up referendums': other examples cited include the 2011 Italian referendum against water privatisation (and Scotland has its own longer tradition of such votes with the 1993 Strathclyde water privatisation vote). These challenge the neo-liberal status quo: a practice which gave great momentum to the Yes campaign (Porta et al., 2017; 2020). Such a politics will be difficult to reproduce in a future vote, but it is a pre-requisite for a successful campaign – putting independence with the grain of how politics and power is shifting in Scotland and across the world.

Fifth, for much of the past 40 years since the rise of Thatcherism, Scottish independence has continually been posed as a 'lifeboat' sailing away towards safety from the wreckage of HMS Britannia: an imagery brought home powerfully in William McIlvanney's notion of Scotland 'surviving the shipwreck' of 1980s Britain (McIlvanney, 1991). From the opposite side, pro-union campaigners have increasingly painted an independent Scotland as a basket case: a Third World country, a 'Caledonian Cuba', a fiscal Armageddon, and a tartan Titanic sailing out into the oceans on its own steam and meeting a terrible fate – a set of metaphors which provided the inspiration for our cover.

Some people reading this may laugh at these caricatures, but they speak to certain audiences, and even more frame the debate in an unhelpful way. This is binary Scotland shaped by black and white choices, being damned or saved. Rather than accept such a language, we need to kick back against a debate defined as escaping in a 'lifeboat' versus sinking in a calamitous, avoidable disaster of our own making: neither of which empower and lift us up.

Rather, the Scotland of the future will be about navigating stormy seas ahead with much turbulence but looking at how we collectively chart that course and address the risks, threats and opportunities which arise. A mindset which positively rejects portraying an independent Scotland in the Manichean terms above is a political community on a journey to maturity, seeing its self-government and self-determination in the context of a shared project. One nurturing the notion of viviculture we have previously talked about – the appreciation and affirmation of life – reweaving the social contract at home and embracing interdependence domestically and internationally.

This book is, we hope, a constructive contribution to that unfolding and critical debate. The settled constitutional shape it takes is still up for negotiation and decision.

References

Anderson, B. (1983), *Imagined Communities: Reflections on the Origin and Spread of Nationalism*, London: Verso.

Church of Scotland (2014), 'Imagining Scotland's Future', *Life and Work*, 4 November, https://www.lifeandwork.org/news/news/post/312-imagining-scotland-s-future-tomorrow

Clegg, D. and Andrews, K. (2021), *Break-Up: How Alex Salmond and Nicola Sturgeon Went to War*, London: Biteback Publishing.

Hassan, G. and Barrow, S. (eds) (2020), *Scotland After the Virus*, Edinburgh: Luath Press.

McIlvanney, W. (1991), *Surviving the Shipwreck*, Edinburgh: Mainstream Publishing.

Martin, C. (2021), *Resist, Reform or Re-run: Short and Long-Term Reflections on Scotland and independence referendums*, Oxford: Blavatnik School of Government, University of Oxford, accessed at: https://www.bsg.ox.ac.uk/research/publications/resist-reform-or-re-run-short-and-long-term-reflections-scotland-and

Porta, D. D., O'Connor, F., Portos, M. and Subirats Ribas, A. (2017), *Social Movements and Referendums from Below: Direct democracy in the neoliberal crisis*, Bristol: Policy Press.

Porta, D.D. (2020), *How Social Movements can save Democracy: Democratic Innovations from Below*, Cambridge: Polity Press.

Sillars, J. (2021), *A Difference of Opinion: My Political Journey*, Edinburgh: Birlinn.

Tooze, A. (2021), *Shutdown: How COVID Shook the World Economy*, London: Allen Lane.

Contributors

BILL AUSTIN worked for HM Customs & Excise (HM C&E) between 1977 and 2007 in the UK (including Northern Ireland), the Republic of Ireland and France. He also served in the Regular and Territorial Army. He researched and wrote on borders, Scottish politics and defence. He passed away in 2021.

SIMON BARROW is Director of Ekklesia, the beliefs, politics and ethics think-tank. He has written and contributed to numerous books, including editing with Gerry Hassan *Scotland After the Virus* (2020), *Scotland the Brave? Twenty Years of Change and the Future of the Nation* (2019) and *A Nation Changed? The SNP and Scotland Ten Years On* (2017), all published by Luath Press.

MARCO G. BIAGI was elected as SNP MSP for Edinburgh Central in 2011 after a decade of involvement with the party. He stepped down in 2016 to begin a PhD in Political Science while continuing to provide commentary and analysis on Scottish politics. He holds degrees from St Andrews, Glasgow and Yale universities.

IAIN BLACK is Professor in Marketing in the Management School at the University of Stirling. He has written and researched widely on environmental issues and politics. He is co-convener of the Scottish Independence Convention (SIC), a cross-party, non-partisan group.

GRAEME BLACKETT is an applied economist with more than 30 years' experience of working with governments, universities, companies and civic sector organisations across Europe, helping them to achieve better economic outcomes and increase wellbeing. He is managing director of a leading economic consultancy based in Scotland and was economic adviser to the Sustainable Growth Commission.

TANJA BUELTMANN holds a Chair in International History at the University of Strathclyde. She specialises in migration and diaspora history and her main research interest is in immigrant community life. In her current research, Tanja examines the role of immigrant associations in shaping the collective actions and identity of Europeans in the UK, taking a longitudinal perspective from c1850 to the present.

MALCOLM CHALMERS is a professor and Deputy Director-General of the Royal United Services Institute (RUSI) and directs its growing portfolio of research into contemporary defence and security issues. He has been an Adviser to the UK Parliament's Joint Committee on the National Security Strategy since 2012, and was Senior Special Adviser to Foreign Secretaries Jack Straw MP and Margaret Beckett MP.

DAVID CLARK is a foreign policy analyst specialising in Central and Eastern Europe. He was Special Adviser on Europe to Robin Cook at the Foreign Office 1997–2001.

LISA CLARK has worked in the constituency offices of two MSPs, and for the Church of Scotland, at both national and local level. She has been a believer in independence for Scotland and an SNP activist since the mid-1980s.

JOHN CURTICE is Professor of Politics at Strathclyde University and Senior Research Fellow, NatCen/ScotCen Social Research and The UK in a Changing Europe

CRAIG DALZELL is Head of Policy and Research at Common Weal Scotland.

MARK DIFFLEY is a political pollster and researcher with over 20 years' experience. He has advised political parties of all persuasions and both sides of the independence divide during his career. He is a regular media analyst and commentator on political issues. Mark established his research and consultancy business The Diffley Partnership in 2017.

MAIKE DINGER is a PhD researcher at the Universities of Stirling and Strathclyde. Her research project is focused on political participation, cultural narratives and media representation during the Scottish independence referendum campaign from 2012 to 2014. She holds degrees in Cultural Studies and Philosophy, and National and Transnational Studies and has previously spoken on connections between national identity, literature and culture.

SIONAIDH DOUGLAS-SCOTT is Anniversary Chair in Law at Queen Mary University and visiting Fellow at Princeton 2020–21. She was special legal adviser to Scottish Parliament European and External affairs committee Brexit inquiries 2015–2017 (and her book on *Brexit and British Constitutional Unsettlement* is published by CUP in 2022.)

GAVIN ESLER is a broadcaster and writer, having most recently completed the book *How Britain Ends* (Head of Zeus, 2021).

SUSANNAH FITZGERALD works as an anti-corruption advocate for Transparency International UK, although her words here represent her own views rather than those of her employer. She works on issues surrounding the flow of dirty money into the UK and political corruption, including the Scottish Alliance for Lobbying Transparency.

ROZ FOYER is General Secretary of the Scottish Trades Union Congress (STUC) and ab active trade unionist. She delivered the 2021 Jimmy Reid Foundation memorial lecture.

DANI GARAVELLI is an award-winning freelance journalist and columnist who regularly writes for a range of publications including *Scotland on Sunday*.

CARON E. GENTRY is Faculty Pro-Vice Chancellor of Art, Design, and Social Sciences at Northumbria University. Previously, she was a professor in the School of International Relations at the University of St Andrews. Her research focuses on gender and terrorism and feminist political theology, particularly the politics of hope. As such, she believes a feminist foreign policy engages in hopeful politics.

STEPHEN GETHINS served as MP for North East Fife, was the SNP's International Affairs and Europe spokesperson and the first SNP MP to sit on the House of Commons Foreign Affairs Select Committee. Before entering Parliament he was a Special Adviser to the First Minister on Energy, Climate Change, International and European Affairs. He is currently Professor of Practice at the School of International Relations at the University of St Andrews and his first book *Nation to Nation: Scotland's Place in the World* was published by Luath Press in 2021.

HANNAH GRAHAM is a criminologist who works as a Senior Lecturer in the Scottish Centre for Crime and Justice Research at the University of Stirling. Outwith the university, she is a member of the Scottish Sentencing Council, an independent advisory body.

SEÁN PATRICK GRIFFIN is a Scottish solicitor with experience practising in constitutional law and human rights. In 2019, he was appointed as Policy Adviser in the Leader of the Opposition's Office to conduct a research project on reforming the UK constitution. He produced a report for the Labour Party on reforming the state, currently works in the Governance and Legal Unit of the Labour Party, is an active member of the Campaign for Socialism and works closely with the Red Paper Collective.

GERRY HASSAN is Professor of Social Change at Glasgow Caledonian University and has written and edited over two dozen books on Scottish and UK politics including *The Strange Death of Labour Scotland* (2012), *Caledonian Dreaming: The Quest for a Different Scotland* (2014), *Independence of the Scottish Mind* (2014) and *The People's Flag and Union Jack: An Alternative History of Britain and the Labour Party* (2019). He has edited three previous books with Simon Barrow including *Scotland After the Virus* (2020) and his writing, commentary and research can be found at: www.gerryhassan.com

KIRSTY HUGHES is a writer and commentator on Scottish, UK and European politics. She was the founder and director of the Scottish Centre on European Relations from 2017–2020. She has researched and published extensively on European issues including the EU's several enlargements and prospects for an independent Scotland to join the EU.

BEN JACKSON is Associate Professor of Modern History at Oxford University and Co-Editor of *Political Quarterly*. He is author of *The Case for Scottish Independence: A History of Nationalist Political Thought in Modern Scotland* (Cambridge University Press, 2020).

FATIMA ZAHRA JOJI is Co-chair of Aberdeen Independence Movement, a Director of 50:50 Parliament and regional lead for Women for Independence in the North East of Scotland; she has previously been a parliamentary researcher to a MEP and is a graduate of Robert Gordon University and the University of Birmingham.

JOHN KAY is an economist whose career has spanned the academic world, business and finance, and public affairs. He has held chairs at the London Business School, University of Oxford and the London School of Economics and is a Fellow of St John's College, Oxford, where he began his academic career in 1970. He is the author of many books and articles: most recently *Radical Uncertainty*, co-authored with Mervyn King, and *Greed is Dead*, co-authored with Paul Collier.

COLIN KIDD is Wardlaw Professor of Modern History at the University of St Andrews. He is a Fellow of both the British Academy and the Royal Society of Edinburgh. He is the author of five books, including *Subverting Scotland's Past* (1993) and *Union and Unionisms* (2008). He has also co-edited, with Gerry Carruthers, *Literature and Union: Scottish Texts, British Contexts* (2018). In addition, he is a regular contributor to the *London Review of Books* and to the *Guardian*.

KAREN LORIMER is a Reader in Social Science and Health at Glasgow Caledonian University. She is a member of the Human Development and Capability Association (HDCA), within which she co-leads a thematic group on gender and sexuality.

JOYCE MCMILLAN is a freelance writer and broadcaster based in Edinburgh, and a critic and columnist for *The Scotsman*. She was Honorary President of Scottish Environment Link from 2015 to 2019, and is currently a member of the Scottish Government's Working Group on the future of public interest journalism in Scotland.

CIARAN MARTIN is Professor of Practice in the Management of Public Organisations at the Blavatnik School of Government at the University of Oxford. A native of Northern Ireland, he had a 23 year career in the UK Civil Service, including 15 at senior level. He held positions in the Treasury and Cabinet Office, and, from 2014 to 2020, put together and ran the UK's National Cyber Security Centre. Prior to that he served as Director of Constitutional Policy in the Cabinet Office. As part of that role, he supported UK ministers in negotiating the Edinburgh Agreement, the basis of the 2014 independence referendum.

PAUL MASON is a writer, activist and filmmaker and the author of several books of which the latest is *How to Stop Fascism* (Allen Lane, 2021).

MARK MULLER STUART QC is the Founder of Beyond Borders Scotland and a Senior Mediation adviser with the UN Department of Political and Peacebuilding Affairs. He is also a Professor in Practice at the LSE where he runs a number of conflict resolution initiatives. Mark regularly advises international bodies on conflict resolution, peace process design and international law issues, including the UN Envoy to Syria and the EU. He is also a co-founder of the Delfina Foundation, a member of Doughty Street Legal Chambers, the Faculty of Advocates and a Fellow of Harvard Law School.

PHILLIPS O'BRIEN is the Chair of Strategic Studies and professor in the School of International Relations at the University of St Andrews. He has written extensively on 20th and 21st century defence policy and strategic history, with a particular expertise in grand strategy, US-UK relations, and, air-sea power. His books include: *How the War was Won: Air-Sea Power and Allied Victory in World War II* (Cambridge University Press 2015) and *The Second Most Powerful Man in the World: The Life of William D Leahy, Roosevelt's Chief of Staff* (Dutton, 2019).

MICHAEL ROY is Professor of Economic Sociology and Social Policy at the Yunus Centre for Social Business and Health, Glasgow Caledonian University. He has published extensively on the health and wellbeing impacts of social enterprises, on policy ecosystems, and on innovative (and contentious) funding mechanisms for social welfare programmes.

PAUL SWEENEY is a Labour and Co-operative Party MSP for the Glasgow Region, having been elected in May 2021. Prior to that he was the Labour and Co-operative Party MP for Glasgow North East from 2017–19.

ANDREW TICKELL is a freelance writer on law and politics, and a Lecturer in Law at Glasgow Caledonian University.

WILLIAM WALKER is Emeritus Professor of International Relations, University of St Andrews. His publications include, with David Albright and Frans Berkhout, *Plutonium and Highly Enriched Uranium: World Inventories, Capabilities and Policies* (1997); THORP *and the Politics of Commitment* (1999); and with Malcolm Chalmers, *Uncharted Waters: The UK, Nuclear Weapons and the Scottish Question* (2001).

ALLAN WHYTE is an independence activist from Glasgow with an interest in self-determination as a mechanism to create a fairer and more equal society. With a background in art and environmental policy, it was after a period of unemployment, then a number of years working with young people in Glasgow's east end, that the harsh realities of a broken system and a desperate need for change led him back to campaigning for independence.

Luath Press Limited

committed to publishing well written books worth reading

LUATH PRESS takes its name from Robert Burns, whose little collie Luath (*Gael.*, swift or nimble) tripped up Jean Armour at a wedding and gave him the chance to speak to the woman who was to be his wife and the abiding love of his life. Burns called one of the 'Twa Dogs' Luath after Cuchullin's hunting dog in Ossian's *Fingal*. Luath Press was established in 1981 in the heart of Burns country, and is now based a few steps up the road from Burns' first lodgings on Edinburgh's Royal Mile. Luath offers you distinctive writing with a hint of unexpected pleasures.

Most bookshops in the UK, the US, Canada, Australia, New Zealand and parts of Europe, either carry our books in stock or can order them for you. To order direct from us, please send a £sterling cheque, postal order, international money order or your credit card details (number, address of cardholder and expiry date) to us at the address below. Please add post and packing as follows: UK – £1.00 per delivery address; overseas surface mail – £2.50 per delivery address; overseas airmail – £3.50 for the first book to each delivery address, plus £1.00 for each additional book by airmail to the same address. If your order is a gift, we will happily enclose your card or message at no extra charge.

Luath Press Limited
543/2 Castlehill
The Royal Mile
Edinburgh EH1 2ND
Scotland
Telephone: +44 (0)131 225 4326 (24 hours)
email: sales@luath. co.uk
Website: www. luath.co.uk